AIRPORT
CONFIDENTIAL

Brian Moynahan

SUMMIT BOOKS
New York

Copyright © 1980 by Brian Moynahan
All rights reserved
including the right of reproduction
in whole or in part in any form
Published by *Summit Books*
A Simon & Schuster Division of Gulf & Western Corporation
Simon & Schuster Building
1230 Avenue of the Americas
New York, New York 10020
SUMMIT BOOKS and colophon are trademarks of Simon & Schuster

Designed by Stanley S. Drate
Manufactured in the United States of America
Previously published in England under the title *Airport International*

1 2 3 4 5 6 7 8 9 10
1 2 3 4 5 6 7 8 9 10 Pbk.

Library of Congress Cataloging in Publication Data

Moynahan, Brian.
   Airport confidential

   Includes bibliographical references and index.
   1. Aeronautics, Commercial. 2. Airports. 3. Air
lines. I. Title.
HE9776.M68   1980   387.7'364   79–24395
ISBN 0–671–40111–4
ISBN 0–671–40119–X Pbk.

For Priscilla

ACKNOWLEDGMENTS

I should like to thank the following for their help with this book: airport staff at JFK, Miami International, Dallas/Fort Worth, Washington Dulles and Houston Intercontinental; British Airways, Middle East Airlines, Pakistan International Airlines, Cathay Pacific, Malaysian Singapore Airlines (now MAS and SIA), KLM and Qantas. I am particularly indebted to British Caledonian Airways, and to John De La Haye and Captain Adrian Ross. Many airlines take the view that the less their passengers know about flying, the better. The above are notable exceptions, who enabled me to ride on flight decks and "fly" simulators around the world. It would not be possible to list all the pilots, cabin staff, air traffic controllers, baggage handlers and others connected with the airline world who gave me interviews. Several informants would in any case prefer anonymity, for obvious reasons. I am, however, deeply indebted to Captain Fres Insole, 747 captain and member of the Air Safety Group, who was kind enough to read the manuscript. Any errors that persist are mine.

NOTE: A useful conversion factor for those readers interested (and equipped with pocket calculators or formidable mathematical brains): multiply knots by 1.1515 to get miles per hour.

Contents

Part Three:
READY, STEADY, FLY

Part Four:
AIRBORNE

Part Five:
EMERGENCY

PROLOGUE

My first flight was from Paris to Portsmouth in 1959. The pilot arrived late, with the stewardess. He wore a double-breasted jacket, blue serge trousers and Wellington boots. The stewardess wore laddered stockings and mirror sunglasses. They both went into the cockpit without a word.

When the English coast loomed up the stewardess appeared in the cabin. She was still wearing sunglasses, but her lipstick was smudged. "Southend, anyone for Southend?" she shouted. The boy in front of me put up his hand.

The aging DC-3 abruptly landed. The boy was bundled out onto the grass field and we took off again. The stewardess went back into the cockpit. As we circled Portsmouth Harbour, I reflected that there was more to this flying business than met the eye.

Experience has proved me right. There is an immense amount of knowledge to be mined from the brave new world of air travel. It is breeding entirely new species: men who scare away birds, who pour whiskey down drains, who balance turbine blades, who smuggle rare birds in shoe boxes. There are new airports, too: Paris' eerie and spacelike Charles de Gaulle, or Dallas/Fort Worth with its Texas vastness and its claim to be the airport of the future. There are airports which are almost choked with traffic, like

Chicago's O'Hare, Majorca's Palma or Tokyo's Haneda; and there are deserted airports like Tanzania's Kilimanjaro, lying beneath the snows of the great mountain waiting for the tourist boom that never came.

The most interesting of them all is New York's John F. Kennedy International Airport, which tops the list of both international flights and international passengers. JFK (its owners, the Port Authority of New York and New Jersey, refer to it as KIA) is a representative of all the great airports.

It exhibits the problems common to all—from overcrowded airspace to overstretched ground facilities to a runaway crime rate. JFK is the center of the nation's parrot smuggling (the birds arrive drugged with tequila); the site of the nation's largest robbery ($6 million from the German airline Lufthansa); the scene of one of the most spectacular air misses (a light plane and the gleaming Anglo-French SST, Concorde).

It is the focal point of the great air routes between Europe and the U.S., and the eastern U.S. and Latin America and Asia. It seethes with all the denizens of this strange world, rich and poor, dishonest and honest. Beyond its 23 million passengers a year, with all their human frailties, it has a full-time staff as large as a city and imbued with more specialized vices and virtues than those 23 million have ever dreamed of.

Brian Moynahan
New York, 1980

PART ONE

AIRPORT

1

Airport International

JFK handles more than 23 million international and domestic passengers a year. Traffic controllers and the pilots of 76 airlines work their way through 316,000 takeoffs and landings. It is a city in its own right, employing 39,446 people full-time, the working population of El Paso. Like all the great airports, it dates back only to the last days of the war.

The site on the marshy shore of Jamaica Bay originally included the Idlewild Beach golf course. It was a wet, rough tideland area, largely abandoned to sea birds, which are still hazardous to aircraft, and to refuse dumps. The grass was short and sparse, the few bushes stunted and warped by the strong winds off the bay. When it rained, the site became a quagmire of sucking sludge, salty and deep, avoided even by bird hunters.

The winds still threaten aircraft, and have destroyed one and all those in it, but a 70-mile system of storm sewers takes care of the rain. The muck and silt have been excavated, replaced with sand fill, and topped off with concrete. The greater part of JFK's 5,000 acres is covered with buildings, runways, aprons and taxiways.

Seaplanes had operated since before the war from the choppy waters of Jamaica Bay. The first aircraft to operate into the new airport, called Idlewild, like the golf course, was on a Peruvian

International Airways flight on July 1, 1948. Idlewild was renamed Kennedy, to honor the late President, at the end of 1963.

The runways are the heart of any airport. JFK has five. There are two pairs of parallel main runways, aligned at right angles, and a fifth runway for light aircraft. The total runway length is nine miles, and the main runways are parallel to those at La Guardia and Newark, which are also run by the Port Authority of New York and New Jersey.

The parallel runway system allows one to be used for landings while the other is free for takeoffs, which leads to a rapid traffic flow. The runways are a standard 150 feet wide. They vary in length from the very short 4 Right–22 Left at 8,400 feet, cut short by Jamaica Bay at one end and Rockaway Boulevard at the other, to the majestic 14,572 feet of 13 Right–31 Left.

The General Aviation runway, which a lot of pilots wish would disappear along with its troublesome light aircraft, is just 2,560 feet long and is, in fact, really part of JFK's 25 miles of taxiway.

The runway concrete is grooved so that tires will bite and not skid or aquaplane in heavy rain. It is regularly washed with detergent, and giant scrubbing machines clear the oil from jet exhausts. Burst tires on takeoff can cause crashes—an East-African Airways VC-10 had a fatal crash at Addis Ababa after debris left lying on the runway punctured a tire. The runways are continually checked by a patrol in a special vacuum-cleaner truck. It sucks up the screws, bolts and other pieces of metal that can fall on a runway. A magnet truck is also used. The patrol also checks the runway lights, which have to take the thump of jets landing 260 tons at 160 mph on them. The lighting systems are crucial, and a big airport like JFK has more than 500 miles of cables.

Besides aircraft, an airport has a bewildering supply of vehicles. There are yellow runway patrol and Follow Me marshaling vans; snow clearance trains with plow blades, brushes and blowers; aircraft tugs that can pull a loaded 747; special fuel trucks which can carry up to 20,000 gallons, or 90,000 liters; high-lift catering trucks and trucks with steps.

Every airport has its own large fire services, with trucks that have the emphasis on a "quick KO"—knocking out the fire with a vast amount of foam for a minute or so while the passengers and crew get out. There are fleets of Quick-Dash Trucks carrying oxygen masks, ladders, axes, first aid and cutting equipment. Large tractors are kept as rescue vehicles to pull out aircraft that get bogged down off the runways.

There are special bird-scaring patrols. Birds are a major problem at JFK. A flock of gulls totally destroyed a DC-10 when they were sucked into its engines. The bill came to more than $20 million and safety experts agreed that there would have been numerous deaths had not all 139 aboard been airline employees specially drilled in the use of escape chutes.

The Federal Aviation Administration has failed to keep birds off the airport. (The FAA has not been helped by the fact that the area at the end of the runways has been officially declared a bird sanctuary.) One scheme, to poison food at nearby garbage dumps that attract the gulls, failed after the Society for the Prevention of Cruelty to Animals objected that gulls might fly off with the deadly food and drop it elsewhere to be eaten by other creatures.

A grid, put over the garbage zone to keep the birds from gliding in, also failed. "The birds just glide in short of the dump, walk under the wires and feed away," the FAA's airports chief noted mournfully. A plan to narrow the garbage pit did no better. "It just changed the eating of the gulls from a natural habitat to a cafeteria style."

It has been estimated that getting rid of the dumps entirely, which take 20,000 tons of New York garbage a day, would cost $600 million. So the FAA insists on frequent inspection teams at JFK. Normally armed with shotguns to frighten and shoot off birds, they can also use cassette recordings of bird distress calls and the shrieks of birds of prey. In addition, the British Royal Navy keeps falcons to frighten birds off its bases. In Canada there are ornithological forecasts to warn pilots. These are based on radar sightings (radar can spot large flocks of birds), migration patterns and the weather.

The problem is considerable. There are some 2,000 bird strikes a year in the U.S., and they can be killers. An Electra airliner hit a flock of starlings during takeoff at Boston, an airport plagued by birds, and crashed, killing 61 of the 72 on board. A United Airlines Viscount hit a swan 6,500 feet above Maryland. The bird lodged in the elevator controls, forcing the plane into an uncontrollable dive. All aboard died. The captain of an Indian Airlines DC-3 was killed when a vulture smashed through the cockpit windshield; the copilot safely landed the plane. Modern windshields will withstand impact with a four-pound bird at 470 mph.

Ninety percent of bird strikes are below 1,500 feet except during migration, when there is dense bird traffic between 1,500 and 2,000 feet. One particular danger is that vibration from jet engines at airports brings worms to the surface, attracting birds. However, geese have been sighted above 15,000 feet.

The bigger the aircraft, the more likely is a hit. A 747 averages 10 hits per 10,000 hours, a 707 only 1.5.

At least at JFK there is no need for anti-snake patrols. In Kuala Lumpur, and at Manaus in the Brazilian Amazon, they have to make sure snakes do not crawl up into the aircraft. A light-plane pilot in Malaysia found a cobra coming out of his instrument panel in flight. Fortunately the soothing heat and steady note of the engine kept it too soporific to strike.

An airport is as complicated to run as most cities. JFK has its own quantity surveyor, inspector of works, domestic and foul drainage water supervisor, electrical and mechanical engineer, and security chief. It has an engineering staff of 1,000.

The taxiways are so complex, with turnoff points and the crossovers, that there is a special A to Z taxiway guide for pilots, who were getting lost between the runways and the terminals. In fog they still do, although it is possible for a ground controller to talk a pilot from a runway to a stand by using the airport radar. It is so accurate that the aircraft type can be recognized from the screen. The controller normally guides the aircraft in fog with green lights along the taxiways. The captain simply keeps his nosewheel along the lights.

Using radar in an emergency, the controller can tell the pilot to turn left or right, speed up or stop, making sure that he gets safely past other aircraft. The system is also used for vehicles in thick fog. In one crash in the U.S. the wrecked aircraft could be seen only on radar, and the rescue services were painstakingly directed out to it one by one on radar.

More than 10,000 people work in the huge maintenance areas on the east and south sides of JFK. Much of the work on instruments is done in special dust-free rooms, with filtered air and nylon overalls designed to trap fabric particles.

The engine testing areas are surrounded by banks of earth. Maintenance men work through the night to get planes back on line. Airports are sleepless places. They never close. Indeed, it is illegal for them to do so. Although they can advise a pilot not to land because of fog or snow, they cannot stop him; the decision is his.

The fuel facilities have to cope with a demand of 3.5 million gallons a day. Tankers are slow and ponderous for machines as thirsty as the Jumbo, which can swallow 40,000 gallons, so there is an underground network of fuel pipes running from a tank on the west side to hydrants on the aprons. With these, 500 gallons a minute can be pumped into an aircraft's tanks from each hydrant. Where JFK was storing 600,000 gallons in 1948, it now has 32 million gallons in a special tank farm.

The cargo area on the south side is a miniature airport of its own. The freighters never come near the passenger terminals. There are special Customs posts for cargo and enough storage to cope with half a million tons a year at JFK. A typical load on one 707 freighter flying to Chicago: two poodles, eight plastic bags of eels, a box of radioactive thorium X, 5,000 Swiss umbrellas, 500 assorted boxes of goods for a department store, one ton of German cuckoo clocks, six tons of Dutch blankets and $1 million worth of precious stones.

The airport has its own delicate social hierarchy. There are orchids for presidents' wives, rare bouquets for foreign ministers', roses for ambassadors'. The red carpet is only unrolled on the tarmac for heads of state. The President and VVIPs, the Very Very Important, arrive at a hangar area chosen by the Secret Service. The Russians invariably use the Pan Am hangar and are swiftly motorcaded out.

Special staff look after the protocol and manage the conference rooms. These all have telex and television facilities and have been the scene for many dramatic interviews with returning hijack hostages or errant film stars. The prompt boards, left stacked up by the door, also bear dumb witness to the unending stream of platitudinous politicans. "Like it or not this *is* a changing world. We live *in* a changing world. We are on a collision course with the future. Think about it." "At this present moment in time, we must pull *together* in order to overcome these difficulties which *all* countries and not just our own are currently facing." The emphases are italicized.

The terminals are intensely complex. Routes through the building have to be organized carefully so that streams going in different directions do not mix. They must ensure that the dishonest cannot jump ticket, passport and baggage checks. The passenger has to pass through a number of stages in the right order. In terms of control and routing, catching a plane is the most complicated journey most people will make.

During the rebuilding of Cairo airport, the chaos was so bad that I met a man who had failed to get his plane to the Philippines three times. He had been to Geneva twice in error, and once to Beirut. He had also fractured his toe when a basin in the (rebuilt) rest room collapsed on it. In contrast, the design at Dallas/Fort Worth is so sophisticated that the average distance from car to entrance terminal is normally 100 yards and never more than 300 yards. From the terminal entrance to the plane is 120 feet— passengers on a 747 have to walk twice that distance simply to get to the back of the plane, and a half-mile walk is necessary at many airports to get to the aircraft.

Airports are, on the whole, extremely ugly places: hostile, cramped, mean, utterly lacking the flair that went into railway stations like Grand Central. JFK is no exception. It is a ragbag of conflicting passenger terminals, control towers, cargo blocks, hangars, tank farm, power station and gas stations. Apart from the TWA terminal, designed by Eero Saarinen, though not at his best, most of JFK is an architectural mess.

At least JFK is tolerably close to New York. The new international airports at São Paulo and Tokyo are both 50 miles out.

Narita is two hours and $50 from downtown Tokyo. Montreal's new Mirabeau is 35 miles north of the city in the great nothingness that extends up to the North Pole and a few thousand miles down the other side. Dallas/Fort Worth is near neither city and suffers from its own size. As large as Manhattan, the airport has an "Airtrans' Electric Train" system that is supposed to speed passengers around its broad acres, but in fact is temperamental and the subject of $1 billion worth of lawsuits between the airport and the manufacturers.

For the future, far-out airports are likely to include Los Angeles, which holds 17,500 acres in the Mojave desert, 50 miles northeast of its present airport. Atlanta has two separate 10,000-acre sites each 40 miles from Peachtree Street. St. Louis has 18,650 acres across the Mississippi in Illinois.

Airports have advanced from very basic designs in their short and hectic lives. First of all they were linear. There was a long terminal building, which, like Santa Barbara at Islip, on Long Island, was often very pleasant. But it couldn't cope with very many planes, so it started sprouting corridors, or fingers, known as piers. The most famous pier airport is O'Hare. It can deal with a lot of aircraft, but because of the stress of changing flights along its one and a half miles of corridors, O'Hare is known in the trade as Cardiac Alley.

So along came the satellite system. All passengers arrive at a central terminal building and then go through passages, usually underground, to the departure lounges of the various airlines. Los Angeles and Paris' Charles de Gaulle are examples; Tampa, Florida, is probably the best.

Satellites still involve walking. The newest system is the transporter terminal, like Dallas' International and Montreal's Mirabeau. They do not rely on fingers, satellites or moving sidewalks. They revert to the simple old linear building, but with one big difference. Aircraft do not taxi up to the passenger terminal. They park at the fuel and service stations near the runways, and the passengers go out to them.

The passengers check in at the terminal, walk a few feet to a bus and are driven to the aircraft. The body of the vehicle—called a transporter, Plane-Mate or mobile lounge—rises to the level of the aircraft door and the passengers board. Airlines do not like the system because the transporters cost a minimum of $350,000.

There are variations. Houston's Intercontinental has roof parking and passengers go down to the terminal by elevator. This is a neat way of taking the long walk out of the parking lot and putting it into the building. Los Angeles has an extraordinary Futuristic Theme Building, which serves no purpose at all. Miami's International has a phenomenally long terminal and passengers should allow extra connection time, especially between Delta and National. The District of Columbia's Washington National Airport, for reasons best known to itself, has located its rent-a-car pickup point down some extremely tricky outdoor concrete steps which do not take baggage carts.

Perhaps the only elegant airport in the U.S. is Dulles International at Chantilly, Virginia. It was designed by Eero Saarinen, who said: "Maybe this building will explain what I mean about architecture." Well, almost. The most efficient is Seattle/Tacoma (Sea-Tac to locals), with Tampa not far behind. The most imaginative is Dallas/Fort Worth.

JFK is none of these things. It mixes the linear terminal piers and satellites with abandon, and throws in Plane-Mates for good measure as well. But it does function more or less.

A more serious criticism than design is that when JFK does break down through strikes or bad weather, there is so little for the passenger to do. There is nothing too unpleasant about being delayed at some European airports. Frankfurt, for example, has more than 50 shops selling everything from bratwurst and lederhosen to minicameras and microphones for industrial espionage. The terminal covers a huge range of activities. Frankfurt has two sex shops (favorite item, black suspender belts; best customers, Turkish migrant workers), three movie theaters, one given over to nonstop porno shows, twelve restaurants and bars, an automobile dealer and a dog kennel.

Two passengers could buy a diamond ring on the spot, announce their engagement in the airport newspaper, rent a tuxedo and a wedding dress, make out a gift list at airport stores that would furnish their love nest down to the last chair and pillow, get married in the airport chapel, hold a reception for 500 in a banquet room and spend their honeymoon in the bridal suite of the luxury hotel attached to the terminal by a covered walkway.*

JFK, by contrast, offers very little. There is an exhibition of paintings, sculpture or photography, changed four times a year, in the TWA terminal. The International Arrivals Building has some Dali lithographs and works by Miró, Calder and Hans Arp. A Hoffritz shop sells cutlery and games, and there are a couple of bookshops, some shoe-shine stands, barbershops and coin-operated TV sets. Passengers feeling rich can check into nearby hotels at day rates and get a room, TV and the use of a swimming pool.

Spiritually, the place is not quite a desert. There is a Tri-Faith Plaza, inspirationally placed in a parking lot near the control tower. Services are held only on Sundays and holidays at the Protestant Chapel, though daily at Our Lady of the Skies and, Saturdays excepted, at the International Synagogue. This Synagogue has an intriguing little museum with old maps, a Yemeni wedding dress and Torah breastplates.

Passengers pin up their hopes on scraps of paper. "Jeanette come back safely we love you." "Lord keep the Russian Orthodox Church safe." "Please God don't let my old father find out nor any one of my family or work people and please keep it out of the papers God please." What desperation is behind that girlish trembling script?

Air traffic controllers work around the clock in the nearby control tower to bring the aircraft in. The air in the tower is cool, the calm icy, the controllers in shirtsleeves. The curtains are drawn against the sun, the lights are green-shaded so that eyesight adapts to the instruments. The only conversations are the controllers'

---

*I agree that the idea of airport honeymoons is appalling. But they are surely inevitable. As many as 7,000 couples at a time have been stranded at their home airports for several days by a series of work slowdowns by Spanish air traffic controllers on the honeymoon isle of Majorca. Sooner or later, one couple is going to consign the airplanes to hell, and settle for the airport.

instructions and the pilots' acknowledgments as they repeat them.

An aircraft passes through up to four controllers during the landing sequence. The first controller guides the aircraft in along the airways from an Air Route Traffic Control Center. The airways stretch out like thin interlocking fingers, from 5,000 to 30,000 feet high and up to 10 miles wide. The ARTCC guides the aircraft to one of the holding points for the "stacks."

Then an approach controller takes the aircraft off the stacks. He steers them on radar toward their landing runway, keeping a three-to-four-mile interval between them and the aircraft in front and behind. A distance of six miles is kept free behind a 747, which creates so much wash, or wake, in the air that it can fling smaller aircraft out of control. The wake can also send birds spinning into the ground.

Approach control finally establishes the plane on its landing path. At a few airports, such as Hong Kong and Bermuda, an airport controller can check it down on Precision Approach Radar. The set has two screens. One shows if the aircraft is on the center line for the runway; if not, the controller will steer it left or right. The other shows if it is on the correct glide path, descending at the correct angle so that it will be at 200 feet at the runway threshold. The controller orders it up or down.

Normally, the pilot uses the Instrument Landing System, where an instrument in his cockpit tells him is he is on the right approach to the runway.

After landing, a ground movement controller takes over to talk the planes through taxiing. He also gives them permission to start engines and gives priorities. Many pilots accuse certain airports of blatant nationalism in giving their own airline priority over others, so that it keeps to schedules and others don't. Worst in this respect is Tokyo, which also gives the best cruising heights to Japan Airlines, forcing others to fly at lower, slower and more expensive heights. Canada has a reputation for helping Air Canada. The ground movement controller also controls all the vehicles on the airport, from the bird scarers to the big grass-cutting machines and the conga line of snowplows.

Farther out toward the perimeter, the catering kitchens are alive around the clock, producing 30 million meals a year, consuming cattle by the herd and sheep by the flock. The Airmail Unit is close by, with a security truck to take any suspicious parcels to the decompression chamber on the other side of the airport.

The slightest breeze along the airport starts the senses. The sharp tang of hay and dung from the pens of the Animalport sets the eyes to watering. The scent of juicy steaks and the oily musk of smoked salmon drift from the flight catering kitchens. There is a clatter of machinery from the printing shed where embossed first-class menus in deep reds and blues, with epaulets and tassels of gold braid, are finalized, with Wild Duck à l'Orange for a flight to Chicago, Poached Turbot and Shrimp for West Africa.

A police patrol car moves out, strobe lights spinning. The airport police number 248 in their smart two-cell station, with its drug-sniffing Labradors and bulletin board with pictures of world terrorists. The station has an armored car, leased from the Purolator security firm, which, armed with two M-16-toting police, accompanies every El Al flight from its landing run until it is empty.

The armored car also leads aircraft with bomb threats to the two holding points, one at the end of 22 Right by Jamaica Bay, the other by the blast fence on the run-up of the same runway. A mobile X-ray truck is used to check luggage for bombs and there is a decompression chamber to simulate the effect of an aircraft at height on altimeter bombs.

The police spend much of their time on traffic. JFK has more than its share of abandoned cars, and there is a dump by the cargo sheds. Hundreds of cars a year are stolen, although there has been nothing quite as ingenious as a car-hire racket that flourished at London's Heathrow. The villains worked in an off-airport parking lot and knew how long each car would be left from the date of return by the customers. The cars were hired to unwitting passengers at rates well below Hertz and Avis. The culprits were caught only after a series of accidents brought in the police and all long-term car parks now ask owners to read their mileage to prevent such rackets.

Police must also be present at all security searchings of

passengers. Trained as fire fighters, the police also run the Emergency Services. From their main base and a satellite garage, the fire trucks can be at any part of any runway in three minutes.

The lowest grade of emergency is a 3:2, or nonrequest, where a pilot reports he has a problem but does not ask for aid. One Quick Dash Truck, a light water and powder vehicle, is sent out together with a massive $350,000 Chubb F.40 with 4,000 gallons of foam and water.

A 3:3 alert responds to a request by the pilot. The police "roll both houses" and Quick Dash Trucks and Chubbs go out from both the main and satellite garages.

A 3:4 is an actual crash, and everything rolls, including ambulances. An alarm rings automatically in the Medical Office, the two garages, the operations center, the health and hospital center, the New York City police and fire departments and the U.S. Coast Guard.

There is a mobile emergency hospital, a huge truck on two levels, with a complete operating theater on the upper level. It is manned by doctors who make their bread and butter out of general practice for the airport workers' compensation suits and for specialist checks of pilots. Donated by United Airlines, the mobile hospital has fortunately had little use.

JFK works through emergencies at the rate of around 7 a week in winter and 15 in summer. The busiest time coincides with the airport's own peak from 2:30 P.M. to 9:30 P.M.

The foam and cutting trucks link up at special rendezvous points with ambulances. The drivers start as the aircraft crosses the threshold markers of the runway. That way they will be with the target for the longest time, as they have calculated, so that they will not overshoot the crash spot and have to turn back, nor undershoot. Timing is vital, for a fuel fire is an uncontrollable and poisonous thing. Flooded with foam, a fire can be suppressed for a minute while the cutting teams get the passengers out.

Beyond the fire center is an old, blackened airliner. Its engines have been removed. The undercarriage has collapsed. But every month, it is set on fire with thousands of gallons of kerosene, the warm, sweet-smelling jet fuel that permeates the air of every airport. The airport police then practice putting the fire out, awkward in their heavy asbestos suits and breathing equipment.

Many experts feel that commercial airport fire facilities are hopelessly inadequate compared with those of military airfields. With the military, giant fire-fighting helicopters reach aircraft that crash a few miles from the airport in a minute or so. They carry fire fighters, doctors, nurses, medical equipment and foam-throwers. No civil airport is equipped on this scale, even though the numbers involved in an airliner crash are normally far greater than in a military accident.

The public is a major menace at any crash. Looters and sightseers often beat police and ambulances to the scene. They cause such serious traffic jams and hamper rescue work to such an extent that it has been suggested television and radio should withhold news flashes about accidents until the emergency services are in control.

Almost every trade and profession is represented at a great airport. Some are not on any official payroll, but certainly earn their livelihood from airports. In the spring come the international pickpockets, following the great society migration. In the high summer months, as the airport fills with its maximum flow of tourists, smugglers put in their greatest effort.

The summer also sees the check and credit-card con men at their height. Teams operate in fours. One man steals a wallet or handbag, looking more for checkbooks and credit cards than cash. He immediately passes the booty on to another man. If he is challenged, he will be "clean." The second man takes the valuables and dumps the rest in a waste bin or toilet. The checks and credit cards are passed to the "cashers," the man and girl who use them to get cash from banks or easily salable items like jewelry and watches. Some items like cashmeres and tweeds are ordered by a fence at their home base before the teams leave for abroad.

They travel on airline tickets bought with credit cards stolen in their last port of call. Airports give them mobility, victims, plenty of shopping and banking opportunities, plus a jet-speeded exit.

One gang arrived at 8:30 A.M. The members never left the airport. By midday, they had accumulated 10 checkbooks and 38 credit cards, and departed for Sweden. Their haul was $1,400 in cash from airport banks, $4,000 in traveler's checks, and $18,000 worth of perfume, fabrics, cameras and watches from the duty-free shops, They were caught eight airports and three countries later.

Prostitutes, "call-button girls" as they call themselves, roam from airport to airport, operating from the airport hotels.* Most claim to be airline stewardesses. This is both a cover for the hotel and a come-on to the customers, since stewardesses are international sex symbols. There is a well-known bar on the Ginza in Tokyo where all the girls are dressed in the uniforms of the great international airlines. The allure of flying is great enough to ensure the bar's success.

Smugglers are locked in endless battle with the Customs. For the professionals, it is a battle of skill, with invoice forms and cargo manifests the keys. A minor change in description can alter the duty rate from 50 percent to zero. For the amateur, it is often the grin in front of the hidden spy holes on the far, "safe" side of Customs that gives away the man with the odd camera or extra bottle of Scotch. Glances picked up through the two-way mirrors in Immigration provide other clues.

With more than $10 million in cargo and passengers' valuables disappearing every year, some of the staff are also there for more than their salaries.

Few workers do their relaxing at the airport. The aircrew goes to the hotels that mushroom outside it. Some have small "key clubs" frequented by pilots. Aircrews are forbidden to drink eight hours before a flight. They avoid bars when in uniform because the public cannot tell whether they are coming back from a flight or going out on one. Clubs avoid this sort of problem.

Airports spawn pretty girls: the biggest concentration of beauty in any country will be found at its major airport. They work in the big hotels or the aircraft or the check-in desks, in the duty-free

---

*Protesters at Dallas/Fort Worth made it clear what they thought of airports. They took out advertisements in the local paper. "Is this what we want? Cheap taverns? Honky-tonks? Go-go dancers? Gay bars? Crime? Dope? It can happen here." They failed to stop the airport.

shops, the departure bars and restaurants, for the car-hire firms and travel companies and banks. There are girl pilots.

Their public consists very largely of temporarily liberated men, away from home, footloose and fancy free. The girls quickly get bored with this. "After a day of every passenger trying to flirt with you, the last thing you want to do is see them in the evening," says an air girl. Hence the key club and room parties with visiting crews and stewardesses in airport hotels, in an attempt to relax away from the customers.

2

Into the Jungle

The traveling public is continuously, if surreptitiously, watched by the citizens of the airport—at times with a view to fleecing the passenger, at others to prevent the passenger fleecing them. This jungle is seldom neutral.

The whole process begins with the buying of the tickets. On some flights it is possible that no two passengers have paid the same amount. Fares have become so complicated that there are more than 25 different rates on the North Atlantic alone. Within the U.S. there are regular, first, coach and night fares, 30-day advance purchase fares, group fares, package fares and any number of promotional fares. The cost depends on how early you book, how old you are, at what time of year you want to fly, how many weeks you will be away, whether you are traveling with a group of friends. The time of day and the day of the week also make a difference, as does where you buy the ticket.

Many passengers pay too much, which is not surprising. Who in his right mind would assume that the cheapest way of getting to Calcutta from New York has been to fly to Bangkok, 1,400 miles farther on, and then to buy another ticket for the 2,800-mile round trip from Bangkok to Calcutta?

And many pay too little. Airlines, anxious to fill empty aircraft, sell their tickets at less than the internationally agreed rate.* On many routes in the Far and Middle East and South America, no local would ever dream of paying the correct fare. These cut-rate tickets are marked "Non-Transferable" in the bottom left-hand corner. There is also, as we shall see, a flourishing trade in stolen tickets.

Once the ticket has been acquired, preferably in a legal manner and at the minimum price, the passenger must get to the airport. This can be difficult for those traveling in their native country. Many airport taxi drivers strongly object to driving their fellow countrymen, motivated not by concern for the foreigner but by the prospect of picking up a "mark," someone who can safely be overcharged.

The cab racket at JFK is relatively straightforward. Limousine drivers hustle passengers in the cab line. They offer a flat $25 fare to Manhattan, claiming the standard cab fare to be $20 rather than the actual $14 or so. Once the mark is in the limo, he finds it contains three or four others, thus making the driver upward of $100 for a single trip into town.

Things can be worse abroad. Sometimes legitimately: the $50 charge for the ride from São Paulo's International and Tokyo's Narita airports reflects the prodigious distance from town rather than the driver's dishonesty.

More often, illegitimately: take the case of George Leggett, the amazing New Yorker who saw London on $1,500 a day. Mr. Leggett had the impression that pounds were worth much less than dollars. He spent $200 each way on taxis to and from the airport, remarking that "the drivers looked very pleased." He tipped a waiter $10 for a meal that cost $5 and ran out of money in 36 hours.

---

*They are regularly fined by the International Air Transport Association (IATA) for doing so. British Airways was fined $144,000 for making improper discounts to the traveling public. Other airlines fined in 1976 included Iberia, down for $74,850, KLM for $71,000, Air France for $31,750, Sabena for $28,450, Pan Am for $24,000 and Egyptair for $22,000. Americans could justifiably feel aggrieved that the big U.S. carriers were being so honest at their expense. *Business Traveller*, Winter 1976.

Mr. Leggett's final words were: "I am going home now because I think people could have been more helpful."

Airport cabdrivers throughout the world are rightly mistrusted. Most passengers realize that they should only take a licensed cab with a working meter. There have been plenty of warnings about "pirate" or "gypsy" cabs, where a man with his private car turns up at an airport or downtown terminal on the chance of catching a mark.

But people do strange things in strange countries. They get embarrassed, they do not speak the language, they do not know the currency. All this is instantly summed up by the cabdrivers. There have been so many cases of people being charged up to 40 times the correct fare on the short trip from the West London terminal to Piccadilly Circus that British Airways started putting spiked wheel clamps on any pirate car that turned up at the terminal. Airline buses have warning signs about nonlicensed "taxis."

Nationality is an important clue for drivers. "The Japanese and the Americans are the easiest," says one pirate. "The Japanese normally stick together in big groups, but if you get one on his own, it's easy. They are very polite. They don't like scenes, especially if there are a lot of people around which there always are at an airport or hotel. If they hesitate, you make it quite clear that there will be a hell of a row on the spot if they don't pay up pronto. They always do.

"Americans above all want to be loved when they are abroad. They stick their hand out full of money and tell you to take the fare. Half of them don't know the denominations."

Luggage is also a guide to the mark. "If the suitcases are all covered with labels, gaudy hotel ones from exotic places like Hawaii and Hong Kong and the Caribbean, then that's perfect. I picked up one couple—pink matching luggage, stuck all over with stickers from the Mandarin Hotel, Hong Kong, and Aloha, Honolulu. Luggage like that is lots of cash, no taste and wide open to flattery. You have to be nice and servile, that's all," says a driver, extorting 10 times the normal fare.

"You notice people who keep airline labels on their briefcases, sometimes a great wad of them. Now, that doesn't make sense for someone who travels all the time—every time you close it you get the labels mixed up in the locks. So that means the owner is vain, and you can always play on vanity.

"The one you steer absolutely clear of, that you run from, is an old leather case with nothing on it except the remnants of a shipping line marker. Those people know it all backwards and they won't hesitate to call the law."

The ideal victim comes off a long-distance flight, preferably one that has crossed several time zones. He will be disoriented as well as tired. The pirate will help him change money at the terminal bank.

"You'd be surprised how many people arrive without local money. Once you help them change it, you've got a moral hold on them. They have to trust you. Not only that, but the denominations won't have to be explained to them. If they were on their own, they would ask. Because you're there, they don't," says a driver at Palermo Airport. The tricks of the trade are as international as flying itself.

Women are less easily fleeced than men, because they can instantly query a fare with a policeman, doorman or even a passerby without losing face. This enters the fare equation the driver makes of nationality, sex, baggage and exhaustion.

The moral pendulum swings on arrival at the terminal. It is now the passenger who may be up to no good. The ticket may be stolen or falsified. The passenger may have bought the return half of someone else's ticket, thus getting the benefit of a return rate on a single journey. He may be trying to travel before he has been away long enough to qualify for an excursion fare. With some concessionary fares a quarter the normal rate, the incentives to "bend" a ticket with a little date alteration are great.

A passenger is a potential hijacker as well as a thief. There are several traits that indicate trouble to the check-in staff. The ordinary citizen should be carrying the average amount of luggage for the journey. Hijackers, many of them acting on the spur of the moment, often turn up without any luggage at all. The clothes should tally with the destination. It is suspicious to ask too many questions about the flight and the aircraft.

Concealed weapons, oddly enough, are no guide since so many

non-hijackers carry them. A one-month haul at Le Bourget airport, Paris, comprised 96 rifles, 10 revolvers, 8,100 rounds of ammunition, 56 daggers, 480 sheath knives, 28 screwdrivers, 19 forks, 75 medical syringes and 21 paper knives.

A passport is a more accurate clue. Many political hijackers travel on Arab diplomatic passports. Embarrassments happen. One "terrorist" was relieved of his Bond-style gun, a loaded and gold-plated Walther PPK valued at $6,000. He turned out to be Prince Kalifa bin Ali Al'tani, the brother of the powerful and oil-rich ruler of Qatar. His temper did not improve when the police officer who took his gun managed to fire it accidentally through the floor of the terminal.

Great care must be taken to ensure that Arabs do not get on flights which fly via Israel, and vice versa. One Bangkok-bound charter flight was diverted from a refueling stop in Dubai when it was realized that an Israeli woman was aboard.

If a potential hijacker is spotted, it will be at the check-in desk. The procedure is well established. The check-in man quietly stamps QQ against the seat number on the visual display screen. QQ alerts the security men at the flight gates for thorough searching of the marked passengers.

An AL after a name suggests a drunk. The captain will take a long look at the passenger before deciding whether to let him board. The cabin crew is told to keep a special eye on him, as it would if he was a CM, a "compassionate case" after bereavement, or an NE, a "non-English speaker," or a UC, an "unaccompanied child."

Not all security arrangements work. Pan Am allowed a young bearded man on board a Puerto Rico flight. He was wearing a combat jacket and a beret with a Cuban badge on it. Not surprisingly, he wanted the plane to overshoot Puerto Rico for Havana. The next day Marlon Brando was removed from an aircraft merely for wearing a combat jacket.

The rules for sick passengers are strict, at least in principle. Thus women who are more than seven months pregnant should not fly. The pressure changes could affect the baby. This is as difficult to enforce as the rule that passengers must be able to walk

150 yards unaided and without needing a rest. "If a woman says she isn't seven months gone, what are you supposed to do about it?" a ground hostess points out. "And can you imagine what would happen if I asked an old dear to walk a hundred and fifty yards before she got a boarding card?"

So occasionally babies are born in midair. When a Russian woman gave birth in a Jumbo over the North Atlantic as she sped back to Moscow from Washington, Pan Am said there was no means of proving the length of pregnancy.

Ground staff must turn back passengers with wired jaws or eye injuries. Broken jaws could choke someone who got air-sick; damaged eyes are very sensitive to pressure.

The "No Go" list also includes contagious disease, heart attacks of any strength in the preceding eight weeks, anemia, chest complaints, pneumonia and incontinence. The major hazard is pressure change: a mild "chest cold" can turn into serious altitude sickness on a long flight.

Incontinence seems a strange reason for grounding a mature passenger, since babies can travel freely. However, states KLM: "Changes in atmospheric pressure produce unexpected activity in those conditions and the resulting odors may be aesthetically offensive to other passengers in the enclosed cabin."

Death is also frowned upon. "The death of a passenger in flight," writes KLM's Kanelis Vaandiagen, "may cause serious delays and in some cases has produced international complications." Now you know.

In a place as curious as an airport, even baggage is of interest, partly to the airline, if there is too much of it. Hiding a pile of heavy hand luggage while weighing in a single suitcase is an old trick. If the flight is not too full, most airlines will ignore this. They should not. Their own regulations strictly limit the amount of hand luggage that can be taken aboard. This is because bags and shopping strewn over the cabin make it much more difficult to get out of the aircraft in an emergency. It has little to do with weight: modern jets are powerful enough to carry much more than the prescribed 45 pounds per passenger.

If excess baggage is charged, an airline will inform all other airlines flying that route. There is thus little point in a passenger storming off and trying another airline. Cooperation is not a hallmark of the airline industry, but it is applied in this area.

A more probing and less welcome interest in baggage is shown by thieves, some of them employed as baggage handlers to load the aircraft.

"Something happens to people when they get to airports," says a security man. "They wouldn't dream of letting a suitcase out of their hand, let alone sight, at a subway station. At an airport they'll leave it and go for a stroll or buy a paper. They seem to think that because flying is expensive, you only get nice people at airports. Alas, nothing could be further from the truth."

Far from the problems coming to an end when the baggage is handed over to the airline, that is often when they begin. Consider the cautionary tale of Alwin Schockemoehle, champion German show jumper. Herr Schockemoehle was flying home from London after a most successful week of prize winning in England.

His smart black leather briefcase, with its two differently numbered combination locks, contained the evidence of his equestrian skill. There was a gold watch won in the Nations Cup, another watch as a present for his wife, $800 in small notes for traveling expenses, a spare shirt and most of his winnings from international competitions—$1,000 in tens and $5,000 in ones and fives.

The British Airways flight to Bremen was delayed an hour. Herr Schockemoehle became a little worried: "There were crowds of people around and I thought there was a chance the case might have been stolen. I thought it was safer to give it to British Airways."

All he got at Bremen was his case, with the locks ripped off, and his shirt. Herr Schockemoehle was not aware of a fundamental airport tenet: any unusual or lavish baggage is likely to be stolen.

His baggage fell into both these categories. Briefcases are seldom sent as cargo, normally being carried aboard as cabin luggage by the owner. Briefcases made of black leather with combination locks indicate a certain lavishness. The baggage handler who opened it may well have thought that the case was being sent as cargo because the owner was smuggling out money and did not wish to take it through Emigration himself.

Shockemoehle was perfectly entitled to export that money. But often passengers are not. Passengers smuggle millions of dollars out of U.S. airports every year: money that is hot because it comes from organized crime, or because no tax has been paid on it, or because it evades currency regulations. Favored destinations for hot money from JFK are Zurich, Geneva and the Bahamas, with a second choice of Montreal, London and Frankfurt.

Elsewhere in the country, IRS agents and thieves check out flights from Los Angeles to Taiwan, Hong Kong and Mexico City. The Texas abhorrence of socialist blood money, known as taxes to other citizens, has caused the IRS to publicly deplore the flow of hot money from Texas to the Cayman Islands. More privately, the IRS double-checks baggage leaving Houston's International and Dallas/Fort Worth for Grand Cayman.

So do baggage thieves, for this is a near-perfect crime. Few owners are likely to report their loss, for to do so invites investigation and possible prosecution by the authorities. The thieves keep a sophisticated eye on exchange rates, tax levels, currency regulations and other factors that indicate a flight of money out of the country. "You get a run on the dollar," says a JFK policeman, "and some of it is going to run through an airport."

With huge amounts of cash being used to buy drug shipments, baggage on flights from all U.S. airports to Colombia is of considerable interest to others than the owners.

Currency also comes into the country. While it is legal for it to arrive, it has often illegally left a country with strict regulations. Thus 1979 saw a flood of cash coming through U.S. airports from Iran and the Republic of China. Indians, Argentinians, Chileans and South Africans are others who can take only a very limited amount of cash with them, and who may all be traveling with a wad of notes in their suitcases.

Baggage, or the absence of it, is also used by check-in staff as the ultimate sanction against rude passengers. It is "accidentally" dispatched to Nairobi or Nassau. According to airline legend, luggage mistakenly sent to either of these places has never been found. Neither has much luggage sent there deliberately.

Some passengers are immune to such treatment, no matter how rude they are. They are members of the exclusive airline clubs. Magical things happen to a club member.

He can check in at a first-class counter, even if he is traveling economy. Before takeoff, he is entertained to free drinks, free TV and free charm in a hospitality suite. Extra-swift personal service speeds him through the formalities. If the aircraft is delayed, free telex and telephone ease the annoyance. Once aboard, the stewardesses call him by his name.

Clubs are not restricted to flight privileges. One gives automatic membership at 25 golf clubs from Gleneagles to Bermuda and Corfu, and automatic discounts from hotels like the George V in Paris, the Grosvenor in London, the Plaza in New York. Club members usually qualify for a "Q" (high credit) rating on their Air Travel Cards. This enables them to obtain unlimited numbers of tickets to any destination in the world on any of 140 airlines with the piece of green plastic. The ATC "Q" is perhaps the world's classiest credit card.

Most airlines have their clubs—Pan Am's Clipper Club with its Clipper Skippers, TWA's Ambassador Club, Northwest's Top Flight Club, American Airlines' Admiral's Club, United's Red Carpet Rooms, Eastern's Ionosphere Club. Election depends on how much is spent or how far is flown with the airline, with qualification normally being around $10,000 a year or 100,000 miles. Most airlines review membership annually. Pan Am, however, is good to those who travel less. Their memberships are for life.

Some airlines sell membership for $30 a year. This entitles the traveler to sit in the VIP lounge away from the airport hassle. There is normally a lounge bar and a room for small business meetings, with desks and phones available.

Ordinary passengers may resent the way others sail through a line on the strength of a tie or a special baggage tag, blue for British Airways, silver for Pan Am, marked "Service Plus" for Air

France. Consolation is available from a French businessman. Befriended and unaccustomedly jovial in a German nightclub, he thought that a good way to cement his friendship with his seven new friends would be to fly them all to Tahiti on his "Q" card. By the time he had sobered up, all eight of the happy throng were airborne on first-class tickets. A grand gesture, costing some $14,000.

3

The Black List

It is chilling to listen to pilots describing the many airports they do not like. "High, bad lights, difficult approach—with a strong southerly blowing you can keep it, thanks" is one pilot's view of Ankara. Another says of Gothenburg: "Short runway, prone to bad weather, surrounded by hills; I'll never fly it with an inexperienced crew."

Or Boston: "At night, you have to come in over Boston Bay and you may have to land with a tail wind." Or Los Angeles: "Noise abatement can have you taking off right into a fogbank at night."

"Teheran has the most dangerous conditions I came across," says a long-haul pilot. "A combination of physical danger and human inefficiency. You have to descend close to high mountains with strong winds. The VHF radio is the worst of any major airport. It is virtually unintelligible, although I suppose that could be a blessing in disguise since the controllers are so bad you are better off without them. You find the lights going out, the navigation aids going out."

No pilot enjoys flying to Rhodes at night when there is a westerly wind. He has to approach over a high col between hills only a mile and a half apart, and gusts can blow him off course.

The International Federation of Air Line Pilots' Associations (IFALPA) sums up this very busy holiday airport in alarming style: "Inquiries have indicated that it is not possible to improve this aerodrome and that a completely new one should be constructed. High minima should be considered necessary, especially in high winds and gusty conditions."

Malaga and Alicante, gateways to the Spanish Mediterranean coast, both have high ground to the north. They are tricky when southerlies blow at night. Corfu has hills dangerously close and is badly affected by gusts. Gibraltar is dangerous for purely political reasons. The Spanish, who are reclaiming "the Rock" from the British, forbid aircraft to descend in Spanish airspace and a tricky letdown over the sea results. Ibiza has neither radar nor ILS despite the tourist invasion and the consequent flow of night landings.

Naples has very short runways, with Vesuvius waiting at one end and an area where there is a "cone of radio silence" that affects navigation instruments. Alitalia lost a Viscount with 45 aboard on Vesuvius. At Palermo, in Sicily, pilots complain that there are no proper approach aids, despite the high ground immediately to the south of the airport and the frequent thunderstorms in spring and autumn. An Alitalia DC-8 hit Mount Lunga on the approach in bad weather and 115 died. Venice, Milan and Bari are other Italian airports where inadequate equipment or landing aids have been criticized by the International Civil Aviation Organization.

The same weather pattern affects the Greek holiday airport at Corfu—another spot where IFALPA wants an entirely new airport built. "It is difficult to see how this aerodrome can be improved," the pilots' federation reports. "Unless and until a new aerodrome is built, pilots should only operate here to high weather limits." Innsbruck, a major airport for skiers, is at the end of a valley. Radio aids bounce off the mountainside and lured a propjet with more than 80 skiers into a peak in bad weather. Nicosia has sudden weather changes. Mist shrouds the heights around Lima. The Athens runways "begin in the sea, end in the sea and have mountains at the side," says an American pilot.

Pilots are disturbed by ground controllers unwilling to take responsibility, notably in the Caribbean. The controllers do not like guiding pilots in with an instrument approach where they could be blamed if something went wrong. They prefer pilots to fly visually, where the whole liability rests on the pilots. "You could circle Jamaica and Trinidad until you run out of fuel, and they won't give you instrument approach," a British pilot says phlegmatically. "If you don't go visual, you don't get down."

IFALPA marks airports which its members reckon to be "critically deficient by international standards" with a black star. Other airports, considered unsafe but less dangerously so, are classified with red and then orange stars.

Some famous international airports qualify for black stars. Boston's Logan International is a busy center, but the pilots say that new noise-control rules mean that planes can be forced to take off or land downwind at night and require departing and arriving planes to fly toward each other on the same runway. At Los Angeles, noise rules mean that aircraft must land and take off over the ocean, forcing some planes to fly downwind rather than into the wind. A TWA 707 crashed while attempting a downwind landing in poor visibility.

St. Thomas, in the Virgin Islands, is given black-star status because its runway is too short for jets. An American Airlines jet ran off the end of the runway while trying to abort its landing. Pago Pago, in American Samoa, is slated for heavy rain and sea spray on the runway. There is no approach lighting in one direction and the runway and taxiway lighting is inadequate. Navigational aids and weather information are held to be poor. An optical illusion by rain was held partly to blame for a Pan Am crash there.*

Nassau, in the Bahamas, is blacked for severe runway irregularity, poor runway and taxiway markings, no sea rescue launches, lack of navigational aids and obstruction lights on Runway 14.

---

*All survived the TWA crash on January 16, 1974. The American Airlines crash, on April 27, 1976, was also survivable. The Pan Am crash, on January 30, 1974, was not.

So is Kai Tak, gateway to Hong Kong, positioned in the heart of bustling Kowloon, with flats and hotels only 50 feet under the flight path. IFALPA has noted a deterioration in air traffic control, inadequate runway length (several aircraft have landed in the harbor after overshooting), and inadequate separation between runway and taxiway. Surrounded by soaring, steep-sided hills, subject to mist and low cloud as well as typhoons, and with overflying of the Chinese mainland prohibited, Hong Kong is already a difficult enough place to fly to. And it is one of Asia's busiest tourist and business airports.

Colombia is peppered with black stars. Bogotá, Barranquilla, Cali, Cartagena, Leticia, San Andres Island and Medellin all need more and better fire and safety equipment and all those except Cartagena need more navigational aids. Bogotá is very high in a mountain bowl that is subject to sudden mists. "It's called Bogotá Eldorado Airport," says a long-haul pilot. "It's very apt. You feel you've struck gold just by finding it."

The normal flying standards in Australia are high. But flight charts warn pilots to beware of kangaroos and birds on the runway at Learmouth, and Kalgoorlie and Meekatharra are considered inadequate alternates for international flights.

Medan airport in Indonesia is one to miss. The controllers' English is poor, the taxiways are narrow, the fire equipment and firemen are inadequate, flight control clearances are "unrealistic," landing control is "virtually nonexistent," there are often pedestrians on the runway and gliders operate without control. Ujung Pandang, not far away, is not much better—difficult to contact by radio at night, short of qualified flight controllers and with poor communications equipment.

In Italy, Alghero has inadequate approach lighting, fire-fighting equipment and air traffic control services. Rimini, which has very congested traffic, needs approach lighting, a visual glide slope and runway identification lights.

Osaka, in Japan, has taxiways that are too close to the runways and the runways themselves are slippery when wet and need their approach lights altered. The navigational aids are inadequate and the missed approach procedure could result in a collision.

Penang, the holiday island off Malaya, has a rough runway surface, inadequate runway markings, pedestrians along the runways, an "unrealistic" approach procedure, deficient navigational aids and no radar or wind-speed indicator. Fua'amotu, on Tonga, has navigational aids that are either "unsatisfactory" or "missing."

Mexico City, Bombay and Nassau are amongst the busy airports that get red stars. So does JFK, for poor snow removal, unsafe noise control necessitating a curving approach, and too many maintenance trucks about. Honolulu has no runway grooving to prevent aquaplaning and there are no approach lights for landing. Anchorage, halfway point on the Polar Route from Europe to Japan, gets its red star for danger during crosswinds.

Standards on isolated islands should be particularly high. Aircraft carry additional "island reserves" to give them extra circling time, as they have no alternative. Some pilots "top up for Mom and Dad," putting on extra fuel to get them to an alternative, such as New York from Bermuda. Bermuda is very isolated in the Atlantic. Yet it is criticized for approach and landing lighting, and for shortage of navigational equipment. Both Bermuda and Darwin, another "island airport" in Australia, have only one runway. If the plane in front crashes on it, those following would have nowhere to land. An "island airport" is categorized in terms of isolation. Thus Darwin qualifies even though it is on the Australian mainland.

St. Martin, in the Leeward Islands, had no precision approach equipment when an Overseas National Airways flight approached it in bad weather. The pilot bit deeply into his fuel reserves during three attempts to land in torrential rain. He ditched in the sea 30 miles off St. Croix when he finally ran out of fuel, killing 23.

Even lonelier is Easter Island, in the Pacific. Yet it has no weather forecasts or reliable navigational aids. There are no obstruction lights in the dangerously high terrain on both sides of the runway. The approach lighting is bad, and the runway length substandard. Communications with Santiago and Tahiti are poor. There is no crash or salvage equipment, no first aid and no search and rescue facilities.

To cap it all, reports IFALPA, "there is just not enough information from the French about radiation levels after nuclear experiments."

Farther into the Pacific, Suva-Nausoui, on Fiji, has a narrow runway and unreliable navigational aids. Pools of water collect on the runway after heavy rain and cattle are frequently reported wandering in the airport.

Addis Ababa collects its red star for an unsatisfactory runway surface, poor communications between Addis and aircraft in the Sahara area, and a shortage of navigational aids. Khartoum, the only other airport in this wild area of mountains and desert, has poor approach and runway lighting, bad air traffic control and "antiquated, poorly sited and maintained equipment."

Manila is scored for everything from unswept, dirty runways to lack of fire-fighting equipment and poor electricity supplies. The radar is unreliable, is frequently out of order and should be used for training only. Weather briefings are inadequate, and there are frequent navigation and lighting failures. Manila's primary alternate, where the aircraft will go in the not unlikely case of something being wrong with Manila, is Mactan, also in the Philippines. At Mactan, "the power supply is unreliable, subject to failures, affecting all aids, including runway lights."

A pilot diverting here from Manila would already have some problems.* But he could easily find himself over Mactan with no runway lights, no airport lights and no town lights. When the airport darkens, so does the town. "You could very easily not know that Mactan existed. It's better blacked out than anything in the war," says one pilot.

In Germany IFALPA has awarded a red star for a shortage of safety equipment on one runway at Frankfurt, Europe's second-busiest airport. Bremen, Stuttgart and Saarbrücken have also been starred.

The busy airport at Djakarta, capital of Indonesia, is savaged by the pilots. "Air traffic control procedures are in need of vast

*An alternate should expect different weather from the main airport. This is usual if it is on the other side of high ground or inland instead of coastal. If it is on the other side of a city or industrial area, simultaneous fog and haze is less likely.

improvement; the taxiway and runway surface conditions are deteriorating rapidly; runway extension is required. Navaids and radar required; search and rescue facilities have inadequate coverage." At one stage Australian pilots refused to fly there.

The control towers of Turkey's two major airports at Istanbul and Ankara lost all contact with planes in flight for more than two hours in October 1976. At that time there were 20 aircraft that were airborne and dependent on the towers. Contact with them was only re-established through the Turkish military.

All the aircraft got down safely on that occasion. But a Turkish Airlines captain was on the approach to Istanbul airport on a January night in 1975 when all the lights and beacons went out. Although emergency power was restored later, he crashed the F 28 into the Sea of Marmara and all 4 crew and 38 passengers died. Portland, Oregon, gets an orange star for poor runway lighting.

The predictable troubles with airports are lack of navigational aids (navaids), runway length and closeness to mountains or high ground. All these can be dangerous.

Delhi, for example, has long been notorious for bad navaids. Four aircraft crashed on the approach to Delhi in two years. A Qantas pilot* said he and his 150 passengers were lucky to survive after nearly being steered into the ground. He said the airport "cannot be depended upon at any stage." He survived only by ignoring ground instructions and landing visually.

Cairo is disliked by many crews. "If the controllers have got one aircraft in the sky, that's enough. They can't cope with two," says an American pilot. Cairo became so bad that IFALPA refused to make night landings there after two crashes, one of which, a Pakistan International 707, killed 119 people. The airport was said to have insufficient fire fighting equipment, inadequate landing aids and high ground on the approach to the runway.

Japanese radio controllers are overanxious and often difficult to

---

*Captain McManus, the Qantas captain, said that the control tower had given a cloud base of 700 feet when it was in fact less than 500 feet. Commenting on the incident, Reuters noted that four aircraft had crashed on the Delhi approach in the past two years.

understand. English is the international language for air traffic control, and the Japanese have particular difficulty in pronouncing numerals clearly. Pilots flying to Japan have special lessons in poor English, which ranges from "flight" becoming "fright," to the more serious inability to pronounce words like "vector" and "steer."

Air traffic controllers in French-speaking Canada went on strike to force pilots to use both French and English, and Air Canada was ordered to translate flight operation manuals into French, as part of the language tension there. Air Canada pilots complained that the issue threatened safety.

Moscow has notoriously sloppy controllers with very poor English, though the standards improve markedly farther east on the routes from Europe to Japan. Moscow has no civil airport to divert to, and Western pilots are not given any details of military airfields for emergency landing. "It's get in or die at Moscow," says a British pilot.

Caracas can be fatally misleading. "You don't realize the mountains are so close at night. You have to point in toward them before turning left for the runway. Some people have kept going too long," says a charter pilot. The combination of mountains and sea produces sudden mists. Rio de Janeiro also has an approach toward mountains that is dangerous in bad weather.

Building work at an airport can be dangerous. TWA's prestige Flight 800 from Rome suffered a reversed engine on its takeoff run. The 707 slued off the runway. It then hit a parked steamroller and burst into flames. A DC-8 crashed at JFK airport because a small stone being asphalted on a new taxiway was thrown up by the engine wake onto the tail as it taxied past. When the pilot pulled back the elevator on takeoff, the stone jammed the tail. The aircraft stalled and crashed.

Strong crosswinds sweep across the runways at Bermuda, Prestwick and Hong Kong in winter.* The maximum crosswind allowed for most jets is a steady 25 knots. Any more would risk

---

*There are three main types of winds created by local topography to avoid: valley winds, with Innsbruck an example; mountain gap winds, as at Genoa; and headland winds, which affect Gibraltar.

bursting tires through the sideways pressure on them. But pilots often have to fly on the maximum to Bermuda and Hong Kong, as the diversionary fields are far away in New York and Bangkok. With gusting winds, pilots must add up to 23 mph to their approach speed to insure maximum control during the gusts.

High buildings are as dangerous close to airports as high ground. But large hotels have been built close to airports and on flight paths in Majorca, Miami and Beirut.

Pilots are still anxious about Tokyo's new international airport at Narita. Although the $2.8 billion facility is well equipped, pilots remember that the Japanese Transport Minister ordered 13,000 riot police to protect him from opponents when he opened it. The radicals have subsequently fire-bombed it and cut air traffic control cables.

The most embarrassing airports to pilots are those that are side by side. Sharjah and Dubai in the Persian Gulf, Bombay and Juhu in India, and London Heathrow and London Northolt are the best examples. They have similar looking parallel runways. In one week, five jets landed at Sharjah thinking it was Dubai. Jets have landed accidentally at both Juhu and Northolt. A Pan Am 707 landed at Santo Domingo's military airport instead of the civil airport seven and a half miles away in 1977.

Perversely, although almost everything in the air is regulated by international law, there are no international standards at all for the most important ground installation of all—the airport runways. Local authorities design their runways as they see fit. Aircraft are limited by length of runway, and by the degree of up-and-down slope, but not by the general design.

Why such a vital part of safe flight should not be regulated passes comprehension. Research shows that runway design has a profound effect on pilots' visual judgment, particularly when approaching in bad weather with only a few seconds of decision time to set up a safe landing. Fat, short runways make a pilot feel he is lower than he actually is, so that he may put on full power and overshoot. A long, thin runway creates an even more dangerous optical illusion. The pilot thinks he is higher than he is, so that he reduces power and may crash short of the runway.

As for facilities, a long-haul pilot was taxiing his aircraft out for takeoff at Bangkok. He noticed sharp metal debris in front of him and stopped his laden 747. "That is potentially disastrous debris," he says. "It could slash your tires and put you out of control on the takeoff run. I radioed through for the emergency services to clear it. By normal standards, there would have been a fire crew there in ninety seconds.

"I radioed eight times over a period of twenty-five minutes. Nothing. In the end I got through on our company frequency and our station manager had to come out and clear it himself. Never, never crash at Bangkok. And if you do, pray you never catch fire."

Binoculars have replaced radar at some airports. Things became so chaotic during the rebuilding of Cairo Airport in 1979 that the radar was out of use for most of the time. The air traffic controllers took to using binoculars to keep tabs on aircraft.

One binocular-guided Egyptair 737 pilot found himself taking off directly into another jet that was landing from the opposite end of the runway.

"I lifted my head in time to see an Arab 707 rushing toward me," said Captain Safwat Ismail.* "I was taking off and he was landing into me. We were both over runway 23. I took a fast swerve left in time to get out of his way. He just kept on coming."

The controllers, searching the sky through their binoculars, thought that the 707 was coming in to land in the same direction as the Egyptair was taking off. They could not pick it up in their binoculars. This was not surprising since it was in fact flying in the opposite direction, straight toward the 737.

Captain Ismail commented: "Cairo airport radar seldom works and the radio system is weak. I think that the three hundred passengers and myself can count ourselves rather lucky." A truly Anglo-Saxon understatement.

Cairo Airport admitted that there was some room for improvement in safety standards. "It does appear," said an airport spokesman, "that binoculars are not a complete substitute for radar."

---

*Al Ahram, Cairo, July 18, 1979. The incident took place in broad daylight and excellent visibility on July 17, 1979.

Things are not always that bad, of course—which is borne out by the fact that flying by commercial jet in the U.S. is now 15 times safer than driving in a car. Insurance companies charge pilots no more for policies than bank clerks.

And there are airports that pilots positively enjoy. In the U.S., they go for Dallas/Fort Worth, Minneapolis/St. Paul, Kansas City, Miami and Dulles International. They like the lack of congestion, the wide spaces between runways and taxiways, and the general lack of tension. Abroad, they like London's Heathrow, Amsterdam's Schiphol, Paris' de Gaulle and Frankfurt.

But for pure and perverse danger no airport can compare with Kerman Airport in Iran. Captain Moini, flying over it in his Iran Air jet, could get no reply from the control tower. He radioed the police to find out what was wrong. On entering the tower, Police Inspector Dohwar found it deserted. A note was propped up on the main control panel: "I am leaving. My time is definitely up."*

*_Teheran Journal,_ October 12, 1977.

4

Crime: Simple as JFK

"This airport," according to Queens District Attorney John J. Santucci, "is a playground for the underworld. Any crime is possible here." He was referring to JFK, but the same could be said of many other airports across the U.S.

Santucci revealed that members of his staff had been able to buy a wide selection of radios, stereos and tape recorders, cameras and guitars for 10 percent of market value. They had even been offered bulletproof vests and telephone debugging gadgets.

This particular racket involved a corrupt airport policeman, a delivery service manager, an airport truck driver, a freight shed foreman and an airport dispatcher. Although it also involved the theft of stock certificates in a multimillion-dollar operation, Santucci found that neither the airport nor the airlines, nor even the FBI, wanted to know.

"The FBI is part of a group telling me that there's no crime at Kennedy Airport," he says. "I don't know why. At every meeting we are told that Kennedy is a Garden of Eden. Nobody cooperates in those investigations. If I want to fandango, I go to a dance, not to meetings with those law enforcement officials."

The FBI can point to the permanent staff of 12 agents it maintains at JFK to prove that it takes the problem seriously, but there is much truth in what Santucci says. Airports are riddled with thefts. It happens right around the world: Her Majesty's Judge Edie, a man after Santucci's own heart, said when sentencing a loader at London's Heathrow for stealing from passenger baggage, "We have to deal with airport loaders, handlers and other people who seem to steal all the time. I sometimes wonder if they do much else. The place has literally become a cesspool. Dishonesty at airports is an international scandal."

A major reason is that, as Santucci says, much of the crime is never reported. Airlines, shipping concerns, manufacturers and labor unions frequently collude and fail to report thefts. "They only report it to their insurance companies, which pay them and everybody knows that the consumer pays with higher rates," says Santucci; "somewhere along the line, people find it profitable not to report thefts."

Airlines, for public relations reasons, prefer to describe items as lost rather than stolen. Airport police, keen to minimize crime figures in their bailiwick, are all too happy to go along with this.

The unwritten airport motto is: "Say it didn't happen or at least say it didn't happen here." For often, of course, there is no evidence as to which continent a theft took place on, let alone in which part of which airport. A million-dollar consignment of diamonds found empty on delivery in New York City had been flown from Johannesburg via Amsterdam. "You don't know whether to start in Africa, Europe or in the U.S.," says a harassed investigator.

He mentioned $78,000 worth of polished diamonds that failed to reach Hong Kong on an aircraft that had stopped at London, Frankfurt, Teheran, Delhi and Bangkok on its way. Each airport shuffled and said that since there was no proof of what had happened, no crime had been committed.

If this applies to freight, it applies even more to passenger baggage. The essence of catching loaders who rifle baggage is speed and the speed of travel itself works against detection. Flights are turned around in an hour or so, roar off thousands of miles away, and what airport police call the "jet blur" sets in. By the time a theft is discovered and it filters back to JFK many hours will have passed. The passenger's baggage may have passed through foreign Customs, through foreign loaders and airport taxis or buses, to a foreign porter in a distant hotel before the passenger is aware that anything is missing.

Who, then, can say the thief is a JFK loader, when it could be a Japanese bellhop?

The fact that many thefts are not officially reported, let alone investigated, explains the shockingly high real crime rate. Many loaders are on the "lucky dip"; just how lucky they can be is seen in the typical case of Louis Gagliardi, a JFK cargo handler arrested for the alleged theft of more than $80,000 worth of items.

Almost any suitcase can be opened by one of three keys or a piece of plastic. The combination-lock suitcase did not fool the loaders for long: it is dropped on its corner and obligingly opens.

Favorite targets are the Japanese, and passengers from countries with financial problems. The Japanese normally travel with suitcases well filled with valuable photographic and electronic gear, and entire tour groups can be stripped. Travelers smuggling money in their cases are unlikely to report theft. They include all passengers from countries where only a small currency allowance may legally be brought out, so loaders are, at present, very interested in Iranians, Taiwanese, Argentinians, South Africans, Indians, Brazilians and Congolese.

Cash is the most attractive target. Bank notes are negotiable with a fence at 70 percent of face value, whereas precious metals and precious stones fetch only 15 to 20 percent. Stones may have to be recut. Metals have identifying numbers on the bars, but if they are melted down, the stamp of purity will be lost. Furthermore, many countries have regulations against individuals' holding bullion. Gold coins like Kruggerrands do not have these disadvantages and are thus popular.

Although bank notes, traveler's checks and gold coins disappear in the U.S., they are difficult to dispose of in less sophisticated areas. Clothing is the stock-in-trade of loaders at airports in Africa and the Far East, with cameras and tape recorders as targets of opportunity.

Luggage for expensive destinations like Las Vegas year around,

Miami and Geneva in winter, Rio at Carnival and Nice at Cannes film festival time is widely looted. The villains know all the events in the international calendar. Thus Lewis R. Wasserman of Universal Pictures checked in via London for a flight to Venice. The film festival was on, indicating booty—in this case $80,000 in jewelry.

"You combine luggage and destination, and make an educated guess," says a loader. "Gucci luggage bound for L.A.—you could dip lucky from a movie mogul's old lady. Pink leather matching cases, February, destination Bermuda, Seychelles or Nassau—I'm not choosy—you could dip some rocks. Particularly if they have first-class tags. Now, April, Paris, discreet brown leather, a bit old, that could have some really classy stuff but you wouldn't expect it to travel first. People with old cases and old money travel tourist.

"That's outgoing. Incoming, Iran and Taiwan provide hot political money. You keep a good eye on any quality luggage from Nicaragua, Guatemala and San Salvador, particularly if it originates from out there and isn't a returning American. It's amazing how many people put their name and address on the outside of their bags. What's in a name? Everything. You put a Gomez or whatever and a local address on a first-class case out of Managua or Guatemala City and there's a good chance it'll be stacked.

"Same with a lot of Caribbean countries. A rich traveler from a poor country is a crook's delight. Not only because these travelers are often very successful crooks themselves, having ripped off an entire nation through politics or plantations or whatever, but also because they are very trusting. They just load up their cases and it never occurs to them that anyone would steal from *them*. Probably nobody would, back home: he'd get shot. Here, things are different."

Sometimes, the size of a theft at JFK makes it impossible to write it off as a "loss." Thus, the largest cash theft in U.S. history took place at JFK late in 1978. It proves, beyond much doubt, that the Mafia has operated at JFK for years and has a strong grip on it.

Two weeks before Christmas, six armed men in ski masks paralyzed one of the world's most sophisticated security systems with all the ease of inside knowledge. Without shooting or seriously hurting anyone, they awarded themselves America's biggest pre-Christmas present, and disappeared into the dark of the early morning, unseen.

The robbers arrived early on a Monday, at 3:05 A.M., in a black Ford delivery truck. They cut the chains on the heavy steel plates that led into the Lufthansa freight area. Once they had driven in, they carefully reshut the gates.

Lufthansa employee Kerry Wheelan saw the truck drive up on the freight ramp. The six men in the woolen masks were carrying revolvers and a rifle. Wheelan and eight workers in the Lufthansa canteen were rounded up.

The robbers had to get the solitary shift worker on the second floor. They shouted that there was an important phone call for him from the head office in Frankfurt. He promptly arrived and joined his colleagues, lying face down with hands tied on the canteen floor. By 3:20 A.M. all the Lufthansa night staff were seized.

The alarm on the main entrance door was turned off and the black Ford was driven inside it. The robbers knew exactly what to expect. There were jewels worth more than $850,000 in 35 registered packets, including gems, watches and Italian goldwork. There were boxes with $5 million in unmarked dollar bills. Other boxes contained gold bars, bought by U.S. servicemen in Germany and being transferred from the Frankfurt Kommerzbank to the Chase Manhattan.

An accomplice in Lufthansa had told them that the valuable freight was to be left lying around over the weekend. The whole plan had almost gone awry the Monday before. Given the zealous nature of air crime, it was perhaps not surprising that $2,000 was stolen by somebody else that weekend between Frankfurt and New York. Lufthansa tightened security and the gang, after turning up and sitting in their van by the gate for 90 minutes, was frightened off. They returned the following Monday.

Opening the strong room was no difficulty. The gang ripped the shift leader's wallet from his pocket, held the picture of his family in front of his eyes, and warned him that he wouldn't be seeing them again unless he turned off the alarm systems and opened the strong room. He obliged.

It is hard work loading more than $6 million and it took the gang 40 minutes. They drove off in unflustered calm. The Red Baron Caper, as it has been named in deference to Lufthansa, the German flag carrier, was a total success both in conception and performanace. The gang messed it up later but that is another story.

Even before the Red Baron Caper, Santucci had warned: "If we don't do something soon, then the criminal rackets will get so big that no man will be able to control them."

It is all too easy for the Mafia to recruit the labor force at JFK and other U.S. airports. "It's a three-step procedure," says an airport policeman (not all of whom are sky-blue incorruptibles themselves). "Those who aren't in debt already are encouraged to get into it. They are tempted to indulge in Mafia-controlled gambling, prostitution and narcotics. Huge interest rates then squeeze the debtor. Either he tries to pay off the money by stealing on his own or he goes to the Mafia and steals from the freight sheds for them."

Santucci followed one consignment of Minolta cameras that arrived at JFK from Los Angeles with United. They should have gone to Berlin with Pan Am. In the meantime, they were stored in a freight depot.

They never made it to Berlin. Transferred to another airport depot, they were sold off by Mafiosi Patty Coco and Pasquale Rainone on the black market at 10 percent of market price. The word "theft" was never mentioned in the insurance claim.

Fur robberies at JFK became so bad that an air freight company refused to truck fur shipments to the airport. Thefts of registered mail from the airport have amounted to many millions of dollars. In a three-year period, from 1967 to 1970, it was estimated that $70 million in negotiable and nonnegotiable securities had been stolen.

To stop the thefts, the U.S. Postal Service has had to start a security system similar to the old Wells Fargo stagecoaches. It is called Con-Con, short for Concentrated Conveyance. Armed guards accompany every shipment of mail to and from the airport. Postal security officers, wearing .38 caliber revolvers, accompany the mail trucks out to the aircraft and check the shipments into the holds.

Registered mail sacks are held at JFK under guard until the flight is ready. After takeoff security men in destination cities are warned. They meet the flight and guard the sacks to the post offices. Use of night flights was eliminated to make thefts harder. All registered mail to JFK travels only in daylight.

This has been good for the U.S. Postal Service, but bad for everyone else, since the gangster's greed is now concentrated on them. During a typical four-month period at JFK, a wide variety of air cargo was stolen—pharmaceuticals worth $136,000, industrial diamonds, Wyoming jade, raw furs and leather, Italian sunglasses, cigarette lighters, baby foods, tape decks, wigs and machine tools.

Two murders occurred at JFK within a month in 1970, at the height of an airport crime wave. A barman was shotgunned by thieves for not emptying his cash register quickly enough. A rich businessman was robbed and shot.

A Permanent Senate Subcommittee set up to investigate crime at JFK heard evidence from a master mail thief who admitted stealing more than $100 million between September 1960 and September 1970. Robert F. Cudak said that he had received $1 million for his share, but had wasted it all gambling. Most had been stolen at New York and Florida airports, but Cudak said he had also "hit" airports in Las Vegas and Los Angeles.

He began stealing mail shortly after starting work as a ramp man for Northwest Airlines at JFK. He left Northwest, where he said he had been employed despite a prior criminal record, for a full-time career of theft. He was so successful that he employed "chopmen" who drove to the airport to collect stolen goods.

No photographs of Cudak were allowed at the hearing, and it was said that he would have to be given a new identity and a completely new life to avoid a revenge murder by organized crime at the airport. John B. Eaton, a witness in a conspiracy case involving $43 million stolen at JFK, was shot dead near Miami International Airport.

Airport theft has become so sophisticated that almost anything that is stolen can be sold. In a typical case, an importer flew in a large shipment of doeskin gloves to JFK, where they vanished. To his fury, the importer discovered in a few weeks that the gloves were being sold on the West Coast.

The gloves had been flown from JFK to Tijuana, Mexico, and sold as legitimate merchandise, at a reduced price, to a West Coast jobber. The jobber had then sold them to one of the largest department stores in San Diego.

Mafia control at JFK was so great that the leading world airlines were forced to use Mafia trucking companies. An independent trucker known as Direct Airport Service, Inc., tried to break the Mafia stranglehold by hauling freight to the airport. National and Northwest Airlines, anxious to break the racket combine, attempted to use Direct.

Direct discovered that 38 tires on trucks it had parked at JFK had been slashed and ruined. A Direct truck on the crowded Long Island Expressway went out of control when its rear wheels came off. Investigation showed that the lugs on the wheels had been loosened. When the same thing happened to another Direct truck a few days later it was obvious that the largest airlines, whatever their wishes, could not use Direct.

Other airports are as bad. Captain Robert L. Herzog of the Massachusetts State Police echoed the old complaint that airlines were not reporting thefts at Boston's Logan International Airport. He sent some detectives, disguised as truck drivers, to the airport and filmed them in action "stealing cartons of freight, driving away a truck loaded with freight." The film was shown to the airlines—which took no action. Chicago and Montreal, where stock thefts have reached $2 million and $500,000 respectively, are also crime-ridden.

Theft, the police say bitterly, is "as easy as JFK."

The U.S. is not alone. Newspapers have christened London's Heathrow airport "Thiefrow." It is the daddy of them all.

Thefts run at more than $15 million a year with the sort of slickness that enabled $88,000 of Bank of America traveler's checks to be cashed in downtown London before anyone knew they had been stolen.

Despite Heathrow's miserable record, the same Garden of Eden attitude is taken as at JFK. Researching this book, I was summoned by a British Airports Authority public affairs official. "A little dickeybird tells me," he said with a face both straight and sullen, "that you have been sniffing around the police station and talking to people about crime. We would hate the public to get the wrong impression, to think there is a crime problem here. Because there isn't one, apart from the odd, tiny crime you could get anywhere."

One gang stole $400,000 worth of bullion in a week. Another took $388,000 in diamonds over a period of two months; a third lifted $600,000 of platinum over a year; a judge has called the place a cesspool. But what is cess to a judge, to the devoted airport official is as sweet as roses.

When industrial diamonds worth $212,500 disappeared in a four-day spell, so sensitive was Heathrow to the charge they had been stolen there that the insurance company was refused permission to post reward notices, although it posted them everywhere else the planes had touched down on their way from South Africa to Holland.

The airport attracts some of the keenest criminal minds. Scotland Yard has described the robbery of one bullion van on its way to Heathrow as "the most perfect crime of the century."

The van was on a regular run to Heathrow from a City vault. Its cargo was $218,000 worth of bullion and jewels destined for overseas flights. It was going along Pall Mall, the heart of London's clubland. Outside the austere Athenaeum, the van was blocked by two men arguing with each other, their cars stopped in the middle of the road.

They moved off, shouting at each other through their car windows. The van went up St. James's, past Overton's and Lock's, turned left at the Ritz Hotel and drove down Piccadilly. At Hyde Park Corner, the van dipped out of sight down the underpass that leads to Knightsbridge and on down the Cromwell Road to Heathrow.

The two cars stopped, blocking the van again. The drivers did not argue this time. They threatened the bullion van crew with guns.

On the surface, at the start of the underpass, another two cars stopped. The drivers leaped out and carried on a furious argument. This blocked off the underpass, and a massive traffic jam built up back along Piccadilly. Even if the police had received an emergency call from the van, they could not have gotten to the scene—and the van's radio was ineffective, since it was 20 feet below the ground.

In four minutes, the van was stripped of its cargo and the crew was tied up. The loot disappeared along Knightsbridge in the cars. The drivers causing the Piccadilly jam settled their dispute and drove off. Apart from the empty van and crew, there has been no trace of anything since.

Other crimes have been as breathtakingly simple. A hitchhiker, dressed in an airline parka, stopped a British Airways van on the airport in 1973. He said he wanted a lift to another part of the airport. Once in the van he pulled out a revolver and escaped with its cargo—diamonds from a Ghana Airways flight and platinum from South African Airways, just arrived from Johannesburg. His haul was worth $934,000.

Union shop stewards have advised their members to treat plainclothes policemen on aircraft as hijackers if they refuse to identify themselves. The bad relations between police and workers have been conducive to nothing but further crime. The arrest of three loaders in 1976 led to a strike by 90 others. A police hotline was set up so that anything suspicious could be reported. So far, it has only been instrumental in solving the theft of a passenger's box of cigars.

The easiest crime netted the thief $4 million. He was working for an American air courier firm. One summer day in 1976 he went around to the firm's clients, picking up the packets of money and valuables due to be forwarded by them. He then got on a plane and flew to Switzerland with the $4 million. His previous criminal record had not prevented his employment as a courier of bank notes, although the flashy behavior that had tipped off police to his earlier crimes soon alerted the Swiss police.

A Swiss insurance company has put a 100 percent premium on cargoes going to or transshipping at Heathrow. Things have gotten so bad with diamonds and currency that the mining corporations and the big dealers now send couriers with the gems: the air fares are cheaper than the premiums.

The couriers fly first class, in sober business suits, with an occasional glimpse of metal chain between immaculate shirt cuff and briefcase.

Other areas have difficulties. The most famed of them all was the Airborne Loader of Orly, one Fernand Romain, who had himself loaded in a packing case onto Air France flights. This gave him uninterrupted time to "faire le lucky dip" before climbing back into his packing case on landing. On his last trip he successfully stole $44,000 worth of gems on an Orly–Algiers flight before an underworld informant ended his career.

Passengers themselves can be highly dishonest, blaming loaders for stealing nonexistent but highly insured valuables. Kamuel M. Solomon, an Egyptian citizen domiciled in Frankfurt, checked four cases weighting 73 kilos onto a Paris–London flight. He paid the excess baggage charges.

He arrived at Heathrow to find his baggage had "disappeared." The baggage tags with the excess amounts were firmly stapled on his ticket. He claimed that handsome shoes, overcoats and suits befitting a gentleman had all vanished. He produced receipts for his typewriter, Polaroid camera outfit and a woman's fur coat.

The coat receipt was found to be fraudulent. That alone ended the lucrative career of Mr. Solomon and presumably of his anonymous accomplice, who simply took the same flight as Mr. Solomon and "stole" his luggage at the destination airport by walking out with the cases. Mr. Solomon had previously made claims against Alitalia, Lufthansa, Libyan Arab Airlines, Air France, Sabena, KLM and Swissair.

Sometimes passengers pick up the wrong suitcase quite inadvertently, with startling results. An Australian girl flew to Shannon on an Aer Lingus flight from Copenhagen. Also on the flight were $77,000 worth of diamonds intended for the South African-owned Shannon Diamond Company. Her luggage was wrongly labeled by SAS in Denmark. Instead of her case with her clothes, she left the airport with the diamonds.

Airborne crime is not unknown. Professionals flew the airlanes between Entebbe and England and Canada during the Ugandan

Asian crisis. Many Asians were smuggling out money. In a typical case, a professional confidence trickster struck up a conversation with a Ugandan refugee.

He found the man had $6,000 concealed underneath photographs in a family album and in the frames of large wedding pictures. "Aha," said the con man, "it's illegal to bring in that sort of money, but I understand these things. I know how you have to fix those Customs officers. I'll be delighted to take it through for you." The Ugandan was convinced and handed over the valuable photo collection.

There are airborne pickpockets, taking advantage of the casual way people leave jackets heavy with wallets, traveler's checks and passports when they go to the lavatory. People are seldom as loaded with valuables as when they fly, and seldom so off their guard.

What hope for the honest passenger? Common sense, say the police. It is absurd to travel with valuables in a suitcase. The suitcase can be lost by the airline just as easily as it could be rifled. Yet time and again women travel with jewelry, and men with cameras, in their suitcases. If a passenger has to put valuables in his luggage, experience shows that the safest thing is a cheap suitcase with plenty of string around it. Loaders are not likely to start playing round with knots when there are fat Antler or Samsonite cases around.

Do not put name and address on the outside of a case where it may suggest potential loot to a loader or reveal an empty house at home. Put name tags inside.

Or you could take the advice of Caesar B. Pattarini, who runs the three big airports in the New York metropolitan area. "You shouldn't travel with bags anyway," says Mr. Pattarini. "You should have a set of clothes your size waiting at the other end, like Onassis used to."

The airlines are partly to blame for the public ignorance of the high crime rates at airports. Police have tried to get warnings printed on tickets and baggage tags without success. In the same way that many airlines refuse to admit that a crash is a possibility, most prefer to pretend that crime does not exist.

Some thieves specialize in "sob snatches"—taking luggage while the owner is tearfully saying goodbye or being joyously reunited with his family, without a thought for his possessions.

Thieves inhabit the oddest corners of airports. JFK has had tires stolen from aircraft. A bulldozer disappeared from a building site. "We haven't had an aircraft stolen yet," says a policeman. "But it's happened at Miami and I expect we'll get it here soon enough."

The easiest field is tickets. Ticket frauds are becoming commonplace.

The Mafia and organized crime have exploited the complexities of ticketing to make an estimated $50 million a year in the U.S. alone. It takes, on average, six weeks for a ticket to be checked out by the International Air Transport Association's (IATA) ticketing headquarters in Montreal.

IATA is the center of international airlines, regulating fares, routes and services. Every flight coupon is individually cleared. This is when the airlines adjust payments to each other to take account of passengers who switch flights and airlines. It is most unlikely that any irregularity will be discovered until the ticket has passed through the IATA machinery.

The criminals must first obtain blank tickets. These may be stolen directly from printers or the airlines. It is not unusual for criminals to infiltrate a failing travel agent, promising the owner cash if he turns a blind eye to his ticket stocks. He is kept in business for a few weeks.

The crook makes out properly routed tickets and sells them at a discount to travelers, without paying the airline, relying on his six weeks' lead time. More simply he can make out expensive tickets and cash them in for refunds, as "unused."

This is not confined to the U.S. One of the largest frauds came to light at Heathrow when an observant Pan Am check-in clerk noted an alteration and a fare anomaly on a British Airways ticket.

It had been issued in the name of P. de Tilly. This apparent aristocrat turned out to be a former Canadian ticketing clerk, Galvin Brian Humphrie.

De Tilly's career as the "phantom freak" of the world airways had begun with a modest cash purchase of a ticket from Manchester to Europe. Humphrie's knowledge of ticketing enabled him to alter the route to one of higher value. He then told a clerk that he wanted it altered back to a less expensive destination. The difference was made up with MCO's, Miscellaneous Charges Orders—good for any air transport purchases, and if refunded, as good as cash.

With his MCO's, Humphrie purchased another low-value ticket, altered that to a longer route and extended the spiral. He swapped airlines with exotic ease, getting "free" tickets from JAL, British Airways, Pan Am, Air France, TWA, Qantas, KLM, Eastern, Northwest Orient, United, Austrian, Sabena, Finnair and Varig.

The destinations included Sydney, Bombay, Kabul, Athens and New Delhi. On one ticket alone a rebate of $2,413.40 was paid when Mr. de Tilly decided that he wasn't going to Bermuda after all. When he did travel, which occasionally he did for pleasure, he altered Y to F (economy to first) on his ticket and stayed in some of the world's best hotels at airline expense.

British Airways alone was taken for $90,000. The total in a few months of operation was well in excess of $200,000. Humphrie and an accomplice, Gary Schiano, were sentenced to four and one years' imprisonment respectively. An Englishman claiming to be a British Airways employee took advantage of staff discounts to get tickets at 10 percent of normal cost. He girdled the globe several times, conning the airline for more than a decade but was eventually caught and fined $2,000.

Check-in clerks are trained to look for obvious forgeries. Paper, print and inking on tickets are scrutinized. But the airlines do not help matters by habitually flouting their own fare rules, particularly in outlying areas.

A new variation is based on credit card counterfoils. Instead of the bother and risk of stealing the card, the crook simply gets the card number and the name of the user from a counterfoil obtained by an accomplice in a restaurant or shop. He then calls the airline and orders a ticket through the mail on that name and debited to that card number. Since no card has been stolen, the airline's check with the credit card company will reveal nothing odd and the ticket will thus be issued.

People within the industry dream up similar tricks. "Interline" tickets give an employee of one airline a reduction of from 50 to 90 percent when he is traveling on another line. He can simply write "staff 90 percent" on the ticket coding, and SUBLO on the status ("subject to load"; if the plane is full, you don't fly, in preference to the other passengers, who, in theory, at least, should be paying full rate), and sell it at a good profit to a member of the public.

Travel agents get a reduction, the "AD 75," or the 75 percent off for an agent discount. They can get OK (firm booking) on the status. Every agent can get two 75 percent discount tickets per airline. It is highly tempting to sell them to the public.

This does not prevent the public from trying out its own cut-rate schemes. The most common is taking advantage of ITX, the very cheap Inclusive Tour fares. To qualify for this, the passenger should be on a fixed package tour to a hotel. There is, however, no way of proving that a passenger is a businessman with no intention of going near a beach or a package hotel. Flying as a package tourist saves a businessman more than $750 on a trip from the U.S. to Johannesburg.

Schemes for saving money are greatly helped by the chaotic state of IATA's price-fixing. Excursion times often vary between different towns in the same country, let alone from country to country. To qualify for an excursion to Paris, for example, a passenger must stay 4 days—but in Prague 12. A passenger commuting between cities may not stay long enough on any air trip to qualify for an excursion fare. But if he knows the dates, as he will, he can buy a series of excursion tickets in advance.

By alternating outward and return halves, it will appear that he has stayed longer each time than he in practice has—thus qualifying him for considerable discounts. The saving is commonly on the order of 50 percent.

No scheme is foolproof. Once a new system is recognized, the airlines and IATA find a way to counter it. Nevertheless, there is so much confusion over airline fares that anyone who pays full fare is entitled to feel bitter. The ultimate in discounts, package tours, fly-drive, advanced bookings, winter breaks and other excursion fares has now been reached. Airlines have recognized that the few passengers who are paying the "normal" full rate should travel in a special "executive cabin of their own."

The basic ticket form is dictated by international standards. It is a more complicated document than it looks. Airline liability for death or injury is archaic, still based on the quaintly named Convention for the Unification of Certain Rules Relating to International Carriage by Air, signed at Warsaw in 1929. The subject is controversial and very confused. Damages vary greatly depending on airline, the place of the accident and where the ticket was bought.

In general, as we shall see, tickets claim a limited liability of $75,000 where a flight goes to the U.S. and $16,580 for injury elsewhere. Settlements for dead American passengers are an average of 500 percent higher than for others. This does not reflect higher American incomes, since European and Japanese travelers earn the same and Gulf Arabs much more. It reflects the disgraceful inability of other countries to depart from 1929 standards and catch up with the more realistic U.S. settlements.

The ticket contains a great deal of information for the check-in clerks. It is not transferable and the passenger must be the person whose name is on it. This is exceedingly important, since it would otherwise be easy to sell the return half of an excursion ticket. In fact, names are rarely checked, and many people take advantage of this, buying a return ticket on an excursion discount but using it only one way themselves.

The fare basis shows whether a passenger is F, first class, or Y, economy. It also shows if the ticket can be used on another airline, YR means it can be used only on the airline which issued it, YO that it can be used on any airline. This will also be written out in the special Restrictions and Endorsement section.

A "status" section shows the strength of the reservation on a flight. OK means a confirmed booking: the passenger has a definite seat on the flight. SBY or WL means that the passenger is on standby or on the "wait list." This is when a flight is full of reserved seats but "no-shows"—people with reservations who do not turn up—are expected. Seats that have not been taken 30 minutes before takeoff are allocated to people on the wait list. Check-in clerks have to be on their guard against knowledgeable passengers who have altered their reservation status to OK. Airlines, however, often overbook their own flights. Gulf Air in the Persian Gulf holds the record, having booked 390 passengers on a flight to Muscat. The aircraft capacity was 42.

A box shows the form of payment, by check, cash or credit card. This can be stamped Non-Ref, meaning that it can be refunded only after the issuing office has cleared it. Similarly, a series of numbers shows that is is part of a package holiday, when it is again nonrefundable. The letters CY next to the fare show the currency which was paid, an important item with floating currency rates.

Probably the most imaginative user of an air ticket was an American who flew his wife and two children around the world for 18 months before being apprehended. He paid in traveler's checks which were in every way genuine, except that he had invented the bank on which they were drawn, and designed and printed the checks himself. Bank clerks being more attuned to forgeries than to nonexistent banks, and with more and more small banks now issuing their own checks, it took a long time for authority to discover that it had been had.

5

Security

International airports are faced with every modern crime from credit card abuse to hijacking. They are sensitive to the slightest suggestion. A clairvoyant's dream has been enough to start a massive security check. A man told police that he had "seen" a Jumbo with flight number 743 being hijacked with a machine gun over France. An immediate check revealed that a Pan Am 747 on a round-the-world trip was at Frankfurt in transit for New York, Flight PA 743. The airline decided on especially strict security measures.

Three more airlines were affected. TWA's Los Angeles jet Flight 743 had just changed its number to 811 at Boston before going transatlantic to London, but was still searched. So was Qantas' Sydney to London 743 and BA's Copenhagen to London BA 743. An official commented with dignity: "Airlines operating flights with this number have been informed and countersteps have been taken. Security officials have been given details of the dream."

All calls have to be taken seriously, as do bomb threats. These are almost always sparked off by a press or TV report. All the big airlines employ security staffs, or hire private firms. A chart on the wall of the security office marks off the bomb threats. Threats to specific aircraft are marked in red: the caller mentions an actual flight number or route. Nonspecific threats are marked in blue. Yellow on the same square indicates that the aircraft is on the ground, green means that it is in flight. Ground installations are marked in brown. Clearly a combination of red and green is the most worrying: a threat to a specific aircraft in flight.

Airlines do not like talking about bomb threats, with good reason. The incidents go in very distinct waves, and the crests are always when bombs are much in the news on TV or in the press.

JFK has a decompression chamber, in an isolated corner of the airport, where the pressure can be lowered to reproduce that of an aircraft in flight. Suspicious parcels are put into it to see whether they explode as "height" is reached—the chamber is in a heavily sandbagged bunker. Most aerial sabotage is done with altimeter bombs, set to explode when a certain height is reached.

The control tower at JFK has been totally evacuated on occasion, although the hoaxers would be disappointed to know the landings are handled from an emergency trailer. Generally, says one security man, "You just weigh it up. If you get a young male voice on the phone saying, 'There's a bomb on one of your planes,' you put it down as nonspecific. If you get a mature voice with a pronounced national accent and a particular flight in mind, then you're going to pay a lot more attention.

"Unfortunately, people with the hoax mentality exist. It's something we have all learned to live with."

Airport anti-hijack networks have often been shown to have holes in them. A spokesman for a pilots' union was able to clamber unhindered at night over aircraft at Heathrow despite his beard, spy-type epauletted raincoat and an international hijack scare that was on at the time. A dinner-jacketed figure was found at the controls of a parked jet (escaping the breathalyzer that would certainly have pursued him had he stuck to his car).

An eleven-year-old successfully stowed away on a transcontinental flight despite airport security. Derek Stillwell got aboard an American Airlines flight from JFK to Los Angeles. The cool youngster was only caught by police when he tried to check into a Los Angeles airport hotel.

The situation is not helped by the splits in the responsibility for security at many airports. There is doubt as to who guards what, and argument over who pays for what. In theory the airport authorities are responsible for runways, parking areas and buildings.

The airlines have accepted responsibility for all passenger and baggage security. For example, the airlines themselves pay for and lay down the standards of passenger search. Thus El Al uses entirely different techniques, including written questionnaires, from most airlines. The airport authorities have nothing to do with direct passenger security and so airport security is as weak as the weakest airline.

Airport police concede that American standards are higher than elsewhere in the world. In Europe, Zurich is probably the only really well-looked-after airport.

Some airlines carry armed men for protection.* Tarom, the Rumanian airline, carries up to three revolvers on every flight. They are sometimes carried by stewardesses. On arrival the guns are locked in a box which is riveted to the floor of the flight deck. Aeroflot carries guns on all flights, domestic and international. Up to five Russian-made automatic pistols are carried, and they have been used in one aerial shoot-out in which both pilots were killed and the plane crashed. The guns are distributed throughout the plane in flight, and pilots and navigators are always armed.

El Al carries three guards on every plane. They are Israeli government employees and are armed with Belgian automatics. Two submachine guns are carried in specially adapted briefcases which look like ordinary businessmen's cases. On the Arab side, Royal Jordanian Airlines carries six armed guards on its jets, all revolver-carrying serving members of the Royal Jordanian Army.

The Iraqis pack plenty of punch: three guards with pistols and, as a backup, two machine guns in briefcases. Ghana Airways carries two armed men, as does Ethiopian Air Lines.

The Carriage of Arms for the Protection of Aircraft, HM Government, London.

6

Anything to Declare?

Customs men the world over know what to expect on particular flights. People returning from England will be laden with woolens and cashmeres, silver tableware and fine china. From Hong Kong and Singapore come cameras, tape recorders and hi-fi equipment. From South America, there will be emeralds and alligator handbags, and from South Africa diamonds and animal skins. From Mexico there is onyx, and from the U.S. new electronic gadgets which will later be copied and come in from the East.

And from the Far and Middle East, North Africa and South America come drugs. The big syndicates rarely use passengers as carriers. Freight is safer. But semiprofessionals still use suitcases. If they get a few pounds through, the profits will keep them going in the U.S. for a year or more in style.

False bottoms are not in great demand now. The entire suitcase is built around the drugs, which line it top, bottom and sides. There was a fashion for taking the handle and maker's nameplate from Samsonite cases and building the drug carrier around that. Then it moved to American Tourister. Today, Customs agents look out for Grasshopper cases.

"Any Grasshopper case I come across," says Pat Solan, a senior inspector at JFK, "I automatically test the sides of the case to check they are not packed with drugs. All too often, they are."

Drugs are by far the largest problem for U.S. Customs. The big new duty-free allowances for goods bought abroad have slashed traditional smuggling items, like jewelry, furs and fashion clothes. "Air France 077 was a terrific flight for seizures," says Pat Solan. "Haute couture, fur coats and all types of jewels. El Al was riddled with smugglers too—diamond smugglers. But the new allowances have stopped all that. In a way, I'm sorry because that Air France 077 was fun. I could spot them coming a mile off."

A good nose, or what the victim might consider sixth sense, is vital. Customs agents call it "smuggler's eye." It is indefinable, and cannot be taught at the Customs training school in Georgia, but it is that quality that makes a really good Customs agent as he screens hundreds of passengers passing through on the six-hour shift. Or she: many of the best agents, like Pat Solan, are women. The smuggler's perennial ploy of approaching a woman agent because she looks weaker and easier to fool has often proved disastrous to the smuggler.

Every guilty passenger has telltale traits. The normally timid become overboisterous, the placid bite their lips, the domineering are ingratiating, bossy women turn sweet. The "eye" is mainly a question of feeling who is acting out of character.

The process starts much earlier than most people realize—at the moment when they pick up their luggage off the conveyor belt. It is there that Customs agents weigh up their attitudes. Smugglers like to go through Customs in the middle of the line. If their bag comes up first, they will often let it go around on the conveyor belt and only pick it up after other passengers from the flight have started off through the channels. Likewise, they get agitated if the bag is late and they have to go through at the end.

They also visibly relax when they pass through the Customs hall without being challenged, not knowing that plainclothesmen mingle with the crowds in the terminals. An international drug smuggling gang was caught after a courier, an attractive and well-educated girl, ordered a large brandy in a terminal bar after clearing Customs. Young girls do not normally travel alone or take stiff drinks. Drugs were discovered in special compartments in her bra and wig. She was being paid $2,000 a trip to smuggle. Bluestockings, who would have passed unchallenged 10 years ago, are now commonly used as drug couriers.

Baggage tags indicating the airline and origin of the flight are important. "We get people off a South American flight who will hang around and come through with people on a flight from Europe," says Pat Solan. "They're actually surprised we pick them up."

It is not only drugs that are smuggled. Money is, too, as we have seen, hidden in condoms and tubes of toothpaste.

So are sausages, olive trees, soil from the Holy Land, fruit and other articles that cannot be imported into the U.S. "The Alitalias are sausage flights, and you get olive trees on the Olympics. The Greeks stick them down their trouser legs. You see them limping along with the branches sticking out," says a Customs agent.

"The Italians drop sausages into cans of olive oil, or scoop out a cheese. On the flights up from Kingston, we get a lot of Jamaicans with mangoes. They really get upset when we confiscate them. But the real junk flight is Dominicana 902 from Santo Domingo— roasted fruit, hot pepper sauce, chicken, barbecued meats, all the foodstuffs that are banned. The biggest rows tend to be over furs from endangered species, and ivory. We had a shocker with Zsa Zsa Gabor about a leopard-skin coat."

Although all commercial film is held for scanning, pornography is not the hot smuggler's item it once was. "We don't make the decisions, a court does," says a Customs agent. "And the way the courts have been going, nothing is pornographic now."

Drug smuggling is the big business, growing every day. "I remember the old marijuana days, eleven years ago," says Pat Solan. "People would pour off the Avianca flights with big vests full of the stuff, wearing ponchos to hide it. You had to see them to believe it. I made eight seizures one night with twenty-five pounds of the stuff. All from people wearing ponchos."

The big amounts come in as cargo, by ship or by special aircraft. Individual passengers carry 5 to 6 pounds unless they are in the diplomatic racket, when their bag can be full of 40 pounds or more. Diplomatic passports, normally Latin American but including some European and Middle Eastern countries, and United Nations passports are being widely used. They are particularly used in getting Customs preclearance for the U.S. in Canada and Bermuda.

Some smuggle for their own use, but most are "mules," paid $1,500 or so a trip. They are frequently paid in counterfeit money. "They come in all shapes, sizes and colors," says a JFK Customs man, one of 300 at the airport. "Most are from the twenty to forty-five age group, but we've had grandmothers, and mothers who have hidden stuff on infants." Mules have included a former Los Angeles probation officer, a priest and several doctors.

There have been all sorts of hiding places—the soles of platform shoes, vests, under hats and wigs, inside candy bars, in leather saddles and bongo drums, sewn into clothes.

Cocaine can be dissolved in liquor or perfume, and is easily recovered after passing through Customs. Water containing dissolved cocaine can be soaked into cotton clothes and the cocaine retrieved days later with a loss of only 10 percent.

The profit can be very great. Anyone flying in from Bogotá can make $10,000 tax free selling a pound of cocaine, no bigger than a paperback book. Or he can get three years to life.

The most used flight into the U.S. for cocaine is Braniff 922 from Bogotá to Los Angeles. A favorite ploy is for the passengers to hide the powder on the plane, clear Customs in L.A., get back aboard for the connection to San Francisco, and collect the hidden drugs there. Eight pounds of unclaimed cocaine were found in the nose cone of one DC-8. Panel bolts on others are worn from smugglers' screwdrivers. Los Angeles-bound smugglers also use Avianca 080.

There is a clear pattern to drug-smuggling routes from Colombia. On direct routes, JFK Customs agents take a hard look at the Avianca 727 on Flight 204, and Braniff's 908. At Dallas/Fort Worth an eye is kept on Eastern's 990, which connects with drug flights from Miami. In Chicago, Eastern's 78 is checked out.

Even closer to the source of supply, some smugglers fly out of Cartagena on Avianca 068 to Miami. They can connect on to Houston with National 53. Or they fly from Medellin to Miami on Condor 144.

But direct routes are losing their appeal. "We still get numb-skulls who haven't figured out that we take a keen interest in anybody who flies in from Colombia," says Pat Solan. "But some of them have gotten the message. We had three recently who came into JFK on Pan Am 800 from Tokyo.

"Pan Am is an interesting airline for us. You get a mixture of everything and everybody. The unexpected is always happening. Unlike, say, TWA or British Airways, which are more straightfor-ward. But you wouldn't expect much on Pan Am from Tokyo. And the first guy was a returning military man, normally very clean.

"But he didn't fit the profile. The profile says two bags. He had eight. The profile says sets of clothes. He only seemed to have shirts. Sure enough, he had heroin. That's the new thing—the smugglers position themselves to fly in from a really innocent-seeming city."

Besides Tokyo, there have been cases of smugglers flying from Bogotá to Madrid and Brussels, and then going on to the U.S. More commonly, and less expensively, a number will come in via the Caribbean. Pan Am 436 from Santo Domingo to Miami has aroused interest, as well as American 658 to New York. Haiti is equally suspect.

A near foolproof scheme to bring cocaine into the U.S. was found in Port-au-Prince and Santo Domingo. Four women would book a one-week Caribbean cruise out of Miami or Caracas. The liner would make a stop at Santo Domingo or Port-au-Prince, where the women would return to the cruise ship carrying 12 kilos or more of cocaine in wicker baskets or shoulder bags.

When the cruise ship stopped at Puerto Rico, the cocaine would be taken to the distributor who had arranged the deal. The women couriers would return to the ship and continue the cruise. The cocaine was then put into suitcases and flown to JFK on normal commercial flights. There are no Customs examinations of flights from Puerto Rico, so the smuggling carried almost no risk.

One gang is thought to have made more than $4 million in two years with this scheme. The women couriers operated on Commo-dore Cruise Lines' *Boheme,* Chandris Lines' *Amerikanis* and the Yugoslav liner *Istra.*

Even safer has been the use of diplomatic passports. In one

case, involving high Panamanian officials, 175 pounds of heroin valued at $20 million was found by Customs agents on a passenger arriving at JFK on a Braniff flight. Rafael Richard, the son of the Panamanian ambassador to Taiwan, claimed immunity by way of his diplomatic passport. That would normally have put an end to it, but agents found that he did not have full immunity and was subject to arrest.

"Normally, there's not a damn thing you can do to a 'diplomat.' And remember, the whole goddamn Embassy gets immunity—drivers, switchboard clerks, cooks, cleaners, the lot," says a Customs agent. "They get very cheeky. They know you can take the stuff off them, but you can't touch them. I had one who had cocaine in 35-mm cameras. I asked him what it was for. 'For my nose,' he said, as cool as you please."

The agents sniff out smugglers with the help of the "profile" of the normal traveler. "Simply put, the average traveler is very average. He has two cases, and the things in those cases accurately reflect his position in life and his journey. Let's say he's a businessman back from Europe. He may have had a rather complex journey, been to a few capitals over there. His cases will have a fair bit of paper work in them. He'll have a couple of pairs of shoes, good shoes, and a Brooks Brothers suit or whatever, three or four silk ties, and a good selection of shirts and socks, all neatly laundered by a hotel. There will be a little stack of laundered handkerchiefs and a couple of hard-cover books.

"Now, if he's an oilman, even a fairly senior one, he'll be very different. If his travels have taken him to the North Sea, he'll have bought a couple of tartan rugs—for certain, they all do. He's going to have slacks, maybe a plaid jacket, and sports shirts, and a pair of boots. He may have a paperback and a shooting or hunting magazine, and almost certainly a couple of bottles of straight malt whiskey. Don't ask me why oilmen have dirty laundry—maybe Scottish hotels won't do it. But they have it, as certainly as really starched shirts tell you the man in front of you is, depending on the maker, a U.S. merchant marine officer or a British military type," says an agent.

"People think I'm boasting when I say I can tell a Midwesterner, a New Englander or a New Yorker purely from his luggage, but I can. I've spent my working life looking at people and their luggage. A New Yorker will have English shirts, from Harrods or Mr. Fish. A New Englander will have one from New York, and a Midwesterner from Sears. New York women pack everything carefully so the label shows: you don't get New Yorkers creasing labels, not if they are good labels. Whereas California and Texas women just chuck clothes in. They are much less finicky than Easterners.

"When we get somebody whose luggage doesn't match his appearance, or his story, or his route, then we get curious. Like with Pan Am 800. Why should people carrying light clothes, slacks and short-sleeved shirts be coming from Tokyo in February? Why should they have suntan oil in their toilet kits? Because they started out from Colombia.

"They may claim to be students. What is a student doing in Tokyo in February? He's surely not on vacation. So where is he studying? Or a businessman. So how come he's not carrying lots of papers, commercial samples, sales aids?

"Smugglers never accumulate all the rubbish in their cases that an ordinary traveler does—phrase books, torn street maps, half-filled-in postcards, used rolls of film, hotel receipts, book matches, curios, presents for the children. And they can make real fools of themselves. They'll say, 'Colombia, where's that?' And then you point out that their shirt wrappers—back to shirts again—are labeled Bogotá Hotel, or that their toothpaste or shaving cream is Colombian.

"You get some who are so stupid that they don't even fill their suitcases. They seem to think that we won't find it odd that they are traveling with an empty case. Those who fill them often get the mix wrong. There will be masses of clothes, but not heavier shoes or books. The clothes themselves are often suspicious: shirts of different sizes, trousers that don't seem they would fit the passenger, labels with little giveaways—Ind. Col., Colombian made. Or all the other clothes will obviously be new. Or they don't suit the personality of the owner. We had one, a macho type, and he had all dull gabardine trousers and chunky sweaters. Totally out of character, though the cocaine we found wasn't. It takes a lot of skill to fool a man who's been looking at suitcases for fifteen years."

But most major drug smuggling does not involve face-to-face confrontation with Customs. It uses air cargo. There are some clues for Customs. Large consignments of low-value items are natural targets: air freight is expensive and is used normally only for high-value cargo. Half a ton of meat tenderizer revealed 200 pounds of drugs.

Imported foodstuffs can contain drugs—chili pickle from Bombay, pickled mustard plants from Hong Kong, egg jam from Singapore, coriander leaves from Cyprus.

"Sometimes the smugglers almost dare you," says a drugs expert. "We thought there was some heroin in some priceless carvings from Hong Kong. The ivory was flawless and very valuable. We took the risk and broke one open. The powder had been injected."

Most seizures like this are based on tip-offs. Consignments are followed step by step from the poppy fields of Turkey and Lebanon, or the "Golden Triangle," on the borders of Thailand and Burma, where private armies still hold sway, to the departure airports at Beirut or Bangkok. The "informers" are usually business rivals.

"Foolproof" schemes are discovered through jealousy. One was to send tatty suitcases, supposedly containing an immigrant's personal effects, to await collection at airports in Europe. The suitcases would lie in bond, unexamined, until they were claimed by the "immigrant" on his arrival.

In fact, they were stuffed with drugs, but while in bond they were safe from detection. They were not claimed for some time, and gradually were pushed to the side of the freight shed. They were then replaced with identical suitcases, the original labels switched, and driven out of the bonded area.

The substitute suitcases were full of precisely chosen effects, cheap Indian clothes, tatty shoes, cooking vessels. When they were claimed by the "newly arrived immigrant," the Customs check revealed nothing.

It was too good a scheme not to upset other drug dealers.

One method has been used many times. The smuggler puts identical suitcases onto the aircraft—one with the merchandise, the other quite "clean," with clothes and so forth. On arrival he picks up the suitcase with the smuggled goods. If challenged when going through the Green Channel, the smuggler says he has picked up the wrong case. On returning to the luggage pickup point, he will, of course, find "his" identical suitcase filled with innocent items.

This system can fail, as Henry Patrick Solomon discovered. A former Nigerian police officer from Lagos, he was ambitious enough to try to get $80,000 worth of cannabis through Heathrow.

Things went wrong. The case with the cannabis was accidentally misrouted at Madrid onto a KLM flight. When Solomon arrived at Heathrow, there was no sign of it on the conveyor. He panicked and left without even the "clean" bag. He later returned for the "clean" bag, but Customs agents were suspicious, since they knew by then that one bag on the flight had accidentally been sent to Amsterdam. Solomon was arrested on its arrival. It was opened, and he got three and a half years, all because of a baggage handler's inefficiency in far-off Madrid.

Another old favorite is the secret compartment in an animal cage. Whenever Customs agents are suspicious they call in an expert to look after the animal while they search the cage. The hauls have included heroin in a tank of coral snakes and hashish in an oversized dog basket.

A growing development is the use of entire aircraft to smuggle drugs. No less than 10 tons of marijuana were seized at Trenton-Robbinsville Airport aboard a DC-4. Drug enforcement agents are trained to use the Air Force's new AWACS airborne warning and control system planes to track aircraft flying from Colombia.

Near El Paso, small squadrons of executive jets have come screaming across the Texas border. Only one aircraft contains drugs. The others are decoys. Drugs are dropped from aircraft by experienced bombardiers. A plane fitted with 1,000 pounds of Colombian pot, however, did fall victim to an airborne patrol near Fort Lauderdale, Florida, and was picked up after landing.

Another plane landed in a Florida pasture being used by local politicians for a turkey shoot. The crew were arrested. A DC-3 was seen to crash at Newton, Georgia,* by a helicopter crew. The pilot was admitted to a hospital with a broken hip and upper leg wounds. Interviewed by police, the resourceful lad claimed to have had a motorbike crash. The landing field, marked with flashlights on stakes, was found along with the marijuana and the wreck.

Some more ambitious but equally incompetent smugglers used a four-engine DC-4.† They landed in an open area of the Everglades near Monroe Station, Florida. The ground was soft and the nose collapsed. About 3,720 pounds of marijuana, compressed into balls, was found nearby.

Mostly, the pilots get through with their loads of marijuana, cocaine and fake Quaaludes. Ten tons of marijuana, landed safely, is worth $6 million, so the profit is vast even if the aircraft is abandoned. Pilots are paid from $20,000 a trip. They fly down to Colombia from the U.S. and, if the Colombian authorities find them, claim to be lost. "Gosh," said a former Michigan State Police employee, copiloting an old DC-6 the Colombians seized, "I don't know what all the activity is about. We were headed for Costa Rica from Florida when our navigation went out. We were down to our last drop of fuel."

One item of lost property at JFK shows the uneasy relationship between aviation and drug-running. A battered and torn suitcase found at the airport was handed in to the NYC property clerk's office. It contained $593,000. One Heribelto Castro and his wife, Fanny, were questioned by police after showing up at the airport to collect the suitcase. Both maintained that the cache belonged to a person named "Juan." Lucky Juan, if he is still alive to enjoy it. Lucky NYC, if not.

Drugs are a far cry from the traditional staple of airline smuggling, gold. The freeing of the price of gold knocked

*DC-3 N38AP, June 13, 1977.
†DC-4 N174DP, March 3, 1977.

smuggling of it on the head, although it has been showing strong signs of revival in Iran and India of late.

Gold smuggling grew up with aviation, and bars of gold dumped by frightened couriers have been found on many planes. It will flourish as long as countries restrict gold hoarding. During the halcyon days of the "golden stewards," cabin crew and passengers smuggled gold by the vestful into India and Pakistan.

The demand for gold in those countries is insatiable. It alone represents security and status, and smuggling became a major industry with profits of more than 200 percent. One "courier" could make $40,000 a trip. Aircraft flew into India with parts of their stabilizers made of gold; typewriters with gold space bars were brought in as hand luggage. Gold pellets replaced the stones in dates carried by pilgrims from Mecca to Karachi.

Couriers were recruited by vaguely worded advertisements in leading European papers promising quick money in return for travel. They were then flown to Zurich, where they were trained by a woman in a broken-down house near the Hauptbahnhof.

The first priority was to get the reluctant adventurers fit. An early courier was arrested in India because he sat down while waiting to go through Customs. Tired and weighed down with 80 pounds of gold above his belt, he was unable to stand up again. His successors could be seen jogging around the early-morning streets of Zurich, practicing the knees-bend-with-straight-back that was vital to their trade.

Even so the weight on the long flights to the East could be crushing. One man dropped two bars of gold down the lavatory of a 707 while adjusting his load an hour out from Delhi. The lavatory jammed, and the $8,000 mistake was discovered.

Couriers were instructed to dress "English," with collar and tie, and to avoid casual clothes. They were told to be polite and relaxed with officials—but never humble. A nine-page list gave them such advice as "Immediately before arrival, it is a good idea to *have a wash and shave* so that you may look as fresh and as lively as possible."*

---

*A former gold smuggler, who was imprisoned in India, told his detailed story to *Town* magazine.

To stop people bumping into their golden torsos, they were told to carry hand baggage or a camera. Rule 6 in the list pointed out that "this is to give you distance from any person touching you while in a line or when in the gangway of the plane." Further advice encouraged them to "sleep with your head toward the aisle so that the steward will not nudge your chest to wake you up for food or a transit stop."

Rule 13 was more comforting: "In certain transit stops such as Karachi a gentleman in uniform may come onto the plane and stay there while the native cleaners are on board. This gentleman, no matter how ominous he looks, is there to make sure the cleaners do not pinch anything. Completely ignore him and go to sleep."

Once trained, the courier is fitted with a special canvas vest that will accommodate more than $150,000 worth of gold. It has 40 small pockets and one gold bar of slightly more than 2 pounds will fit in each. The gold is bought quite legally in Europe. From Switzerland, it will be stamped with the name of a bank; in London, with the name of bullion dealers, such as Johnson Mathey. In both cases, the bar has the magic number 999 engraved on it—proof that it is 99.9 percent pure gold.

A few couriers made golden nest eggs and retired. Others still languish in prisons in the Indian subcontinent. The big operators made fortunes. Some had a working capital of more than $2 million and could afford to write off seizures of $200,000 as acceptable business losses. But the change in gold prices and the difficulties of getting couriers through routine anti-hijack searches have affected the business.

Not only things are smuggled. People are too, in what has become one of the most lucrative and fast-growing commodities of all, the illegal immigrant.

The aerial traffic in illegal immigrants is largely restricted to Europe. It is a big business in the U.S., but it is land-based. Sitting mesmerized in a car in El Paso, I have counted more than 70 people in an hour passing through a single hole in the so-called fence that runs along this section of the so-called Rio Grande. Apart from some jostling, since this was a relatively small and fresh hole, although it was growing visibly, the scene was good-natured and commonplace.

Later, with the Border Patrol, I watched "illegals" by the score being taken off railroad freight cars and from the trunks of cars with Illinois and Michigan license plates. With people-smugglers being paid upwards of $250 to get a Mexican over the border and into a job in a northern city, this is a multimillion-dollar business. In El Paso alone, 800 illegals have been caught and deported in a single day. The numbers are prodigious.

Other than the regular patrols at El Paso airport, picking up illegals with enough money to fly north, however, this immigration does not hinge on airports and aircraft. It thus has no place in this book: it occurs to me that anyone wishing to enter the U.S. illegally is ill-advised to do so by air, when he can so easily do so by foot.

The U.S. Immigration Service does turn some passengers back. Each officer has his "lookout book," which has details of some 25,000 prohibited or suspect aliens under 20 different codes—political, morals, criminal suspect and so forth. This weeds out some, although not everyone in the "lookout book" is banned from entry. The Immigration officer checks with Washington before entry. Diplomats must be admitted, even if they are suspected of spying: Czech diplomats currently head the list of presumed spies. If a diplomat on the lookout list appears, the Immigration officer notifies the diplomatic passport section in Washington for surveillance.

But no U.S. airport has the illegal immigration problem of a British airport like Heathrow, with its flood of would-be Asian immigrants. One maneuver was a four-day "See the England of the Bard" tour from Sweden to Stratford via Heathrow. Many Shakespearean fans on the trips turned out to be Pakistanis, who would drop off the coach and out of sight long before Anne Hathaway's cottage was reached.

The cost of illegal entry into Britain is now running at about $5,000. Punjabis and Sikhs are highest on the list, and the schools for would-be immigrants are getting so sophisticated that the Immigration Service has established its own Intelligence Unit to get knowledge on racketeering, particularly checking Karachi, Delhi, Bombay, Dacca and Sylhet.

Several methods are used. Stolen British passports can be bought for $150 in India. Doctoring them requires skill and a very sharp razor. The already filled-in Description page, with its photograph, is cut off—not wholly cut out of the passport, but cut off through the thickness of the paper, like a slice of cheese.

A new Description page with photograph is delicately pasted on top. The plastic seal over the photograph on new passports is intended to make this more difficult.

Alternatively, an awkward page on a legitimate passport, one that, for example, restricts the holder to a stay of three months, can be "reconstituted" in the same way. "Completely forged passports are rare," says a senior Immigration officer. "It is too easy to steal a genuine one, although it has to be used fairly quickly before it gets on the stolen list."

Reconstituted pages can be spotted. They will probably be fresher than the other pages. The Description page will normally be particularly well thumbed by IO's, hotel receptionists, banks and so forth. Suspicion is aroused instantly if this page is in good condition. Switched passport photographs can be checked by prizing the corner with a knife to see if the stamp indentations on the picture agree with those on the paper underneath.

Suitable doctoring of a returning Indian resident's family passport can enable them to bring in an extra child. Children under 16 are entitled to admission if they are accompanied by a parent, and greatly overaged sons, nephews and cousins still try to come in. X rays of the wrist bones are used to verify real age. Pregnant women frequently slip in as tourists for short visits—and leave after their children are born in Britain and thus entitled to British passports.

Airports of origin for the short-haulers are Frankfurt, Paris and Amsterdam. Any Asian with a ticket booked directly onward from the subcontinent to Heathrow via any of these European airports is almost automatically suspect.

Visitors' restrictions can be "laundered." One worried London travel agent checked with IATA after he had issued several hundred tickets to Asians, which had been returned for full refunds. IATA confirmed that the tickets had not been used fraudulently. Why should individuals buy so many tickets and then not use them? Because with a ticket to a European country they could approach foreign embassies and obtain visas. Once they had filled up their passports with visas, fresh passports could legitimately be obtained from their High Commissions and embassies. And the fresh passports would *not* show the original three-month restriction on stay.

The latest scheme, particularly with Indians—and the Immigration authorities rely a great deal on nationalities consistently using the same method—is a ticket through to Canada, with a "holiday stopover" in Britian to visit relatives while en route to a new life. This gives the illegal immigrant the chance of trying Britain—and if that fails, going on to Canada for another attempt.

Pakistanis favor the "returning resident" approach. They are rehearsed with street maps, National Insurance documents, and details of their jobs at a travel agent's "school."

Turks are known to have a flourishing business with forged work permits. "It is good work, fresh printed, not altered. Like a lot of papers that give people away, they're too good. You don't expect an Indian birth certificate to be perfect. Much less do you expect the typing and spelling on a Turkish permit to be exact to the nearest comma," says an IO.

All non-British passengers, including Americans, are held at a gate before being told which IO's desk to go to. This enables behavior to be seen. "There's normally the stool-pigeon IO, the one who looks an easy touch, just as there used to be with Customs before the channel system. If you see anyone hanging back, being overly nervous, then you start checking."

Luggage is often a considerable clue, though it must be opened by Customs. The IO has no such powers of search. "If you find someone has his school reports or job references or exam results in his suitcase you can be fairly certain he's not just on holiday. People get upset when we read diaries and letters—but there are a lot of clues you can pick up."

Suspect waiters are asked to show their tickets. As they pull them out, the IO looks for blisters, short nails or other signs of manual work. If they are there, he can and probably will get the terminal restaurant staff to bring a table and cutlery into the room and ask the passenger to lay the table.

A German girl was recently suspected of being a prostitute. A search of her luggage revealed a whip, riding hat, boots and spurs, and a letter confirming accommodation in a luxury apartment. "But of course she just said she liked riding, and she got in."

PART TWO

SKYPEOPLE AND OTHERS

7

Pilots

The typical captain is 43, married, with two children, a dog and two cars. He lives in a house with a large garden within 30 miles of his home airport. His only real interests outside flying are golf, fishing and gardening. He will be politically and socially conservative. For recognition he has four gold bars on his sleeve. First officers have three.

It is a very reassuring profile. Unfortunately, as Dr. Herbert Haynes of the FAA points out: "We have no effective screening methods to make sure pilots are sane." Pilots are rigorously, although not always successfully, checked to make sure they are in the pink of physical condition. They are examined for every imaginable ailment; their physical health must be excellent but nobody challenges their sanity.

At St. Louis airport a stewardess was boarding her plane when she heard snarls at her feet. She felt teeth bite her calves. The captain was on the floor, in full uniform, on all fours. "I like to play dog," he said.

The captain of a United Airlines scheduled flight from San Diego to Seattle was told by the stewardess that the last hot dinner aboard had been served to a passenger. Furious, the captain announced that he would make an unscheduled stop in San Francisco for "resupply." He put the big jet down in San

Francisco, had a restaurant dinner, and then rejoined the plane to take it to Seattle.

An instructor pilot, who was examining another airline pilot on a Boeing 707, suddenly wrenched the plane into a steep climbing turn and yelled: "Damn Japs down there are putting up a lot of flak. Guadalcanal will always be a tough target." He was over Oklahoma City at the time. The crew had to knock him out.

A Boston-based pilot counts the colored passengers who board his aircraft and delays the flight by ten minutes for each one. A French pilot who had a radio argument with a flight dispatcher lost his temper and hitchhiked 370 miles home, abandoning his passengers on the aircraft.

The captain of an Alitalia DC-10 stormed off the plane, which was waiting to take off on a flight from Rome to Bangkok, when the airline refused to let his daughter take the flight on a 10 percent discount ticket. It was August 1976, and Alitalia does not allow staff discount in the peak season. Another captain had to be found for the pilotless plane.

Passengers on a Brazilian Bandeirante in January 1978 reported a violent quarrel between the two pilots as it took off. They were shouting at each other so much that neither was concentrating on piloting the plane, which flew into a tree, killing both of them.

An expert British doctor, L. T. C. Hayward of Graylingwell Hospital in Chichester, has written an "Assessment of Stress Tolerances in Commercial Pilots."* He reports: "There is some reason to believe that many pilots, at the peak of their physical health and outwardly calm and composed, are inwardly suppressing a seething sea of emotional turbulence born of domestic worries, administrative frustration, technical hazards, and operational fatigue."

They certainly seem conservative enough, feet firmly planted on the same bits of ground. Gregarious among themselves, if not with outsiders, pilots tend to flock together in communities just beyond the normal suburban belts. They are not tied down by the boredom of daily commuting and their considerable free time

*Flight Safety I 12-18. 1967.

allows them to live close to the outdoor sports most of them like—notably sailing, tennis and skiing.

Thus Lake Mohawk, a New Jersey town some two hours from the Long Island airports, is so filled with pilots that locals call it "Pilotsville, N.J." and even the real-estate agent turns out to be a United Airlines second officer by night.* Other areas they favor are the hills of northwest New Jersey, the Connecticut shoreline and Bucks County, Pennsylvania. Pilots flying out of Los Angeles, Atlanta, Chicago, San Francisco and Miami also prefer living right out on top of their recreations—ironically it seems to be only in the Big Country that pilots like to settle in the cities, Dallas and Houston. Lake Mohawk is just 20 minutes from the ski center of Hidden Valley—itself started by a group of pilots and home of the American Airlines ski team.

The Lake Mohawk image is stability, conservatism and a lot of quiet money. The pilots are considered excellent for business by hardware, lumber, sporting goods and electrical dealers. They are forever improving their houses, and real-estate values in the neighborhood have soared.

They have gone into local trade: two are now TV repairmen, another runs the local Radio Shack, another is a jewelry wholesaler. They have built up and run the town's recreational facilities— tennis, Little League, football, volleyball, skiing and water-skiing. With their odd hours, pilots help man the local emergency ambulance unit, snow plows and the volunteer fire brigade.

They are forever helping one another on major renovations to their houses, most of which are worth well over $100,000 and furnished with antiques and exotica acquired on international flights.

However, pilots are not that popular with other locals. Restaurateurs complain that they seldom eat out because they do that often enough on the job. Regular commuters envy the large amounts of time they have off, the foreign vacations their children constantly take, their very large salaries. Most people find them cliquey.

*The New York Times, July 20, 1978.

But some strain does accompany this sober, sports-filled, outer-suburban existence.

The pressures on the older pilot are clear. His contemporaries are often beginning to achieve recognition and power in their late forties. His career is virtually finished at 50. Above that age, it would be too expensive to retrain him on new aircraft.

He may worry about crashing, perhaps to the point of obsession. The danger periods to a pilot are said to be three hours after the first solo, and with 300, 3,000, 13,000 and 23,000 hours. Few pilots get in enough to qualify for the last, which represents more than two and a half years in the air. But many worry badly about the other danger points. Pilots who have made it to retirement warn the younger generation: "There are old pilots and bold pilots, but there are not old bold pilots." They are all supposedly dead at one of the danger points.

A pilot is put through at least five tests a year. Failure in any one can end his career immediately. Twice a year the FAA requires the airline to check out his proficiency. Also, an FAA inspector—completely unannounced—can show up just before takeoff, sit in the jump seat and "lift" the captain's license on the spot if he detects a major failing during the flight. Every six months there is an FAA physical, and a company check annually.

Strain is great since the pilot's career and family are both dependent entirely on his passing his tests. Pilots are not the totally self-confident figures, serene and godlike, that they seem to passengers. The insecurity of employment means that many take up second jobs, which can be tiring. Pan American pilot Jim Zockoll says: "No matter how fit I feel, I always get the collywobbles every six months when I go for my medical. And that goes for nearly every pilot. There's this terrible inbuilt insecurity." So Zockoll started a company that unblocks drains, Dyno-Rod, which now has branches in three countries.

British pilots have a peculiar penchant for chicken farming. Others go into real estate, travel agencies and yacht building.

A typical pilot, Captain David Ferguson, started a chicken farm. "He was pushed into his second string with chickens eighteen years ago when he was thirty-four and did lose his license," said his wife,

Betty.* "He needed an operation for a stomach ulcer and his license was lifted for six months. There was no guarantee at all that he would ever get it back, and this is the fear that haunts pilots. They all dread that day when some doctor is going to turn around and say: 'Sorry, it's not on, not anymore.' "

Very occasionally a substandard pilot can get by and still fly. A United Airlines captain, Gale C. Kehmeire, received a poor report when he was being trained to fly DC-8's: "A review of Captain Kehmeire's record still indicates unsatisfactory performance in the areas of command, judgment, Standard Operating Procedure, landing techniques, and smoothness and coordination. On the basis of the above I recommend Captain Kehmeire's DC-8 transition be terminated." This unsatisfactory showing in almost every aspect crucial to flying notwithstanding, Captain Kehmeire was later in command of a United Boeing 727 when it crashed at Salt Lake City.†

The tension is international. The divorce rate for pilots is high, especially those on the long-distance routes. They are away from home much of the time. When they come back, they have to spend days reacclimatizing to the new time clock.

A wife gets the compensation of duty-free gifts, a high salary, the latest gadgets and foreign holidays at very little cost. But many of them tire of being left alone to struggle with the children, house repairs, medical emergencies. Some are former stewardesses, which does not quiet the nagging fear of their husbands' infidelity on a trip.

Pilots can also seem very authoritarian. They are notoriously sticky about status. A former airline chairman called them "spoiled children." They complain about trivialities: stewards' getting gold bars on their sleeves—because the passengers might think that diminished the pilots' importance; other pilots calling air traffic controllers "sir"; being checked out by younger men for

---

Daily Mail, September 28, 1973.

†Aircraft Accident Report. United Air Lines Boeing 727, Salt Lake City, Utah, November 11, 1965.

flying skill; being checked by Customs at all. One captain insisted on having his tea served on a silver tray; another allowed his engineer to smoke two cigarettes an hour—on the hour and the half hour.

A long-haul captain, at 43, will probably have spent the last 20 years of his life on endless journeys. But he cannot seek help obviously if he begins to get jaded. He could easily be grounded as mentally unfit.

A pilot who has suffered a recognized psychiatric condition has great difficulty in obtaining reinstatement to flying duties, however successful his treatment appears to have been. Dr. Hayward writes in *Flight Safety:* "Pilots with self-perceived problems of a patently psychiatric nature are therefore reluctant to disclose them to the flight surgeon, until the seriousness of the developing situation forces his hand." So tired and sleepless men are advised to relax by "drink, drugs or sleeping with the stewardess," as airline doctors put it.

The chief medical officer to the British Department of Trade and Industry, Dr. Geoffrey Bennett, claims that 2 percent of all pilots are alcoholics, shielded by their fellows. He says that they fight a "continual battle against adversity," with unhappy wives, strained marriages and short job prospects. One British Airways captain died of acute alcoholic poisoning less than a month after being in charge of an airliner between Hong Kong and London.

Drunken pilots in northern Ontario caused some of the 89 crashes in the area between 1920 and 1976. "It's like playing Russian roulette when you charter a plane up there," says Constable G. L. Fitzpatrick, a Mountie who wrote a report on the problem. "Pilots drink until late at night and then fly you the next morning still half drunk."

A DC-8 of Japan Air Lines was on a scheduled freight flight from Anchorage, Alaska.* During the 17-minute taxi to runway 24 Left in heavy fog the aircraft entered runway 24 Right at the midpoint of the runway and announced that it was ready for take-off.

*ICAO summary S/77, January 13, 1977.

The tower told the flight of its improper position. After repeated instructions the aircraft finally made a 180-degree turn, taxied to 24 Left and took off. The aircraft lifted off, climbed 150 feet, veered first left and then right and hit the ground 1,000 feet beyond the end of the runway. Three crew and two passengers aboard did not survive.

Toxicological tests on the captain less than 12 hours after the crash showed a blood alcohol level of 298 milligrams percent. Most countries ban drivers with alcohol levels above 80.

The Russian airline Aeroflot breathalyzes all crew members before commercial flights. If anyone is positive for alcohol, the entire crew is changed.

Pilots are subject to the same stresses as everyone else. They can and sometimes do develop severe fear of flying. There have been many cases of blacking out. Vertigo is common. Fourteen percent of all the fatal crashes in the U.S. Air Force are attributed to vertigo. Vertigo accidents are likely when the pilot is under stress and without experience to keep his nerve, typically while flying a new type of aircraft, or in weather conditions he has not met before. Momentary disorientation going into and out of cloud, from flying off instruments to looking out the window, is normal. It takes 45 seconds for the senses to change completely from visual flying to instruments, a more difficult transition than the other way around.

A Pensacola Naval Study revealed surprisingly large errors in judging degree of bank—the amount the aircraft is "banking," or tilting. Some pilots identified 60 degrees of bank as straight and level.

The U.S. Navy logged 14 epileptic attacks to airborne flight crew members. Dr. Hayward records that EEG's give some indication of psychiatric abnormality. One suggestion was continuously to monitor the EEG's in flight, so that if one crew member showed signs of abnormality the machine would warn the others to take over.

It has been established that the human brain cannot judge some apparently simple situations. Boeing was worried after four of its 727's had crashed in quick succession. All had landed short of the runway.

An engineering psychologist and chief scientist for the Personnel Sub System of Boeing's Commerical Aircraft Division began to investigate the landing-short phenomenon using a night-landing simulator. A model of a lighted city was linked to the cockpit controls of the simulator. The pilots flew a visual approach, looking at the city lights, with all the cockpit instruments working except the altimeter.

Boeing used 12 of its most experienced captains who had averaged more than 10,000 hours of flight time each. They thought the exercise would be easy. The model city was projected either on a flat plane with the runway or on a slight three degree upward slope. Eleven out of twelve crashed short of the runway. The twelfth man was a former Navy carrier pilot with a special knowledge of landing on a moving deck at sea.

The pilots were shocked. But it was clear that the problem exceeded human visual ability. The brain cannot work out the right angle of descent onto flat ground at night. The experiment proved vividly that it is indeed possible to fly straight into the ground unless the altimeter is checked constantly.*

The short-haul pilots are tired by heavy concentration on radio messages and frequency settings, and the many takeoffs and landings. The greater speed and the smaller crews mean they cannot get back into the cabin. Most short-haul aircraft like the DC-9 and Boeing 737 have only two pilots, without the flight engineer and navigator of 10 years ago.

Thus the pilots spend the whole flight with the aircraft "strapped to our backside," as they put it, without even momentary relaxation. Backache is the most common occupational disease. The pilots also claim that the absence of contact with the passengers is turning them into automatons.

---

*British Airways Air Safety Review. A high initial accident rate was common with the early jets. Thus the 707 had 18 accidents in its first million hours, dropping to 13 for the second and 8 for the fifth million hours. But the introduction of the new big jets, the 747, DC-10, TriStars and Airbus, has been notably safer than before, even with the DC-10 disasters.

The long-haul pilots have fatigue problems, with upset appetites, sleep patterns and biological rhythms.

The tiredness is obvious. Some flights begin in temperatures of −20 degrees Fahrenheit and end in the hot nineties. Aeroflot pilots on the Moscow-to-Havana routes in winter, or Canadian pilots flying down to Jamaica from Montreal and Toronto, must endure these extremes of cold and Caribbean heat as a matter of course. Pilots often work for 14 hours nonstop, try to shut their eyes in a strange hotel room when their body clocks think it is afternoon, and then put in another long flight.

A Japan Air Lines survey of pilots and engineers shows how many factors affect crew fatigue. In ascending order the percentage thinking themselves "seriously affected" was 34 percent by lack of exercise due to continuous seating, 71 percent by time zone differences, in-flight humidity and sunlight, 74 percent by after-midnight flying and 80 percent by weather.

What do they do on the flight deck on those long stretches across the Atlantic and Pacific? The passengers know they cannot be very busy, and they are not. The tempo on a long transoceanic flight is slow. But they do not have secret drinking parties, or orgies with the stewardesses, or wild card games, as a passenger staring at the flight deck door might think.

All too often, they simply fall asleep. All of them. A British Airways VC-10 captain on a night flight in the Far East found himself nodding off.* He shook himself awake. He found his copilot sleeping peacefully next to him. The flight engineer had slumped on his instrument console and was snoring. The crew had black coffee all around and flew on.

Pilots can, and occasionally do, drop dead at the controls of airliners. Flying is taxing on the heart. Heart rates go up to 140 on takeoff, and a wearing 150 on landing. The norm is the steady 80 of the cruise. An official report on the hearts of two pilots on an actual transatlantic crossing also noted that the rate increased to 100 when the stewardess leaned over with their meal trays. Sitting on a chair in cramped conditions, with it virtually impossible to

*Flight Fatigue. Report of the Special Committee BALPA, London, 1973.

move or take exercise, is not good for avoiding coronaries. Heart ailments are the most common cause for loss of license.

The odds of death in flight are small. But 17 captains died in American airliners in a six-year period alone; all the deaths were caused by heart attacks, but only one fatal crash resulted. Although pilots are trained to cope with this emergency in the next seat, there were five accidents and five near misses. A heart attack to a British Airways Trident captain was a factor in the worst crash in Britain, when 117 died after the plane stalled shortly after taking off from Heathrow.*

More typical is a DC-8 of KLM on Flight 863 to Tokyo. The aircraft was less than 30 seconds from touchdown at a scant 150 feet when the captain died of a massive coronary. He had been fully in charge of the flight at its most crucial phase, when transition to the copilot would never normally be attempted.

With only 12 seconds of decision time left to him, the copilot, Cornelius de Jager, took over the controls. Putting on full power, he was able to go round again. He moved the dead pilot from his seat with the help of the steward and dragged him into first class as the aircraft flew on automatic pilot. The worst danger is of controls jammed by the body, leading to a crash, rather than just the sudden death of one pilot, since a copilot should be able to fly the plane adequately on his own. The copilot returned to the cockpit and made a perfect landing.†

Braniff Captain Lloyd Wilcox, 59, died of a heart attack as his wide-bodied jet with 334 aboard cruised on autopilot from Honolulu to Dallas in March 1979. Even his wife, working aboard the aircraft as a stewardess, was unaware of his death until the aircraft landed in Dallas.

However, four months before the Tokyo incident, on April 22, 1966, an Electra on a military charter flight crashed in Oklahoma after the captain died of a heart attack on the landing approach. Only 15 of the 99 aboard survived.‡ The dead pilot was Captain

---

*CAA report 4173. The crash was on June 18, 1972.
†CAA World Airline Accident Summary 22/66.
‡CAA World Airline Accident Summary 14/66.

Reed W. Pigman. All seven crew died, together with 77 of the 92 passengers. Captain Pigman, who was the founder of the airline American Flyers, had a very serious heart condition of long standing and also suffered from diabetes. He had falsified his medical record to keep his license.

The Federal Aviation Agency estimates on statistical evidence that about three U.S. pilots will die in flight each year.

Food poisoning has ceased to be an acute danger since flight crews were forbidden to eat identical meals in the 1950's.

But crews have been poisoned by things other than food. The crew of a Pan Am freighter died after nitric acid reacted with sawdust in a packing case to produce choking smoke, and they crashed at Boston.* Intoxicated by carbon monoxide fumes from a faulty cockpit heater, the crew of a holiday flight from Manchester to Perpignan flew into a mountain, killing all 89 aboard.†

This is the sort of schedule that a pilot can expect in a typical eight-day period. He pilots from New York to Paris and then "deadheads" (flies as a passenger) from Paris to Singapore. He pilots the aircraft from Singapore to Sydney, and again from Sydney to Darwin. He deadheads home to Europe.

The actual flying hours involved are small, with only 38 hours on duty. But there are tiring time changes and the disorientation of sleeping through six hotels. Flying conditions vary from the lush warmth of Singapore to the vicious gales of the Tasman Sea. As a pilot says: "You're always just on that edge of tiredness where it only needs a whine from the air conditioning to keep you awake all night; where an egg that's overboiled will put you off your food for the day; and one flip remark from a waiter has you snapping your head off in the cockpit eight hours later."

A pilot on a "bus stop" or vacation charter route will be saturated with radio transmissions and complex landings. Aircraft on these routes often get "stacked," kept circling in the air waiting their turn to land in an aerial traffic jam.

A pilot has to retune his radios nine times on the New York–Boston shuttle. The most familiar noise in the cockpit of a

*CAA World Airline Accident Summary 31/73.
†HMSO CAP312.

short-haul jet is not the whine of the engines and the rush of air playing around the windshields in the breathless way of the long-haul jets. It is the clatter as the radio channels switch from one frequency to another.

The vacation airfields in the Caribbean get very cluttered in the winter. Pilots must line up to land and take off, weaving intricate patterns in the sky to the orders of traffic controllers who are often not skilled, above airports that are seldom fully radar equipped.

Punctuality is almost more important on vacation flights than on scheduled services. "The big airlines can always roll out another aircraft if one goes u/s [unserviceable]," says a charter pilot. "We don't have spare equipment. And if we start getting behind, it snowballs. Miss one flight and the vacation bookings for a whole season start snowballing into each other. The hotels can't cope. You have to keep to times to avoid a nightmare. It erodes safety standards."

Most pilots are men. Not all. The first all-woman flight in the U.S. took place in March 1979 on Western Airlines. Flight 514, a 727, was flown by 28-year-old Captain Valerie Petrie, daughter of Clint Walker of *Cheyenne* TV fame. Her copilot was Second Officer Cindy Rucker, another of Western's 11 women pilots. There are women pilots flying for Russia's Aeroflot and British Caledonian as well.

But more than 98 percent are men. And most of them are ex-military pilots, who got their training in the Air Force. They join the airlines with a few thousand hours of flying time, largely on transports or heavy bombers.

The airlines do not approve of nonconservative personalities. So out-and-out fighter pilots are rare, and the nonmilitary pilots who came in from civilian flying schools wear short hair and neat blazers.

Individual sparkle, flair and thoroughgoing experience were the qualities still much needed 10 years ago. The captain of one old transport had to take 26 horses from England to Singapore. For him it was a normal flight but it was also a flying initiative test from beginning to end.

A captain's emergency equipment then comprised imagination,

nerve and a briefcase full of money. The flight was mettlesome. The captain survived four engine failures and personally supervised the repairs. One horse went beserk in flight two hours before reaching Bombay and had to be shot.

The Times of India reported: "On landing, the dead animal posed for the captain a big problem. Its body could not be taken out of the small entrance meant for the crew. Neither could it be taken out of the bigger exit as it would have meant the disembarkation of the other 25 horses. It would have delayed the plane for a few days. After hours of deliberation, a member of the crew hit upon the idea that parts of the animal could be chopped off.

"The services of two butchers from Bandra slaughterhouse were requisitioned. They, however, proved intractable as their demands increased minute by minute when they found that no one else could do the job. The crew, however, refused to oblige them. They secured knives and themselves cut the legs and other parts of the animal and brought it out. The operation took 18 hours."

The captain talked his way out of an illegal landing in Rangoon. He personally bought fodder for the animals en route, paying every bill from fuel to hay himself from the briefcase.

Nowadays there are regular jet freighter services from England to the Far East for racehorses, with a single two-hour refueling stop.

Modern selection is designed to get the stable, level-headed personality rather than the individualist. Lufthansa, which trains its own pilots, has a week of non-stop screening of personality to select the one in eight of serious applicants who will get pilot training.

During the week, the would-be pilots play several games of basketball. The good team player is preferred to the original or creative player: an individualistic approach might lead to friction in the cockpit at a later stage.

A recent U.S. Navy study by Dr. Robert A. Alkov states that in crashes caused by pilot error, the pilots involved frequently had a "John Wayne" attitude about their lives and flying. Dr. Alkov, writing in *Approach* magazine, said that a composite profile of such pilots "reveals an individual who is an egocentric perfectionist with a high opinion of himself." Such a pilot is "resentful of authority [which] he feels puts unfair restrictions on his superior performance. He portrays himself as a sociable extrovert, the life of the party, and a ladies' man.

"He has a low tolerance for tension and is less in harmony with his environment and drinks too much. He feels he is above ordinary mortals and lives by his own rules."*

A system is used to measure personality, aptitude and intelligence. It is a sort of high-school exam, with psychological tests thrown in.

"Pilots rate their skills very highly. They point out that few of their fellow countrymen can take a hundred tons of metal and fuel 3,000 miles through the night and land it like a feather in another continent. But the war showed that a very large percentage of young males are perfectly capable of flying aircraft, even though they may not wish to spend their lives doing it," says a veteran medical officer.

"Basically, if you can pass an ordinary intelligence test, can see and hear all right, and are good at something that requires coordination and judging distances—clay pigeon shooting would be a perfect example, but football or driving a car would do almost as well—there is good reason to suppose that you would make a competent pilot. People think a pilot should be fit, dashing, tall, handsome. None of these qualities is necessary. In fact, they are rather thrown away by leading a life strapped to a chair."

The student pilot spends 21 months flying on single- and twin-engine light planes. By the end of training school, he will have 250 hours' flying time and a grasp of the basics of navigation

---

*The use of such behavioral analysis studies has been criticized by a doctor with one U.S. airline. "Pilots aren't fools. They get to know exactly what we're looking for, and they then turn it on for us. A guy who wants to be a fighter pilot will say he likes driving cars real fast whether he does or not. He talks hairy because he knows it's expected of a fighter boy. The opposite with a transport pilot; a guy who's a drag racer will swear blind he's never broken a speed limit. It's the same with airlines.

"So what happens now? I say to a potential pilot, 'You an extrovert?' No. 'You the life of the party?' No. 'You a ladies' man?' No. 'You like John Wayne?' Hell, no.

"But you need some sort of man to fly an airplane."

and engineering. When he joins the airline, at 19 or 20, his first job is a month learning the nuts and bolts of the jet airliner he will be flying.

His first approach to the plane is to a "cardboard bomber," a mock-up of all the dials and instruments in the cockpit. Every switch, every button, is mocked up exactly as it is on the plane. But nothing works or moves. The pilot sits in the "bomber" on an ordinary chair checking the panels until he knows instinctively and in the dark where each instrument and control is. It is called "cockpit familiarization," the first step in teaching the pilot to fly a jet without the expense and risk of actually putting him up in one.

The next simulator is slightly more sophisticated. The systems instruments "work," the dials move for the hydraulics, fuel systems, engine temperature gauges and so forth. The flight instruments and controls are dummies.

Then the pilot moves on to the big simulator, a machine that is as close to the real thing as several million dollars can make it. Everything works. Indeed, the pitch, roll and yaw movements of an aircraft are reproduced by motors. Pull back on the stick, and the nose comes up just as it would in flight. Push the throttle forward, and the airspeed indicator and fuel gauges and other instruments will react. Even the noise of the engines and the thump of the undercarriage are reproduced.

Accurate models of airports and countryside are mounted on moving belts. Television cameras roam over these, picking up the commands of precise height and angle sent to them from the pilot at the controls. Being in the simulator feels the same, sounds the same, and looks the same as being in a real aircraft.

This is where the pilot learns to fly a jet. Indeed, at the end of the course he acquires an Instrument Rating on the airliner he is to fly—without necessarily having seen one, let alone flown one.

Anything can be thrown at him: multiple engine failure, hydraulic breakdowns and loss of instruments, stalls. The simulator can "crash," signifying this by intense vibrating and banging.

Each simulator represents one particular aircraft type, having that plane's exact performance and criteria built into it. Airlines used to lose many expensive jets, and expensive crews, on training accidents. On March 8, 1971, the training captain of a 707 shut down an engine on takeoff in Scotland.* The aircraft took off normally but immediately afterward started to roll to the right and continued to do so despite full left rudder and left aileron. The captain got a measure of control back by opening up the "failed" engine. On the landing run the aircraft again veered to the right before landing successfully. The strain of the training "emergency engine failure" had fractured the lugs on the rudder power control unit.

On March 31, 1971, a 707 of Western Airlines in California† had a similar simulated engine failure on landing. The training captain advised the pilot to overshoot. The aircraft climbed to 500 feet, rolled to the right and crashed vertically into the ground. The lugs on the rudder unit had fractured.

Thus aircraft and crews are destroyed on training flights that could be carried out safely on simulators. Aircraft which normally carry passengers are subjected to dangerous maneuvers which may weaken them. In this case, three weeks passed without vital information getting from Scotland to California.

To help with air traffic control, simulator training normally builds in garbled messages, broken pidgin English, a very bad radio reception and static. It would be entirely possible for a crew who had never seen a real aircraft to emerge from a simulator, walk onto a flight deck and fly around the world.

Indeed, some pilots have 40 hours on a simulator followed by only 20 hours of base training on actual jets. They then go "on the line" for their first scheduled flight, with 20 hours flying a jet transport in their logbooks. The young copilot of a British Airways Trident had just 79 hours and 5 minutes' flying experience on jets when the immensely experienced captain collapsed in the seat next to him. He would have been expected to fly the aircraft back to safety himself had it not been in a fatal stall.

His inexperience was held partly responsible for the crash. Only two days before the Trident crash, a Japan Air Lines DC-8 crashed

---

*HMSO CAP 361.
†National Transportation Safety Board NTSB-AAR-72-18.

on the outskirts of Delhi, on the banks of the River Yamuna. Crew inexperience was again held to be a cause.

JAL was replacing its senior American pilots with Japanese, and the crew of the Bangkok–Delhi sector of JAL's Flight 471 from Tokyo to London was relatively inexperienced. Approaching Delhi on a very hot, sultry day—the temperature was 116 degrees Fahrenheit and the wind 20 knots on June 14, 1972—with the sky obscured by a dust haze, the aircraft plowed into the ground, killing 86.

The various factors which combined to cause the accident* were so shattering that JAL was obliged to restrict its routes while pilots were trained. An investigation found that a comparatively inexperienced captain and copilot were flying the jet, although they filled the legal requirements. Neither of the pilots was very familiar with the route, and they had misconceptions about the facilities available at Delhi.

They did not follow the laid-down procedures in calling out landing and approach checks, "which shows indiscipline and slackness." In conditions where an Instrument Flight Rules approach was preferable though not necessary, flight instruments were ignored after the pilots had made the first and incorrect sighting of lights.

The aircraft was cleared down only to 3,500 feet. Having come down to 2,100 instead of leveling off at 3,500 feet, the pilot continued to descend on sighting lights and landmarks near the crash site. Poor orientation led the crew to believe they had reached the outskirts of Delhi Airport, instead of a village several miles away.

Further, the copilot was allowed to make the approach, in spite of being inexperienced, by a pilot who himself could not be regarded as very experienced. The total instrument flight time of the copilot in DC-8's was "most inadequate to make an approach to an airport on a route on which he had no flight checks."

The captain did not perform the functions of a copilot after

*CAA World Airline Accident Summary 18/72-19/72.

putting the copilot at the controls. The pilots ignored the altimeters. The aircraft was down to a critical height before it was realized that the runway was not actually in sight. The "overshoot" command at this stage was late, and the engine did not develop full thrust in the six-second time lapse between the command and the crash.

The accident report summed up: "The immediate cause of the accident, therefore, appears to be the total disregard of laid-down procedures, abandoning all instrument indications without properly ensuring sight of the runway by the flight crew. The 'cause behind the cause' was pilot inexperience and pilot error. It was particularly worrying that both JAL and the Japanese Government sought to blame a false glide slope signal being transmitted from the ground. The investigator said this contention is not accepted." It is disgraceful that a national airline and government should have made it.

There is a great orderliness about a pilot's profession, in which promotion and increased salary come through the unwinding of the calendar, and not through particular skill.

And pilots are extremely well paid. Captains on wide-body jets in the U.S. can exceed $100,000 a year and the $70,000-a-year pilot is commonplace. The big European airlines like Air France and Lufthansa pay around the same. The pilots joke that the Jumbo has a great bulbous nose under the cockpit so that the pilot can sit on his wallet. Pilots, as a rule, are among the top-paid 1 percent of the population they come from. They normally retire at 60.

This does not stop them from being fractious and strike-happy. Their international union, IFALPA, first drew attention to the serious deterioration in the relationship between management and pilots back in 1968. The situation has improved little.

"They've got managers everywhere," says a young pilot. "A little guy rushes up and says you're leaving at such and such time, here's your lunch, here's your weather report, here's your passenger list, now get going. You *are* just a bus driver."

Increased speed and increased passenger capacity have cut the pilots off from the public. Chatting with passengers was always thought great therapy. "You walked back from the cockpit," says a

French pilot, "and you knew at least some people thought you were still God. It was very good for the morale. You felt your link with the great sea captains, with the captain's table."

Some pilots made a great art of passenger relations. None more so than the legendary Captain Thompson, a Scot with British Airways. The first edict asking captains to provide "in-flight entertainment" for the passengers came in 1951. Most captains took it as meaning a chat with passengers, preferably adoring girls. Captain Thompson emerged from his cockpit in a kilt, strumming a ukulele and singing "When I'm Cleaning Windows" (a well-known dirty song).

Captain Thompson would always arrive after the passengers had boarded on night flights. He would then tap his way up the aisle, with a white stick and dark glasses. The cockpit door slammed, the engines started. Then the passengers would see him open the door and grope around, pinning up a message. As the door closed, and the passengers could read the notice, he started the takeoff run. It read: "Blind Flying Tonight."

Toward the end of his career, he flew an old biplane on the routes in the Scottish Islands, a plane that had no separate passenger compartment. The pilot merely sat in the very front seat.

Thompson would board with the other passengers, taking a seat at the back, wearing plus fours, a tweed jacket and carrying a hunting cap. He and his fellow passengers would get increasingly irritated at the nonarrival of the pilot. Thompson declared that he had read a book about flying, and thought he could manage to get the thing up and probably down. Indeed, if the damn pilot didn't turn up in three minutes he'd try it.

Time up, he then strode to the pilot's seat. He took off, flying in a deliberately eccentric manner while musing aloud about which chapter had said what about landing.

Nowadays, on a wide-body aircraft, fewer and fewer pilots even bother to point out anything to the passengers over the public-address system. All information is left to prerecorded cassettes. Thompson himself has enjoyed a well-earned retirement in Scotland.

The modern pilot is a rather remote figure, far from legend. He is basically a systems engineer, operating and checking very complex electronic equipment, and only a small part artist. Even his emergency training will have been done, coldly and clinically, in a simulator.

Indeed, some pilots think that it is easier to fly a real aircraft than a simulator. "In a simulator it's tense, with examiners and instructors breathing down your neck. On the actual aircraft you can get navigational assistance from the ground, use the autopilot, all the aids. It's less sweat," says one pilot.

There are criticisms of the artificiality of much training. Young Lufthansa pilots, for example, are taught to fly in the cloudless skies above the Arizona desert. Only ground training is done in Bremen. So clear and uncrowded is the Arizona weather that each training aircraft can fly 1,700 hours in visual weather conditions against an average of 600 hours in Germany.

But, although cloud can be simulated in the air by making a pilot wear a visor, so that he can see nothing but the instrument panel, there is still something lacking in the desert air. German Luftwaffe pilots also train in Arizona, something that has been put forward as a partial reason for an appalling accident rate for German Air Force Starfighters.

"You simply cannot simulate a filthy day over the Rhur. You can almost smell the factory fumes at thirty thousand feet; there is a yellowish grease about the clouds. It's a crossroads for civilian and military flights. There is no way you could reproduce it in Arizona," says a senior captain.

Most of the conversion training to a new aircraft type is now done in simulators. Propeller pilots converting to new jets like the 707 in the 1960's averaged 22 hours of actual flying and 18 hours on a simulator. But a modern 707 pilot converting to a 747 or DC-10 averages 14 hours in a simulator and only 6 actually in the air.

One fatal crash was caused by too much simulator training.[*] The pilot had only practiced overshooting in bad weather on a simulator.

Instruments on the simulator responded immediately and

*CAA 27/65.

accurately to actual changes in attitude. But on the aircraft they took time to register and change. The pilot pulled up in the fog to go around. Nine seconds before the crash, his instruments showed that his speed had not built up although his rate of climb was good. He relaxed his pull on the elevators. With six seconds to go, his speed was still not very fast, although the rate-of-climb indicator showed that he was climbing at 850 feet a minute. He put the nose farther down.

The accident report reveals: "At four seconds before impact the vertical-speed indicator was probably showing a substantial rate of climb, and the altimeter a gain in height, though the aircraft was in fact losing height." The pilot put the nose farther down, and the aircraft plowed into the airport, killing all aboard. If the pilot had trained on a real aircraft, this might not have happened. He would have known the lag of his instruments.

The pilot is expected to do more than simply fly the aircraft nowadays. The modern twin-jets, like the BAC 111, DC-9, Boeing 737, have only two-man crews. The captain, in the left-hand seat, flies the aircraft. The copilot has to work the fuel systems, navigate, operate control levers at the captain's command, and continually monitor radio channels. On larger three-man aircraft, like the three-engine Boeing 727, the third pilot is mainly responsible for checking engine performance and the actions of the others. Most big jets carry only three crew—Boeing 707's, the Airbus, the DC-10 and even the 747 all operate with three. There are two pilots, with a third pilot acting as navigator and radio operator.

Very few aircraft now carry navigators. Getting lost in the air is almost a thing of the past. An aircraft flies from beacon to beacon along airways. Doppler sets work out ground speed, position, and course to steer. With a computer it also gives the distance flown and the distance to go. Distance Measuring Equipment gives the distance to go to ground beacons. Some navigation equipment records the position of an aircraft automatically on a chart in the cockpit.

With Inertial Guidance Systems, a pilot has a precise map display of his position. This is based on gyros. The pilot dials in his position at the start of the flight. So accurate are these systems that he can dial in the exact latitude and longitude of the particular pier he is at. The piers have their geographical position marked on them for this reason.

Thus even on a high-speed run on a vacation charter flight to an underequipped vacation airfield in the Caribbean or Mexico, a plane with 150 vacationers is considered quite safe with just two pilots. One will fly the aircraft. The other will navigate, largely a beginning of the day. Thus there is no room for personal quirks, or for making up others' weaknesses.

Teamwork is equally mechanical. Most airlines do not keep crews together, as air forces do. The pilots on a flight may very well be complete strangers who are introduced to each other at the beginning of the day. Thus there is no room for personal quirks, or for making up other's weaknesses.

The flight deck is a completely professional place, where the cockpit drills are so thorough that a group of strangers can work together safely. That is the theory. But one incident was caused by an engineer closing the throttle when the pilot, whom he had not worked with before, yelled "Takeoff power." The pilot meant him to open the throttle to the power setting for takeoff. The engineer literally took off the power, and "crashed" the plane.

Fortunately, these strangers met on a simulator.

8

Airline Girls

A passenger's life is held in a pilot's hands. However, his more immediate welfare rests with the stewardess. She has considerable power over him, and is backed by well-tested methods of dealing with him should he be rude or difficult or if she is having an off day.

The check-in staff, or "checkers," take the most abuse from the public. They have to relay the bad news that an aircraft is late, that fog has closed the destination airport, that baggage is overweight. They are not responsible for these things, but they take the blame for them.

By nature they may not be vindictive. But years of harassment have built in safety mechanisms designed to get even with those who annoy them. Their prime power is over seat allocations.

In principle, this is on a "first come, first served" basis, with an aircraft layout displayed on the check-in counter for the passenger to choose a seat from those remaining. In fact, the clerks have found that displaying it leads to trouble. Passengers resent their favorite places being taken. Arguments follow.

So many checkers keep the layout concealed on a shelf on their side of the counter. The passenger cannot choose: he takes what he is given. And this lets the checkers punish those who meet with their disfavor. Businessmen are seated with families with children, or next to talkative old ladies. Smokers are put in seats in nonsmoking zones. Those who inquire overstrenuously about the movie will wind up in window seats two rows back from the screen, the worst place in the plane for film-watching.

Experienced travelers will always avoid seats close to the toilets on long night flights, knowing that they will be waked up frequently. The check-in staff are also well aware of this, allocating these seats to those who irritate them. They know, too, that for safety reasons mothers with infants should have the wide legroom found at the ends of cabins near the bulkheads. That is also a very tempting place to seat the unsuspecting passenger who thinks he will get room and the privacy of not staring at a head in the row in front. In practice, he will get a howling infant.

"It is amazing how stupid passengers can be, especially those who pride themselves on being well traveled," says a Paris-based checker girl. "Those are normally the ones we have trouble with, who get arrogant. They fall for the cabin front seat every time. The great thing is that if they do start complaining about the baby in the next seat they are not going to get any sympathy.

"People can be stuck next to each other for fifteen hours on some flights. They know all about window seats, and where the noise is worst. But they simply don't realize that it is the person they are sitting next to or the people they are sitting between who make the real difference to their flight.

"Of course, normally we just let them sort it out themselves. But I had one businessman who was unbelievably patronizing. Knew it all. Off to Los Angeles. He still won't know that it wasn't just chance that had him stuck between a smelly hippie and a merchant seaman for five hours. You get people you like, of course, and you put attractive people together. I often wonder how many love affairs I've started by simple seat allocations."

Weight on modern jets only plays a critical part when a full fuel load coincides with a very hot day at a high-altitude airport—both height and heat make the air thinner and reduce power on takeoff. On domestic flights, the size and not the weight of baggage is the governing factor. But a difficult passenger can expect his baggage to be minutely weighed and excess charged if applicable. His hand luggage is restricted to the legal maximum of one overnight bag, one camera or pair of binoculars, and one umbrella. His boarding card is marked QQ or AL so that he is rigorously searched as a potential hijacker or scrutinized as a drunk.

Once on the aircraft, the cabin crew take over with their torments. His meal is overcooked. The food cart bumps persistently against him as he tries to sleep. He is left until last to buy from the duty-free cart, and is then told that Customs now demands that the duty-free be sealed.

In cases where the cabin crew are out of sorts, or all the passengers annoy them, they can inflict subtle misery by turning the lights from dim to full brilliance at breakfast time, blinding people awake, or by altering the cabin heat from warm to cool and back.

A stewardess's rage can follow the wretched passenger off the plane. She can tell the ramp controller on arrival that he is a suspected smuggler. This is then radioed through to Customs, and his baggage will be searched.

There are warnings on what makes passengers qualify for this inhuman treatment. "I hate the ones who say 'Hey, miss!' and the ones who click their fingers, the ones who poke you, the ones who are always asking what the time is in Timbuktu or where are we," says a stewardess. "Then there are the ones who ask several of us for the same things. I'd like to give all passengers a book of rules. The first one would be: Don't ask more than one stewardess for a glass of water. The second rule would say: 'Occupied' means there's someone in the toilet."

It is not jaundiced opinion that stewardesses are getting older.* It is a fact. During the swinging sixties, the average girl worked in the sky for just 18 months before leaving to get married. By the end of the seventies, it had crept up to 5 years for women and 10 years for stewards.

---

*Stewardesses were first used by Air France in 1931. They were thought of as nurses to deal with airsickness and other problems. Glamour crept in, ironically, in World War II, when nurses were unavailable.

The main reason is that unions have been successful in lifting the ban on married stewardesses. Further, more stewardesses now marry stewards who want them to keep at the job. In the sixties, a higher proportion married passengers, who were anxious for them to give up flying.

The most wizened cabin crew are undoubtedly the stewards on British Airways long-haul routes. Many of them came off the transatlantic liners in the days when BA had a commercial link with Cunard. They average 20 years' service, against the girls' 3½. The long-distance French line UTA averages 15 years. Air India has perhaps the youngest stewardesses, keeping them an average of just 18 months. Others with noticeably young girls include Air California, Braniff, Gulf Air, Japan Air Lines, African Airways.

The revised rules do not please the airlines. One airline journal noted sourly: "Airlines are forced to keep married stewardesses far beyond the period where they are an asset to the airlines' promotional efforts." It embarrasses the airlines when their stewardesses are older than the girls in the seductive "Fly Me" ads.

The airlines do their best to keep them looking fashionable by changing uniform styles completely every three years on average. Since this means buying 200,000 new uniforms, on a world airline basis, it is a highly expensive bit of promotion.

The average age of flight attendants in the U.S. has risen from 22 in 1968 to 30 in 1979. A growing percentage of men are now working as cabin staff—a fact that baffles some passengers. "It wasn't until I saw my first steward," says a management consultant who flies frequently, "that I began to take seriously the fact that those people are there for public safety and not just for drinks and decoration. And I'm still hesitant about asking a steward for something when there's a stewardess around."

The scrapping of the no-marriage rule has dented the image of the swinging stewardess, and length of service in the profession has soared. From a 36-percent-a-year attrition rate in 1968, United loses less than 4 percent now. United even employs a grandmother, Ruth Wagner. Donna Adams, of Eastern, summed up the new philosophy: "People have this attitude that some day you'll grow up and quit. They still have this conception of a stewardess as someone who gets free travel, never works, and is some kind of waitress. That hurts, I go to retraining school each year and I don't plan to quit until the retirement age of sixty-two, if I can help it."

Actors, models, graduate students, dancers and artists are becoming cabin staff, using the job to support themselves while waiting to strike fame and fortune.

If their age has noticeably increased, so has their ill-temper. More than 16,000 flight attendants have broken away from the Transport Workers Union and have joined independent unions to deal with several airlines in contract negotiations. Mary Ellen King, head of the breakaway union at Pan Am says: "The glamour image isn't there anymore. We have a nonstop from San Francisco to Hong Kong which serves three meals and shows two movies. There's nothing glamourous about working that hard for anyone." A stewardess on a flight from JFK to Los Angeles or Paris can expect to walk up to 13 miles during the crossing.

An anonymous TWA girl revealed to *The New York Times* an attitude passengers will, alas, have little difficulty in recognizing: "The big difference is that ten years ago you had a 'customer is always right' attitude. Today if someone gives me a hard time, I don't stand for it."

All too often, asking for a cup of coffee or a bottle of duty-free is taken as giving a hard time. Today, the customer is only right when he is asleep or mute. The most trivial request is met on some airlines, including major American carriers, with hostility and rudeness. "If flight safety had deteriorated as much as cabin service has in the past ten years," says a Chicago businessman, "there wouldn't be many airliners getting through. Cabin staff have become arrogant to a totally unacceptable level."

A major problem is that many stewards and stewardesses are mainly in the game for the massive travel benefits, with nearly free flights and cheap hotels for themselves and their families. A long weekend, with hotel, can be had in Paris out of JFK for $60, $5 more than a weekend in Madrid from Atlanta. This is what they are in it for, and they find the thought of working at the service of passengers demeaning. A poll of 50 stewardesses at JFK, Los

Angeles and Dallas/Fort Worth revealed that all but two "resented the public thinking of them as flying waitresses." Yet, in truth, that is mainly what their job is. They are waitresses, and their refusal to admit it is turning them surly and petulant.

The airlines adopt a superior indifference to the flagrant ill manners of their cabin staff. But they have become a very real problem. A survey by the Airline Passengers Association* is a deep indictment of how rude cabin staff have become. Passengers were given a list of suggestions to improve airlines. Just after the old pleas for more legroom and wider seats, and way ahead of items like better scheduling, more safety and fewer delays, came "more courteous and competent employees."

Eighty percent of the Association's members who voted Eastern as America's most avoided domestic airline† did so because of poor service and lack of courtesy.

Passengers who feel themselves ill-treated should complain to the captain on arrival. This is most simply done by using the

---

*Airline Passengers Association, 800 Airport West Freeway, Irving, Texas 75062.

†Pan Am, in my view, is singularly lucky that the APA restricted itself to domestic airlines. It is said that 10,000 girls a year apply to Pan Am. Given that wide choice, Pan Am's ability to select the pettiest and meanest-minded girls this side of Aeroflot is stunning. With other airlines, some routes are worse than others—like American Airlines' La Guardia–Dallas/Fort Worth ("Relax, will yah—that will dry-clean out, no sweat"), British Airways' notorious London–Glasgow shuttle ("Coffee, sir? Sir must be joking"), Air France's Paris–West Africa ("We 'ave ze right to sleep too, m'sieur"). Pan Am's system-wide lack of courtesy is unique. Only Gulf Air, Kuwait Airways and Air Malawi in the non-Communist world would run as close seconds.

As far as ground courtesy is concerned, despite short tempers and long lines at Miami's International and Chicago's O'Hare in particular, London's Heathrow is in a no-contest situation. The British Airports Authority is in a global league of its own when it comes to slovenliness and hostile incompetence. Despite being the proprietor of the world's largest international airport, the BAA was unable to deal with a snowfall of less than three inches in early 1979 and Heathrow was closed down. Incredible but true. Connoisseurs of airline irony may have noted that Pan Am considered withholding landing fees from the BAA to recoup revenue lost during this bizarre closure. The prospect of the world's rudest airline fighting the world's trashiest airport authority would warm the cockles of many a passenger's heart.

forward exit on disembarking: the flight deck is just in front, and the door is often ajar and usually unlocked after landing. Knock, enter and give the captain details of the cabin staff's names and behavior. A captain is responsible for the whole aircraft, and must take a dim view of sloppy stewards and stewardesses. A complaint forwarded by a captain will have far more weight with the airline than a beef that comes directly from a passenger.

The old standards are unrecognizable today. The Association of Flight Attendants' handbook of 1930* laid service on the line. "Remember at all times when on duty to maintain the respectful reserve of a well-trained servant. A ready smile is essential but never permit yourself the intimate attitude of a traveling companion. . . . Keep the cabin windowsills dusted and use a small broom on the floor before every flight. Swat flies in the cabin before takeoff. . . . Carry a railway timetable in case the plane is grounded. . . . Warn passengers against throwing lighted cigar butts out of the windows, particularly over populated areas. . . . Assist the passenger to remove his shoes, if he so desires, and clean them thoroughly before returning them to him."

Against this, modern flying is incomparably more comfortable than it was. Cabin service in the old days had to be good because so much else could go wrong. A westbound transatlantic flight today is a seven-and-a-half-hour outing once the passenger is clear of the airport and airborne. Before the jet arrived at the beginning of the sixties, one prop pilot never flew London–New York direct in more than seven years, although this was the advertised flight for his Stratocruiser, the Boeing 377.

The schedule was 17 hours but 24 hours was more common, with stops at Prestwick, Iceland and Nova Scotia and frequent diversions to Boston and Montreal. Aircraft would lag halfway and more across the Atlantic—because the prevalent westerlies were blowing the aircraft back toward Europe, the halfway time in a trip happened well after the actual halfway distance—and then "do a 180 degrees and turn back to Ireland."

The aircraft often bumped the whole way across in cloud or

*Quoted in BA ASR, October 10, 1977.

heavy icing conditions as the navigators coped with the captain's point of no return (insufficient fuel to turn around and head back home) and the PLE, the prudent limit of endurance.

Passengers needed coddling.

The job itself is straightforward. The girls check in 80 minutes before takeoff. The first girls are given lists of their passengers and a quick briefing on the likes and dislikes of any VIP's. Economy girls are given just the number of their passengers, together with any of the special categories—Compassionates, Unaccompanied Children, Non-English Speakers.

They get a supply of cash to make change for bar orders. Once aboard, they have to take care of paper work as well as serving passengers. This includes checking for forged currency. The airline business is plagued with forgeries. Descriptions of counterfeit numbers are telexed around the world and are issued to stewardesses on their exchange-rate lists on international flights. The most notorious notes are Italian 10,000-lire notes numbered L171-4117, U.S. $20 bills BO6063685 and BO6073685C, Australian $10 notes with a weak metallic thread, and Argentinian 5,000-peso notes from 457001A to 4583000A.

A special Secret Service group had to be sent to Colombia in January 1979, so widespread has the counterfeiting of U.S. currency there become. Although 70 percent of counterfeit dollars are U.S. made, usually by rank amateurs, 65 percent of the much more sophisticated foreign-made dollars come from Colombia. Smaller amounts, also of good quality, came on flights from Canada, the Far East and France.

With Americans paying out perhaps $25 billion a year for marijuana, there is plenty of need for dollars in Colombia. Secret Service agents seized $18,337,000 in fake dollars in fiscal 1978 before they could be circulated, but at least $4,000,482 in counterfeit money was confiscated after it was on the market in the same period. Of this, almost $1 million was foreign made.

Airlines have to be careful since the last holder of a hot bill takes the loss—there is no reimbursement from the Treasury even if a citizen turns in a fake bill.

One agent caught a middle-aged amateur in Los Angeles who

was churning out counterfeits on an old press with the help of a library book on printing. "He had a hundred and fifty thousand dollars ready to go," the agent told UPI with a trace of admiration. "And he hadn't even returned the library book."

Most counterfeiters still age their bills by soaking them in coffee. Another L.A. loser told agents that his very superior ink had been obtained by lacing it with Jack Daniels.

Airlines, casinos and theme parks like Disney World are favorite places for unloading counterfeits. But, with staff trained to pick them out, they are the worst places to do so.

Stewardesses are not medically trained. The emphasis in the short training period is on personal appearance, and on serving food in a cabin mock-up. On many airlines, the girls have only a rudimentary knowledge of first aid and evacuating the aircraft. Cabin staff panic has been a feature of several crashes.

"What happens if someone dies? Oh, we're trained to cover him up with a blanket so he looks as if he's asleep. We get a half-hour lecture on how to deliver babies, but I've never needed it, thank heavens," says one girl. So it is standard practice to ask if there is a doctor on board if someone is taken ill.

A typical training schedule gives one week on safety equipment, two days on medicine, one day each on fire, deportment, grooming and hairstyling, and three weeks on cabin service.

The stewardesses have two medical boxes. A turquoise box holds the A2 medical kit—aspirin, airsickness tablets, Dettol, bandages, eye drops, scissors. The black A10 box is sealed and locked and the girls can open it only with the captain's permission. It has the heart stimulant nikethamide, the heavy sedative Amatol, and morphine.

The cabin-crew routine is hard. A typical 21-day trip starts with a transatlantic from New York to Frankfurt. There follows Frankfurt to Teheran via Beirut, a 13-hour haul. Twenty-four hours off in Teheran (not a favorite, with its insistent youths and revolutionaries) is followed by a 6-hour flight "deadheading" to Delhi as a passenger. From Delhi, the girl works on the 5-hour trip to Bahrein before getting her next 24-hour rest.

From Bahrein, she goes on to Hong Kong via Bangkok, a 13-hour working day, followed by another 24 hours off at Hong

Kong, From there, the girl jets to Sydney and a three-day stopover before working her way back along the route to New York.

There are compensations. The girls pay only 10 percent of regular air fares when they go on holiday. Big hotel chains, like Inter-Continental, Holiday Inns and Hilton, give a 50 percent discount.

Some hotels in the Persian Gulf will pay stewardesses to stay there, since they drum up bar and night club business from well-heeled locals merely by being there.

Small wonder, then, that the girls look like walking travel posters. Their 10-destination baggage tags are marked "CREW" in red capitals. The hotel stickers on the faded tote bags (new girls leave them out in the sun to fade, much as the pilots do with the gold stripes on their uniforms) read "Antigua, Trinidad Hilton, President Bangkok, Bermuda, Casa Mia Jo'burg, Swinging Seychelles." These status symbols, too, are carefully dirtied and torn, as if they were only there because some irritating hotel baggage boy put them there. Stewardesses are just as big travel snobs as their passengers.

Stewardess parties are a blend of the same self-conscious internationalism. The cigarettes come in all sizes and brands, the liquor out of old, often refilled bottles, the talk and the suntans from many countries.

There is a flight crew camaraderie that encircles the world, with the same vaguely dull jokes and catch names for airlines. It's "dangling the Dunlops" where the layman might lower the landing gear, "dropping the rubber jungle" when the oxygen masks come down in the passenger cabin.

The airlines are Pandemonium Scareways, or Pan Am; Air Chance, Air France; TWA, Try Walking Airlines; Queer and Nice Types of Stewards, or Qantas of Australia. There is Every Landing Always Late of Israel, Sweet and Sexy SAS, Can't Promise Anything of Canada. Hysteria Airlines, or Iberia. Garuda of Indonesia works out as Good Airline Run Under Dutch Administration (the Dutch quit years ago). There is Stay at Home Stay Alive, or SAHSA of Honduras.

Lufthansa becomes Let Us Fondle the Hostesses and Not Say Anything, Delta is Don't Ever Leave the Airport and American

Airlines translates into Amateurs Anonymous. If something is "full of Eastern promise" it means it is going to be late, and if a couple are United they are getting divorced.

Even the practical jokes are international. New girls are asked for a sickbag by the copilot. A can of vegetable soup is poured into the bag. When the girl goes back to collect it, the captain tastes it with a finger—"Ummm, not bad." Or she is asked to put all the air vents at full blow and pointing backward to get additional speed. She will get her revenge on a new pilot with a Junior Jet badge and a baby's bottle.

There is the lavatory flushing routine. The new girl is told the aircraft has no automatic flushing, so it has to be done manually. She is instructed to press a button in the cockpit for 45 seconds every 20 minutes. In fact, this is a circuit breaker nicely positioned above the captain's head so that she has to bend over him to get at it. Another ploy is to fill the demonstration oxygen mask with pepper.

There are RT, radio transmission, jokes for every country. The Frankfurt RT joke shows the standard. Ground: "Vy haf you stopped taxiing?" Captain: "We've just ingested one of your sea gulls into an engine." Ground: "Vich one?" Captain: "Dunno. You've seen one sea gull, you've seen them all."

And airline jokes. The legendary South African Airways pilot Captain van der Merwe is asked for his height and position. Quick as a flash, he radios back: "Six foot two and in the cockpit."

The wit shown by one girl fired by BA has, alas, long passed. "What is the servant situation like in England?" she was asked by a domineering woman in first. "Madam," she replied, "I am sure you will have no difficulty in finding a position."

Stewardesses talk the new language of the air: "no shows," passengers who do not turn up to join the flight they are booked on; "slipstops," points where an aircraft changes, or "slips," its crew; "shooting a letdown," for an approach and landing; "interliners," passengers transferring from one airline to another at a transit stop.

They learn some pilots' jargon as well. "Alternates" are the airports listed on the flight plan to fly to if the aircraft is diverted from its destination. "Holding" is the pattern flown by an aircraft waiting to land; a "stack" is made up of all the aircraft flying holding patterns. "Notams" are the notices to airmen used for route information.

Airports themselves are abbreviated by International Three Letter Codes, although the stewardess will know by now that an airport should always be called a "station." They must be memorized, and they are not logical or easy. ORD is Chicago's O'Hare Field,* GIG turns out to be Rio's Galeao Airport, and an aircraft going to YEG is en route to Edmonton's International.

The abbreviations are important, as they are used on tickets, baggage tags and itineraries. A mistake can mean a passenger or baggage going to the wrong destination. The reason for the confusion is that most airports, unlike seaports, have different names from the parent city, and some cities have three or more airports. Thus Detroit has DTT, DTW and YIP, for the City, Metropolitan and Willow Run airports. Paris comes on flight schedules as ORY, LBG, CDG and ISS, for Orly, Le Bourget, Charles de Gaulle and Issy-Les Moulineaux airports.

Flight numbers help passengers make sure they are catching the right aircraft. It is notoriously easy to get on the wrong aircraft, as Mrs. Shirley McVay will testify. She and her two-year-old son boarded a plane at Los Angeles after going to her father's funeral. She thought it was going to Chicago, although she was puzzled by the time it took and the large expanse of water it crossed. After eleven and a half hours, she arrived in London.

By international agreement, all flights traveling either north or east should have flight numbers which are even, and those flying south or west have flight numbers which are odd. Thus a flight from Baltimore to Dallas should have an odd number since it goes westward, where Chicago to Boston should be even for eastward. Should. Unfortunately this rule is often ignored.

Cabin staff have a developed sense of fringe benefits. An efficient cabin crew can strip a 707 in 20 minutes. They often do so, commonly when the lights are dimmed after dinner and before breakfast on a long-haul flight. Some crews prefer the final approach, when passengers are strapped in and the curtains

*Years ago, it was called Orchard Place Airport, hence ORD.

around the galleys are pulled shut. The restless or observant passenger may notice that the cabin crew are moving softly with large bags to the rear of the aircraft and hovering around the galley area.

Methodically, the stewards first "rumble" the dry stores. "Rumbling" is the professional word for looting. Cans of chicken supreme, minced beef, Dundee cake, instant coffee, tea bags and crisp bread slide into "coat bags."

The coat bag is the greedy steward's best friend, and the reason why he can always outloot stewardesses. It is a large bag into which he puts his starched uniform jackets. There is plenty of room for more than clothes.

The steward cooks his looted meals in his hotel room by using a "dipstick" or a "hot-cup." The first is an electrical filament that can be slipped into any liquid to heat it, the latter a cup-shaped heating pot that will scramble eggs.

By using the dry stores and milk and fruit juice from the galley, a steward can get through a three-day stopover abroad without spending anything. His $40-a-day meal allowance goes straight into his pocket.

He can be more ambitious at home and can stock up for the whole household. The Stilton jar from first, the unused, still-frozen steaks, the vegetables, the fruit, disappear into the coat bag. As the galley is thoroughly done over, liquor from the first-class bar is decanted into plastic bottles. The drinks are free in first, and consequently the airline has no idea how much has actually been consumed by passengers and how much has gone as perks. Plastic bottles are used because the original glass ones have the name of the airline printed on them, and would be incriminating evidence at home.

Even the mixes go. "Some stewards think the war's still on and there's rationing," says a stewardess. "You get back to the galley before touchdown just wanting a couple of oranges, and the men have taken them. I mean, even the yogurt and the cornflakes. They come along with Tupperware all ready for the shrimp cocktails."

After the food and the complimentary cigarettes and liquor have been taken, there is a mad rush for the lavatories. Here at least the girls are permitted by tradition to have first claim on the baby powder, skin tonic, the milky cleanser, moisture and hand lotion, eau de cologne and Tampax. The perfumes and lotions are decanted into plastic containers.

The stewards then clean out the after- and pre-shave lotions, the talc and the Kleenex. The toothpaste is requisitioned. The first-aid kit is denuded of Dettol, aspirin, Elastoplast, scissors and eye drops.

Rumbling is relatively safe away from home base. As long as the liquor and cigarettes stolen are within local duty-free limits, they are of as little interest to Customs officials as the tins of chicken and candy bars. At home base, Customs has no authority either except on dutiable items, but it is far more likely to pass on the names of the rumblers to the airline.

Customs agents swarm onto an aircraft immediately after the last passenger is off. First they check the bar seals, which are put on by the crew before landing, and take the removable stores list. They put their own seals on the bars and check the crew list for declarations. The moment of truth for the crew comes when they go down the steps to the crew bus.

Company security men may be on it, and they can dismiss cabin staff for a stolen can of tonic. The Customs "Rummage Squad" could be there, too. It will take a crew and their luggage, and if need be their aircraft, to pieces. "They're sitting waiting for you in the bus, smiling at you just a little. Then it's straight off in the bus to the Customs sheds, and they go through the lot. And when they rummage they do all of it—squeeze the toothpaste, sniff all your ciggies for hash. Even if there's nothing there they practice on you. Cabin crew are the sort of tame thing for experimenting on. The public wouldn't stand for it," says an American girl.

Perks extend beyond stripping an aircraft. Some cabin crew are basically self-employed businessmen. They have wives or boy-friends running shops and boutiques at home which are stocked with curios they fly back wholesale. An Air France man flies to Nairobi with piles of old clothes bought in the Flea Market. He trades these for wooden carvings which his girl friend sells on the Left Bank.

Each route has its favored goods. Onyx chess sets from Mexico, camel saddles and leather bags from Beirut, cameras and hi-fi from

Hong Kong, crocodile handbags and watch straps from Rio and Buenos Aires, gold from Kuwait—all can be bought, shipped home free and sold at a guaranteed profit.

Free shipping can be overdone. A British airline captain was discovered to be running a flourishing fruit-importing business purely on the ability to freight in fresh fruit jet-quick, and completely free, in the forward freight compartment of his 707. A group of American pilots maintained a chain of highly successful seafood restaurants on the East Coast because they were flying in cheap West Coast seafood at a cost only to their unwitting company.

Both these businesses were uncovered because of the scale of the operation. The 707 skipper was flying an aircraft that was so fuel-thirsty on its return flights from East Africa that a young man being trained by the airline thought he would take this aircraft and crew as a theoretical problem in fuel management.

There seemed no reason for the excess consumption. Why should a captain be "heavy" on the throttles and burn up the fuel only when returning from Africa—not when going out, and not when returning from anywhere else? The aircraft engines were well within maintenance times, and were not normally expensive on fuel. Headwinds were not affecting other pilots.

The aircraft settled out of a leaden winter sky from Africa and was surrounded by security men. The trainee's final theory proved correct, in the form of a ton of avocados, oranges, passion fruit and pawpaws that were not on the cargo manifest.

The seafood pilots were as unlucky. They abandoned a takeoff and the heavy braking resulted in the electrical circuits being flooded. It was a strange experience for the company to find an aircraft full of water. An investigation turned up the lobster tanks, which had spilled over during the emergency stop.

"Freefreighting,"* as it is called, is quite widespread. Employees, including ground staff, are often given a 220-pound freight

---

*It is most common in the military. I met a sergeant in the Delta area of Vietnam who put Milo Minderbinder, the free-freighting star of *Catch-22,* to shame. This ingenious soldier, nominally a machine gunner, hired most of a transport squadron from the pilots. He used it to ferry in neon signs, jukeboxes and bar equipment for the red-light district he was developing.

concession a year for "personal goods." Arabs and Asians working for French and British airlines have used this concession to start highly successful freight and import-export businesses.

Though it does not happen in the U.S., foreign check-in staff will often insist on being paid for excess baggage in cash. There is, of course, no reason why the passenger should not pay by credit card. But the check-in staff will say that the airline does not accept cards for excess baggage because of the charge made by the credit companies. They then simply pocket the cash. Beware those "friendly" types who, having calculated excess baggage at, say, $63.25, enthuse: "Why don't we call it a straight fifty dollars in notes?"

It is tempting to settle for $50. Even if it goes to the employee and not the airline, that is hardly the passenger's affair, and a saving of $13.25 is not to be sniffed at. It is, however, often possible to circumvent the charge entirely. A passenger should be given an excess baggage ticket: issuing this will prevent the employee from gypping the airline since it is traceable.

The instant reaction to a request for a receipt is: "In that case, we'll have to charge the full amount." At this stage the passenger is strongly recommended to call the airline supervisor and to reveal the bargaining that has been going on. The charge is likely to be dropped entirely.

Few passengers do this in practice. That is why ground staff notably in Rio, Rome and Madrid have turned excess baggage into a profitable fringe benefit.

Some cabin crew have in-flight businesses, with the traveling public as the customers. Even relatively crude ideas work. Stewards sell wrapped cutlery sets as souvenir packs for a few dollars, and leave saucers in the toilets for tips. A Royal Air Laos crew rechristened their lavatories "cloakrooms," with well-tipped attendants. Inexperienced holiday travelers often fall for these simple ploys.

In-flight entertainment has given wide and well-grasped opportunities to the crew. Thus earphones are rented out for watching movies or listening to stereo music by the airlines. Many girls are skilled at resealing the packs. The apparently brand-new issue, neatly and freshly wrapped, will in fact have been resealed several times. The money goes straight to the crew.

Some girls "own" their own earphones, accumulated slowly over flights from "breakages" and those "taken off by passengers." They dole them out on a 50:50 basis with the airlines' headsets. On movie flights (popular anyway with cabin crews because the movie keeps the passengers quiet), a girl can make 25 or more rentals of her own equipment, $50 or so of pure profit a flight.

A cursory examination of a steward's effects as he boards an aircraft might reveal the odd fact that he is taking empty miniatures and quarter-liter bottles aboard, together with a funnel and a child's flexible drinking straw.

He needs the empties to start business. During takeoff, with people still strapped in but the complimentary liquor for first-class passengers already flowing and the tourist bar about to open, the steward busily funnels liquor from the first class bottles into miniatures. This is called "dipping." Without taking on his own empties, he would have to wait until passengers drank a first "genuine" round before entering business on his own account.

The miniature market is vast. Pan Am sells more than 12 million a year, BA 8 million, United 17 million, Lufthansa 3 million. Worldwide more than 177 million are sold, some of them purely for the profit of the crew.

An indication can be a solicitous steward who insists on opening the miniature. Breaking the seal can indeed be awkward, though the steward will often "open" it for the very good reason that the seal was broken several flights before, and the bottle is full of first-class gin or whiskey.

The money paid goes straight into the steward's or stewardess's pocket. With a full first-class compartment on a 707 of 16 (cabin layouts and numbers differ), the equivalent of 32 miniatures of spirits and 16 splits of champagne or wine can be siphoned off with little chance of discovery. These are sold to tourist-class passengers for some $60.*

---

*The rewards on the wide-body jets, with their hundreds of passengers, are correspondingly higher. Thus cabin staff call their 747's, DC-10's and 1011's "the Big Dippers."

Enterprising cabin crew also find that they can undercut their employers by selling duty-free cigarettes and liquor. Cigarettes sell duty-free for $2 a carton in Bahrein. Yet most airlines charge $6 for them off the duty-free cart. That profit margin has proved irresistible to many stewards on the great routes which transit Bahrein. They buy their own duty-free cartons and sell them to passengers at the airline price—a 200 percent profit for them. Cartier tank watches sold for $1,200 on flights from the Middle East are bought by the cabin crew for $500 in Kuwait.

In reverse, liquor and cigarettes are smuggled into places where they cost more than on the aircraft. The crew buy up the duty-free from the cart, noting it on the liquor and cigarette sheets as having been bought by passengers. The airline will not query a pleasant upsurge in sales: indeed, it will usually pay the crew a commission on the goods they have in fact bought for themselves.

The actual smuggling is normally left to ground staff and cleaners. A steward might try making $17 a bottle on Scotch in Delhi with four or five in his coat bag. But if he's a serious operator, who has just bought up the aircraft's total supply of perhaps 10 dozen bottles, he will leave a ground operator to get them past Customs and settle for 50 percent of the profit.

Few cabin crew deny what goes on. Flight-deck crew are seldom involved. "It's partly because, with their money and skill, it's not worth the risk," says a steward. "But also it's because we wouldn't let them. Those are our perks. They get enough in salary."

Visits to their apartments show there would be little point in denials. The whiskey bottles are always the same, the label getting more faded as they are constantly refilled from the plastic bottles. The bathrooms are full of colognes and creams, awash with Kleenex and small tubes of toothpaste.

The cigarettes are a wild assortment of brands, tastes and countries of origin. The sugar comes in tiny plastic bags. The pepper and salt come in individual airline packs. The food will be pleasantly out of season, the fruit exotic.

One top rumbler has perfected his perks to the point of fetishism. The cutlery, linen, china, glasses, all come from aircraft cabins, still with incriminating airline motifs stamped on them.

The meal is served from an aircraft first-class cart, which the host proudly explains he was able to "rumble" despite its size.

The wines and liqueurs are poured from bottles bearing the airline's name. The menu is written out neatly. For a small dinner party, smoked Scotch salmon, sirloin steak in white wine sauce, mushrooms and tomato, buttered asparagus spears with *pommes parisienne,* palm heart salad, assorted cheese, fruit basket, *friandises,* all of it rumbled from a plane that day.

9

Passengers

People behave strangely on aircraft. Take this telex message from H. Rodriques, a shift supervisor in Honolulu. It is filed as supervisor report Flight BA591/459:

Prior to arrival Captain Thompson radioed operations advising that he wanted a British Airways senior official to meet his aircraft on arrival at Honolulu. He stated he had two passengers on board the aircraft who were creating problems. What the actual problem was, was unknown at this time. Ops advised Station Manager Mr. Benson, who came out to meet the aircraft.

On arrival Mr. Benson and myself contacted Captain Thompson to see what the problem was. We were advised that a man in seat 25A and a married woman seated 19A got together during flight and were using profane language and molesting one another. They were both in the last row of seats, row 25. Two other passengers seated directly in front of them complained to the chief steward. The CS approached them to control their actions as they were causing an inconvenience to other passengers.

The lady became quite irate and requested to see the captain. This was arranged and the captain advised her that he could not permit these sort of actions on board the aircraft. She told the captain that she was going to kill him on arrival in Honolulu. Captain Thompson advised her to take her seat or he would turn her over to the police on arrival. She returned to her seat but only to carry on where she had left off with Mr.—.

Per Captain Thompson and the chief steward both passengers had sexual intercourse right in the plain sight of all other passengers. Captain Thompson stated once this was completed they both settled down and went to sleep and were of no bother from that point on. As a result Captain Thompson did not feel they should be off-loaded. As far as he was concerned they just needed to get it off and would not be of any more inconvenience to other passengers. Outgoing captain and chief steward were contacted and advised of the situation and both agreed to leave well enough alone. Both of these passengers were traveling JFK/SYD.

The incident was on a British Airways VC-10 flight from JFK to Sydney.

Such sexual escapades are by no means rare. They usually involve passengers who have never seen each other before. "Love at first flight" is how the airlines put it. In the majority of cases, they do not even share the same destination. This is a major attraction: the affair is totally fancy-free, with no chance of complicating follow-ups.

Modern aircraft are less suitable for lovemaking than the gracious giants of the past. The postwar Stratocruisers, huge double-deckers that serviced the North Atlantic, had curtained-off luxurious bunks.

Connoisseurs claim that the last great Five Mile High Machine (the Five Mile High Club being an institution for those who claim to have made love in the air) was the turboprop Lockheed Electra. In the first-class cabin back in the tail was a long daybed which was easily locked off from the rest of the aircraft. The Electra itself suffered from a tendency to shed its wings in flight at one point, but this merely added a wholesome sense of urgency to proceedings on the bed.

Japanese stewardesses took a dim view of their passengers when Japan Air Lines introduced a sleeper service on long-distance flights in 1978. They went on strike to have the service abolished. "Men passengers are sometimes undressed when we serve them drinks," said one stewardess. "At other times, I must face intimate couples in bed." The girls urged the sleeper service be discontinued on "moral grounds."

Passengers with an eye for the stewardesses should remember the cautionary tale of Aubrey Bumguard. A Texas oil worker on leave from the North Sea, Bumguard took a National Airlines flight from London to Miami on January 20, 1977. He slapped two stewardesses, Patti Dewbody and Jane Otto, on their bottoms. Contrary to National's "Fly Me" image, he was reported and charged under the Federal Air Piracy Act in Miami. This makes it a felony "while on an aircraft to assault, intimidate or threaten a crew member or flight attendant so as to interfere with their duties." The maximum penalty is 20 years and an $8,000 fine.

Mr. Bumguard's case was referred to a grand jury, and he got six months' probation and a $586 fine.

First-class travel today appears exotic in the brief moments when the curtain is pulled aside and it can be glimpsed from the economy cabin. The first-class passenger has already checked in at a special counter, waited in a special lounge, been driven out to the aircraft in a special coach and walked up special steps.

The free bar, together with free cigarettes and cigars, starts before takeoff with champagne cocktails. The seats are more like armchairs, deep, with wide arms. On 747's there is an upstairs bar, behind the cockpit and reached by a circular staircase from the normal cabin level. It has casual sofas and coffee tables, and its own barman.

The food is superb, served by the cream of the airline's stewardesses.* IATA regulations allow five courses at dinner and

---

*Most American and European airlines have had to bow to pressure from militant feminists and first-class stewardesses are appointed by seniority, and not looks. As a result, the high payers at the front wind up with some of the more mature girls. The level of service, however, is vastly better than in tourist.

lunch, where only three are permitted in economy. Personal attention is excellent. Buttons are sewn back on, letters and postcards are taken to be posted on arrival, coats and jackets are hung up in closets, and passengers are addressed by their names.

There are free presents, to a maximum of $3, such as cologne, slippers, and sleeping masks, kimonos and golf caps.

But this is not a great deal extra for paying half as much again as the economy passenger. It mainly appeals to businessmen on expense accounts, who now make up 85 percent of first class. This is sad, since it makes first on the business routes a more boring and predictable cabin than economy.

This is not to rule out every first-class passenger as a dullard. Lady Beaverbrook, widow of a newspaper tycoon, refused permission to take her dog into first class (dogs should travel in the hold), promptly chartered the whole plane, an Air Canada DC-8, to take her from London to Canada. It cost her $17,000. Aspiring actresses book themselves first on flights to Venice and Nice (for Cannes) to be near directors, turning the jets at film festival times into casting couches. It is revealing to see how many arrive first at Las Vegas, and leave economy. For sheer beauty and wealth, however, first class on the 747's and Concorde from Paris to Rio in February, for the Carnival, is perhaps unequaled.

People in first occasionally liven things up for those in steerage. Economy passengers on National Airlines Flight 51 were droning through the haul from Miami to Los Angeles on a hot June day in 1978 when a young blonde appeared from first determined to cheer them up. She first stripped, and then climbed nude over six rows of seats. Perched on Row 27, she sipped champagne from the bottle that was her only adornment, and told the cheering cabin: "I've just inherited five million dollars and I'm celebrating."

She then fell fast asleep and, covered with a blanket, dreamed her way to L.A. Said the airline: "We are not aware that she is anyone well known but she does seem to have a desire to be so."

Drunkenness is common to both classes on all but Saudia of Saudi Arabia and Libyan Arab Airlines, which are strictly dry. People drink too much through fear or tension, and the effects are multiplied by the rarefied air of the cabin. This is the equivalent of being on top of a 6,000-foot mountain, with half the moisture of the air in the middle of the Sahara. This combination makes a drink in the air worth at least two on the ground. The effect is even greater on a flight at very high altitude, above 37,000 feet, where cabin air is thinner still.

Particular types get drunk and worry cabin crews the world over. "You recognize the danger signs even if you're dealing with a race of people you know nothing about," says a stewardess. "It's people who are not used to drinking. You can tell very simply. They will always ask for whiskey. It's the only drink that means alcohol to them. And they won't have the first idea of what to put in it: offer ice or water or ginger ale and they'll say 'yes, please' to all three."

A captain can arrest any passenger whose behavior is prejudicial to safety, and the passenger can then be sentenced by a court on arrival at the destination. In practice, however, airlines rarely prosecute their passengers.*

Many people who, for the strictest religious or social reasons, would never normally drink change in the air. Among those most affected are Chinese and Muslims. "Charter flights back from Hong Kong with Chinese kitchen workers can be real hell," says a pilot. "They get very drunk very quickly. They all play Mah-Jongg, which doesn't help because it's the perfect fuel for rows and fights.

"I've been back plenty of times. It's like a Conrad ship—you get them trying to open the doors, fighting, shouting. But the uniform calms them pretty quickly."

Crews are agreed that the ultimate horror is athletes, particularly in teams. The same pilot says he would rather fly a hundred Chinese charters than one sector he did back from Mexico City after the Olympics. "They are all either super-angry because they haven't won a medal after years of training, or super-elated. They are also super-fit. That means they get super-drunk super-fast. It

---

*Admanant nonsmoker John McAward is an exception. Irritated that American Airlines could not give him a seat in a nonsmoking section of the aircraft, he was charged with delaying the jet's takeoff for 45 minutes.

also means you can't push them around. The uniform doesn't do much to that lot," he said.

The most common affliction to passengers is fear. It affects at least 20 percent of those who fly: an Air Canada survey of passengers puts it at 27 percent. It can hit anywhere at any time. A former flying doctor suddenly had phobias: "My personal fear is particularly embarrassing as first, being a doctor, I feel I should be able to overcome the phobia, and second because for nearly three years I ran a 'flying doctor' type service over the jungles of Malaya and Borneo for the Marines, with whom I was a medical officer in the early 1960's.

"Not only did I enjoy every minute of this rather dangerous flying but frequently piloted the helicopters and Beavers myself, including trips to situations under fire from the other side.

"I am sure my phobia originates in a near fatal incident in a British Eagle Trooping Britannia at Bombay Airport. Since then I have looked upon flying as a passenger in abject terror, although I have, in the past, deliberately flown from London to Scotland to test my reactions. I arrive at the destination in such a state of stress that it is no longer worth trying."

This fear is held in common by Mohammed Ali, Doris Day, stuntman Evel Knievel, rock superstar David Bowie, Hermione Gingold: the list is long.

Mohammed Ali, asked on television what he was most frightened of, replied: "Flying. That's the only thing that terrifies me. I'm flying all the time and I feel it's time for one to crash. I don't control the airplane. Some pilot does.

"Say we're between America and England. And the engines stop. Now even if it gets down there without the engines, how am I gonna find my life raft? And even if I do, how are they gonna see me in the dark? And what happens if a shark comes along and rubs against it?"

Few airlines bother to give special training to cabin crew on flying phobia. This is despite the fact that pilots are every bit as prone to the fear as anyone else. The American Air Line Pilots' Association admits to having its own "white-knuckle brigade."

Doctors think there are three main causes: claustrophobia (most passengers are happier in partly empty aircraft), vertigo, and a phobia that the lump of metal cannot stay in the sky. There are societies for sufferers.

There are seminars, often held in hangars, since many people find it difficult just to visit an airport. Pilots give talks explaining how an aircraft works. This often develops into group therapy sessions.

Pan Am pilot Truman "Slim" Cummings originated courses for fearful flyers at JFK. He takes them for an hour-long "graduation flight" on a 707. Those who get through the trip satisfactorily are awarded diplomas and framed copies of John Gillespie Magee, Jr.'s poem, "High Flight"—"Oh! I have slipped the surly bonds of Earth . . ."

A fearful flyer leader says: "Nearly all our members are people who fly frequently. People come with heartrending stories of their children in California whom they cannot see. Or their vacation homes which they want to visit for three weeks and find that the week before they go they are so tensed up it takes a week after they arrive to wind down from the flight. They get one week of vacation, and then the last week of the vacation they are winding up again, getting ready for flight. Businessmen fly out on a trip and find they are in no state to do any business when they arrive."

He hopes that people who suffer from fear may get special luggage stickers and ticket holders. "It would help enormously, both at the airport and in the air, if staff could tell at a glance that someone needed special treatment."

A few pilots take particular care to reassure passengers. Captain Frank S. Hlavacek, who flies a DC-10 on American Airlines' Flight 6 from New York to Los Angeles, explains the noises the passengers will hear in detail over the PA system before takeoff. He points out that the squeals, groans and whistles are part and parcel of normal loading and taxiing. He warns of the heavy thump after takeoff, caused by the retracting landing gear, and the cutback in engine power during noise abatement.

Air Canada's Fear Relief Center in Toronto has six-session courses and claims a 90 percent success rate.

But all too often this huge army of the fearful is sneered at. "We call them caterpillars," says a captain. "You know, he looks up and sees a butterfly. 'Huh! You wouldn't get me up in one of those things,' he says to himself."

There are more than 20 known cases a day of flight hysteria at a big airport like JFK. Others are painfully but quietly coped with by the passengers without being noted. Yet airlines do nothing to help, though they spend millions on reassuring advertising—KLM changed the stripes on its insignia from diagonal to horizontal "to promote a greater feeling of security." However, most major airports have medical centers with special travelers' help units staffed by volunteers from International Travelers Aid, a branch of the YWCA.

The symptoms of the phobia are unmistakable. The mouth becomes extremely dry, the hands shake slightly and seem difficult to control. A nervous habit, such as coughing or scratching the head, flares up. There is an acute sense of panic and an inability to cope. Breathing is shallow and rapid and the heartbeat increases. The best antidote is to do something to break the concentration on panic, reading if possible or talking to somebody else. In extreme cases, walking to the toilet and washing the face with cold water is often effective in switching the mind off panic.

Far from being panic-stricken however, the average passenger tends to be overoptimistic about flying. A test group was asked to choose the number of airline crashes and deaths in one year, with five sets of figures given. The great majority opted for the lowest figures—4 crashes, 14 fatalities. The actual figures were the highest, 19 crashes and 214 deaths.

An international survey of 6,000 passengers revealed an interesting list of their priorities. They put in-flight service first, then public reputation, satisfactory past experience as a passenger, convenient schedules and comfort. Safety was well down the list.

It is difficult to assess which is the safest airline. Airlines never stress their safety records in their advertisements: punctuality, experienced crews, superior engineering, good maintenance and other safety aspects they may mention, but safety itself they do not.

This is partly because it would be tempting fate to advertise an accident-free history, partly because it is thought that it would frighten passengers away, but mainly because IATA forbids it. Airline advertising has to concentrate on the safe trivia of flying, the beauty of the stewardesses, the excellence of the food, or the width of the seats.

But it is certainly possible to see where it is safest to fly if not always with whom. Research shows that United States airlines are much safer than the world average. American flights have been four to five times less likely to crash than the world average.

The Western European airlines are right on the average. Those from Africa are twice as bad, from Asia two and a half times as bad. The airlines of South and Central America and the Middle East are four times worse than average and those from Eastern Europe, though excluding Russia's giant Aeroflot, for which accurate statistics do not exist, are a frightening 10 times worse.*

During 1978 the world's scheduled and nonscheduled airlines carried 765 million passengers, killing just 986 of them. That gave odds of 775,862 to 1 against being killed.

There is not much doubt of the free world's most dangerous country: Colombia. Not without reason do Colombian pilots, alone among Spanish speakers, call a landing not "*aterrizar*" but "*caer*." That means not "to land" but "to fall." The standard reply of Colombian pilots to the question "What is your destination?" is "*Hasta donde caiga*"—"To where we fall."

It isn't that aircraft are unimportant in Colombia. They are vital

*The loss rate of jet airliners shows a marked difference in geographical areas, and a steady improvement from 1965 to 1978, with the exception of Africa. One jet hull (or aircraft) is lost per the number of flying hours given.

	1965	1978
World 1 loss per	265,000 hrs	460,000
Australia, S. Pacific	335,000	2,744,000
U.S.	354,000	761,000
Canada	310,000	469,000
W. Europe	306,000	412,000
Central, S. America	244,000	313,000
Asia	131,000	235,000
Africa	204,000	217,000

in a vast country with mountains up to 20,000 feet. And it isn't that Colombian pilots are unskilled. As the head of their Pilots' Association, Jaime Mejia Soto, says: "It's not the fault of the pilots. If there was a gold medal for safe flying under difficult circumstances, we would win it hands down."

Colombia's position at the bottom of the planet's safety league is the fault of the aircraft, the airports and the operators. Eighty percent of the country's 1,000 registered aircraft are at least second hands: of these, more than a quarter are more than eighth hand. They normally come to the end of their healthy working lives in the U.S. and are sold off abroad from Miami's International, gradually working their way down the fitness scale and the Central American isthmus until they arrive in Colombia.

The airports are so poor that, as we have seen, no fewer than seven appear on the IFALPA black list. This record, in getting every single major airport blacklisted, is also a world first. Few Colombian airports have proper navigation aids. Runways are pitted with holes. Rescue trucks and fire extinguishers are old and unreliable. Air traffic control is desultory.

Operators do not maintain their aircraft properly and habitually overload them. One DC-3 was loaded with a ton of freight and 39 passengers; DC-3's maximum is 2.8 tons of freight or 28 passengers. The Cessna 185 that flies from Villavicencio to Miraflores has two seats: five other passengers cram in on the floor.

An ancient DC-6 of the Caribbean airline LAC rolls for takeoff at Bogotá. It heaves into the air, veers and hits a treetop with its port wing. A fuel tank is pierced. The aircraft, on a newspaper run to the Colombian north coast, explodes. Seven passengers illegally aboard the freighter are killed with the crew. The safety report is a marvel of brevity: "Due to an accident, the aircraft caught fire."

A dozen commercial pilots are killed in a good year—"1973, that was a very bad year," says Captain Soto. "Thirty-nine members were killed." Even in the good years, the record is around 4,200 percent worse than that of the U.S.

One crash can send an individual airline's safety rating slumping far down the table, and individual safety records are thus difficult. *Flight* magazine publishes annual surveys, however, and from these and other sources a rough guide emerges. As of 1978, Qantas and TAP are two of the safest internationals, carrying the flag for Australia and Portugal respectively, though TAP had its first fatal crash involving passengers in 1977. Delta, American, United, Continental and Eastern are domestic carriers with excellent records.

British Caledonian is well up the European list, with Lufthansa, SAS and Swissair. TWA and Pan Am also tie into the table here. None of the world's major airlines gets into the high passenger-death positions, although some flag carriers are there: CSA of Czechoslovakia, Egyptair, Romania's Tarom, PAL of the Philippines and Garuda of Indonesia.

There is a world order of safety for the leading air nations between 1963 and 1972, given in terms of fatal crashes per million flights. The Netherlands is best with no fatal crashes. Australia has 0.785 per million flights, Scandinavia 1.348, the U.S. 1.680, West Germany 2.181, the U.K. 3.620, Canada 4.030, Japan 4.495, Italy 4.705, Belgium 6.787, France 7.090, Brazil 7.620, India 16.238.*

These odds are minute, and the passenger should realize that safety is more a matter of his own conduct than of choosing an airline. In his book *The Safe Airline* (London, 1976) J. M. Ramsden calculates that the odds on a passenger being killed between takeoff and arriving at his destination are three in a million. Taking a flight a day, a passenger could expect to die once every 913 years. Ramsden also lists the smaller air transport countries with excellent safety records. They are, in alphabetical order: Austria, Finland, Iceland, Ireland, Israel, New Zealand, Portugal, South Africa and Switzerland.

A further analysis of Ramsden's figures shows that two countries, the Netherlands and the U.S., have records that are better than might be expected from their volume of air traffic. Australia, Belgium, Canada, Italy, Japan, Scandinavia, West Germany and the U.K. are more or less on a par. France, Brazil and India are worse than statistically expected.

A pilot with a major scheduled airline has a 1 percent chance of

*Flight, May 17, 1973.

being killed throughout his career, compared with 2 percent in coal mining and 5 in construction.

Accident liability is an appalling mess. The family of one passenger can receive $3 million or more, yet the man in the seat next to him could be worth only $10,000. It depends on the nationality of the airline, the country of departure and arrival, the eventual destination and even the country where the ticket was bought.

The first attempt to work out liability was the Warsaw Convention of 1929, limiting the airlines to 125,000 Poincaré gold francs. This sounds a lot, but is in fact worth only $10,000 1976 dollars. It was doubled to $20,000 by the Hague Protocol of 1955, but this was still considered too low. The U.S. government pressed airlines flying to or via the U.S. to sign the Montreal Agreement, which increased the limit to $75,000 for passengers on those routes. In addition, limitless damages can be won if negligence by the airline or aircraft manufacturer can be proved, particularly in the U.S.

The crash of a DC-10 near Paris on March 3, 1974, killing all 346 aboard, gives some idea of the legal complexities. Turkish Airlines, the aircraft's operators, was not even a party to the Warsaw Convention. But the flight was between France and England, both of which are Warsaw-signatory states. And many passengers, who had switched to Turkish Airlines because of a British Airways strike, were on Montreal-based tickets from British Airways.

The aircraft crashed because a cargo door came away in flight and a buckled floor seized the controls. This was variously alleged to be due to negligence by Turkish Airlines, by the U.S. Federal Aviation Administration, which licensed the aircraft, McDonnell Douglas, which assembled it, and General Dynamics, which designed and built the door.

With liability so inexcusably complex and shabby, the wise passenger looks after his own life insurance.

Luggage liability is equally unsatisfactory, with airlines compensating by weight at about $10 for two pounds. Some travelers thus put bricks in their bags to bring the weight up to 45 pounds. Passengers whose baggage has been lost can claim an "overnight bag" from the airline, which must contain slippers, shaving kit, scissors, after shave, soap, pajamas and towel.

If the general safety of the airline and his redress for liability are not in his hands, the individual passenger can look after his own life by listening to safety briefings on aircraft. Most people assume nothing untoward will happen, and ignore all attempts to get them to listen. But the wise passenger always examines the safety leaflet, primarily to memorize the position of the emergency exits. These exits differ from aircraft model to model and from airline to airline. Remembering where the exits were on one 747 is no guarantee they will be in the same place on another.*

He will also see how they open. Main exit doors may have to be pulled inward before they can be rotated and opened. This is to prevent them being sucked out in flight, but passengers have died crushing against doors that needed an initial pull before being pushed. Wing exits are simpler, though they may be unusable if wing fuel tanks catch fire.

There is a simple drill in an emergency which much improves your chances of survival. First, remove any sharp or metal objects from your pockets; a pen or comb can cause serious injury on impact. Put them in the seat pocket in front of you. Make sure the seat belt is really tight, and the seat upright. Take off tie and spectacles. Put your feet flat on the floor, not under your seat or the one in front. The seat could collapse and trap you. Work out exactly what escape route you are going to use, and make sure you have an alternative should the first be impassable for any reason.

When the crash is imminent, try to cover your head with a rug or pillow. Put your arms, with fingers interlocked, over your neck and push your face into your knees, keeping your feet straight down. The aircraft will probably hit more than once in the crash, so don't move from the braced position until the aircraft has stopped. When it has definitely done so, undo your belt and get out of the

---

*There are five types of 747, e.g.: a short-range, high-density-seating model, a long-range passenger aircraft, a cargo-passenger convertible, an intercontinental freighter and a special long-range version.

plane, fast. Once out, run away from it as fast as you can in case it explodes. Do not take any possessions with you, briefcases, cameras, anything. Delay kills.

Obey the crew, but never expect them to rescue you. Rescue yourself. Thus you should work out for yourself how to operate emergency exits, ensure your legs are not trapped, minimize the odds of being knocked unconscious by protecting your head. Never ever inflate a life jacket inside an aircraft. It will jam you in the exit, stopping your escape and that of the other passengers.

Women, children and the old are particularly at risk. In one crash, 32 out of 37 men got out of the aircraft, but only 15 out of 36 women, children and elderly. The aircraft, a TWA Boeing 707, hit a roller at Rome Airport and ruptured a fuel line. There was no noticeable impact at all, but the aircraft rapidly went up in flames. Family groups, women and children, and the old were tragically slow to leave. Such people should take particular care to rehearse mentally what they will do in an emergency.

Above all, the wise passenger knows that he can make it if he does not panic. Most accidents are on takeoff and landing, where the speed is not great and where the impact itself is usually survivable.* It is not the crash in an air crash that kills, but suffocation or poisoning later. The wise passenger, anticipating a crash, remembers: "Impact does not kill. Fumes and fire do." As a rule of thumb he has 60 seconds to get out.

A Boeing 707 of Varig Airlines of Brazil was approaching Paris' Orly on a flight from Rio on July 11, 1973.† There were 127 aboard. Heavy smoke started billowing from the left rear lavatory. It could not be stopped from spreading with an extinguisher. The smoke penetrated up the length of the fuselage. The flight engineer depressurized the aircraft and opened the rear discharge valve, but smoke still poured into the cockpit.

---

*About 60 percent of fatal crashes have survivors. An average of 30 percent of those aboard survive fatal crashes. The percentage would be higher if passengers listened to safety drills and reacted fast and firmly. Even more would live if airlines improved seat fastenings, so that they remained fixed to the floor under greater forces.

†International Civil Aviation Organization (ICAO) Summary No. 54.

The flight crew put on oxygen masks and opened the cockpit side windows. They were finally unable to see their instruments and had to put the aircraft down in a field just four miles short of Orly. The aircraft slid for 600 yards, tearing off the undercarriage but not doing any major damage to the structure. Everyone survived the crash.

The No. 4 fuel tank then caught fire, spreading quickly after the plane had stopped. The seven crew in the cockpit got out the side windows, and three other crew got out from just behind the cockpit. It was left to rescuers on the ground to pull out their passengers, only one of whom survived. One hundred and sixteen passengers died, and most were found still seated and strapped in. The cause of death was toxic gas from breathing poisoned air.

There is a simple moral to this unhappy tale. Passengers who are delighted at surviving the crash impact, and who then sit and wait for the crew to give instructions, die. Passengers who are concerned only to get out of the aircraft, and who know how to do it because they know where the exits are, survive. Ruthless avoidance of poisonous smoke is the name of the survival game in most crashes. Smoke and fumes rise: dropping to the floor gives a chance to breathe and see.

The appalling death toll in the 1977 collision of two 747's on the ground in the Canaries was also fuel-fed. It may eventually be possible to use fuel that cannot ignite in a crash. A chemical is added to it which will not mix or react with the fuel if it is kept under pressure. But if the tanks of fuel lines are ruptured in a crash, pressure is lost and the chemical combines with the fuel to thicken it and make it non-ignitable.

It can make all the difference to be seated in the right part of the aircraft in a crash. The only trouble is that it is impossible to tell in advance which is the safest part. Smoke, like the actual crash, is also unpredictable. In theory, the nose and tail are safest in an aircraft with underwing engines, and the forward part of the cabin in a rear-engined aircraft. This avoids fuel lines which may rupture in a crash.

In practice, the only sensible thing is to know where the exits are. It is also sensible never to put anything heavy in overhead racks, or to take up the cabin floor with hand luggage. The restrictions on hand luggage are not for weight reasons, but to insure that the cabin is not so cluttered as to make evacuation difficult.

Make sure that the seat is firm. Shake it, and if it is loose refuse to sit in it. In a crash you could be hurled forward strapped in a seat that has broken away from the floor fastenings. The seat and belt should hold you firm to an impact of 15g, although US Army Air Force research* shows that the body can survive short impacts of up to 35g. Rear-facing seats are the safest of all; a crash back in 1958 showed clearly that more survived in the rear-facing seats than the conventional ones.

Looking after his physical comfort on the plane, the passenger will keep his seat belt lightly buckled throughout the flight, in case of turbulence.† Two people were killed when a BAC 1-11 hit turbulence near Grand Cayman Island in the Caribbean. They were not wearing seat belts and they hit the ceiling. It is now standard advice on aircraft to wear loose seat belts at all times. Only a fool would ignore it. However, airlines have not yet put seat belts into lavatories even though there is no chance of a passenger regaining his seat in sudden turbulence.

Soft, large shoes are helpful since your feet will swell in the cabin atmosphere. So will your waist, and casual trousers are best. It is easy to catch cold in the thin, dry air and sweaters and cardigans should be worn. Collars will chafe and so ties are a menace.

Effective drugs against airsickness include hyoscine, cyclizine, diphen-hydramine, meclizine and promethazine.‡

*USAAVLAB's Technical Report 66/43.

†A colleague on an aircraft flying over the Caprivi strip in southern Africa suddenly found himself flung across the cabin. The aircraft had hit turbulence and dropped 800 feet like a stone. A stewardess hit him in midair. She broke her leg when she hit his chest, fracturing his ribs. That, at least, is his story and he is sticking to it.

‡Ozone sickness is a new phenomenon that has arrived with very high flights—above 37,000 feet. Its sudden symptoms are labored breathing, hacking cough, sore eyes and a tight chest. Pan Am recorded 164 individual cases of ozone

The comfort-conscious passenger will also try to avoid jetlag. This exhaustion can take eight days to disappear after a long flight. Research shows that heart rate, temperature, blood pressure and breathing patterns are affected. The adrenal glands go out of phase, and potassium loss in urine increases, affecting heartbeat.

The Institute of Psychology in Dublin has prepared a list of hints* to cut back on flight fatigue. Before a flight, a passenger should have a high-protein meal with a minimum of carbohydrates, animal fats and gas-producing foods. Long sunbathing should be avoided. A passenger should drink a lot during the flight, noting that milk reduces tension, that wine in reasonable quantities is beneficial, but that tea, coffee, spirits and dry food should be avoided.

Long-distance flying is bad for the body if only because of the long period of immobility. In one experiment, six healthy "passengers" simply sat in a chair all the time they were not in bed. Within

---

sickness in a three-month period and it also affected stewardesses on United Airlines flights. The problem is considered serious enough for the U.S. Federal Aviation Administration to warrant a new research program to weigh ozone's threat to health.

Ozone is a bluish gas with a sharp, pungent odor. It is called ozone after *ozein,* the Greek "to smell." It is a powerful oxidizer and is used commercially as an antiseptic and bleach. The "ozone layer" is where it is concentrated in poisonous quantities. Its height varies. It is generally lower near the Poles and in regions of very low pressure, like the Aleutians. It shows seasonal changes, seldom dropping below 30,000 feet in summer and autumn but found 6,000 feet lower in late winter and spring.

Ozone sickness was originally diagnosed on Pan Am's Special Performance 747's, whose 45,000-foot ceiling is 7,000 feet above most subsonic jets. Spot checks in the spring of 1978 showed spurts of ozone up to three times the maximum deemed safe by the U.S. Occupational Safety and Health Administration.

Heat destroys ozone. Thus Concorde, despite cruising at 60,000 feet, does not suffer from the problem because the cabin air comes from a rear stage of the engine, whose heat destroys the gas. Pan Am has installed a similar heating device on its 747-SP's. If ozone sickness breaks out on board, the FAA advises the pilot to tell victims to breathe through wet towels or napkins while the pilot takes the plane down to 4,000 feet.

Psychological Aspects of Transmeridian Flying, by Brendan McGann, published by the Institute of Psychology, Dublin, May 1971.

four days, they were all showing symptoms of dizziness, fainting and circulatory collapse. There was also nausea and vomiting.

No flight should last four days, although hijackings have, but a passenger will begin to show mild symptoms after three hours. The young and fit cope best. The Irish study showed that half the pilots under 30 on transatlantic flying actually showed a sleep gain on arrival in New York, whereas 95 percent of pilots over 37 showed a sleep loss. Children hardly notice time-zone changes.

What is good for the pilot, in terms of efficiency and a quick return to normal after crossing time zones, is also good for the passenger. There is research into the body rhythms of pilots* which the wise passenger will note. A group of pilots was required to fly a simulator in what approximated to a holding pattern in a "stack" waiting to land. Their ability to do this was tested at various times throughout 24 hours.

Two performance factors were measured, deviation from speed, range and altitude and the time needed to correct the error. A curve of performance evolved, with a maximum efficiency from 2 P.M. to 3 P.M. Minimum performance at 3 A.M. was 50 percent lower than the total average performance.

Two incidents occurred during the simulator run. These were the equivalent of a sudden increase in weight and the popping up of speed brakes. The time needed to recover from these incidents varied from 53.4 seconds in the afternoon to 103.3 seconds at three in the morning.

Pilot skill is thus severely diminished in the early hours of the morning. A passenger should also try to avoid these flight times where possible, not simply because the pilot is less competent then, but because the passenger himself will arrive more exhausted.

After a long-distance flight of five time zones (Europe to India, Japan to Honolulu, or Dallas to Honolulu are such flights) research shows that it takes eight to nine days for the body to adapt completely and return to normal. Fatigue is probably worst on the

*K.E. Klein et al., "Circadian Rhythms of Pilots' Efficiency and Effect of Multiple Time You Travel," *Aerospace Medicine,* 41 (2):125–132.

third day* rather than the first, although thereafter improvement is rapid.

The research confirmed what many passengers have long suspected. West to east flights on the North Atlantic are more exhausting than east to west. Many passengers who have no problems on other flights complain of restlessness, panic and unease on East Coast to Europe flights. "I go into a cold sweat," says a widely traveled publisher who normally enjoys flying. "I panic, and lock myself in the lavatory and splash cold water over my face. The only way I can get myself from New York to London is by getting drunk."

In fact, what many passengers think is personal weakness is judged by experts to be bad airline scheduling. Brendan McGann, a member of the Aerospace Medical Association, and a former Aer Lingus pilot, blames the airlines for the evening-takeoff, early-morning-arrival timings. In his study *Psychological Aspects of Transmeridian Flying* he writes: "The combination of Circadian effect, sleep deprivation, possible high temperature and humidity, traffic density, night takeoff, holding delays, fume inhalation, and many other factors makes 8 P.M. New York time the worst possible departure time imaginable, from the point of view of flight safety."

McGann says that the major cause of exhaustion after flights from North America to Europe is the policy of night departures. The passenger who flies by day, or at least avoids the hours of maximum sluggishness between 2 A.M. and 5 A.M. will arrive less exhausted and be flown by safer pilots.

Research conducted by the Federal Aviation Agency† has proved that it is time zones rather than the length of trip which count. Passengers flying from Oklahoma City to Rome, across seven time zones, and to Manila across ten, all showed marked

---

*Wegmann et al., "Effects of Transmeridian Flight on the Diurnal Excretion Pattern of 17-OHCS," *Aerospace Medicine, 41, 1003 G 1005*.

†A medically accepted rest formula has been worked out. Devised by the late Dr. Lloyd Buley of the International Civil Aviation Organization, it takes actual flight duration as well as time changes into account. The equation is: rest periods (in tenths of a day) equals flight duration in hours divided by two, plus the time zones passed in excess of four, plus the departure time coefficient plus the arrival

differences in temperature, pulse, blood pressure, respiratory rate, reaction times, emotional tension and urinalysis. In contrast, passengers flying from Washington to Santiago, Chile, across one time zone, were not affected at all.

The real answer to jet lag may have been found by Russian Aeroflot crews. Those on the Moscow–Havana run live on Moscow time in Cuba. They eat breakfast at midnight, and supper at noon, and go to bed in the afternoon. This is easy to enforce, since Aeroflot crews normally stay in their embassies when abroad, with "constant discipline."

An airline is only as good as the flight you are on, but there are indications of whose flights to take and whose to avoid. In a major survey of domestic air travel by the California newsletter *Economy Traveler*, Southern emerged as the least punctual major airline in the U.S. The airline which receives the largest proportion of complaints is Texas International.

Alaska Airlines is the most punctual carrier in the nation, with 90 percent of flights on time or within 15 minutes of schedule.

---

time coefficient. These coefficients are based on social behavior patterns, particularly sleep periods. They are:

(local time)	Coefficient	Coefficient
0800–1159	0	4
1200–1759	1	2
1800–2159	3	0
2200–0059	4	1
0100–0759	3	3

The vital factor is to make the combined departure and arrival coefficients as low as possible. The passenger cannot control flight duration. But he can choose a flight that leaves and arrives at the best time for his biological clock.

Thus, the flying time from London to New York is 7 hours, crossing five time zones. These are reduced to 3½ and 1 by the equation, making 4½. Leaving London at 1700 hours and arriving in New York at 1900 local time adds only 1 to the score, which then gives 5½. This is 5½ tenths of 24 hours, or 13 hours and 12 minutes' sleep. However, a flight that left London at 0700 would arrive in New York at 0900 local time, amassing 7 "penalty" points. Seven tenths of a day gives a rest of 16 hours and 48 minutes. Simply working out these equations should ensure deep sleep. This is a fine alternative to counting sheep.

CAB statistics of major airlines show American, Western, TWA, United and Braniff at the top of the on-time league, with 85 percent of flights on the button or within 15 minutes. Hughes Airwest is just behind with 84 percent and North Central has 83 percent.

Eastern is at 81 percent, Northwest 79, National 78 and Continental 75. Delta is well behind at 70.

Perhaps more to the point than punctuality, in view of its steady decline, is courtesy.* The CAB logs the complaints against airlines per 100,000 passengers carried. TWA is the worst of the big airlines with 6.7 complaints per 100,000. Braniff gets 6.1, Northwest 5.4, Eastern 5.1 and National 4.8. Delta, compensating well for its poor punctuality, is by far the politest with only 1.7.

Of smaller airlines, Texas International is yet worse than TWA with 6.8. Allegheny gets 4.3, Ozark and Hughes Airwest both 3.6. Happiest airline in the nation is the Hawaiian carrier Aloha with a slim 1.6.

The most comfortable aircraft in the nation are Northwest's and Western's DC-10's, whose superior seat width and extra legroom are unmatched by any other airline-airplane combination.

Airlines with wider than average seats on DC-10's and 1011's are American, Northwest, TWA and United. American intends to convert its DC-10's so that the backs of center seats in rows of three are locked down into position as tables at all times except Christmas and New Year.

United is the clear comfort leader on 747's, with as much as 38 inches of seat pitch—4 inches more than most and in seats as wide

*There are several ploys passengers can use to obtain better service. Art Buchwald suggests a broken leg (a fake one is as good as a real one). This means that the passenger is wheeled from check-in counter to the aircraft. He will be first aboard and he will get the best seat with the best legroom. On arrival, he avoids lines and is wheeled again. Readers may consider this unsporting. They should also be careful only to plaster only the lower leg: if too much is plastered the airline may insist on the passenger's occupying and paying for two seats in the name of safety. A much simpler approach is used by an acquaintance of mine. Upon boarding the aircraft, he at once asks for a complaints card. "But, sir, the flight is just beginning," says the stewardess. "Exactly," says he, with menace. Admittedly, this does not save him walking and it does not get him the best seat. But it does marvels for his cabin service.

as any. United does the same on its DC-8's, offering up to 38 inches of legroom compared with Braniff's miserly 34.

The seat pitch on all the 707-720's used by domestic carriers is a reasonable 36 inches. By comparison, all 727's in the U.S. are cramped. No airline offers wider seating than any other: most provide only 34 inches and a flight on an American Airlines 727 from New York to Dallas/Fort Worth was one of the most cramped flights I have suffered. Some National, Northwest and United 727's have slightly more legroom, up to 36 inches.

There are major variations on 737's. The meanest carrier is Air California with 31 inches of legroom, compared with Frontier's exuberant 38.

On DC-9's, Texas International offers a miserly 31 to 32 inches, partly responsible, perhaps, for its poor complaints records. Delta scrapes a bare 33 inches, TWA and Eastern 34, Allegheny from 34 to 37.

The best legroom on wide-body jets is the central section of United's 747's. The most comfortable narrow-body jets in the U.S. are Frontier's 737's.

These figures are based on CAB statistics and there is more to choosing an airline than legroom and complaints alone. Several useful polls exist on the subject, including a survey of the members of the Airline Passengers Association in Irving, Texas. Eastern emerged as America's most shunned airline.

Eastern polled 820 votes as the outfit to avoid, chiefly because of poor service and courtesy. Delays, cancellations and reliability rated well below plain bad manners. Allegheny was the next most unpopular with 393 votes, with poor service again counting more than anything else.

Asked which airline they would travel given the choice on any domestic route, 26.7 percent opted for American, 25.5 for United, 15.1 for Delta and 14.3 for TWA.

That is what expert travelers make of the domestic airline scene.

Moving abroad, the airlines with most room on the North Atlantic, with 9 abreast instead of 10 economy, are Air India, El Al, Iranair, Pan Am and TWA.

Six thousand passengers in the East chose the worst 10 airlines in that region in ascending order: worst, Tarom of Rumania; second worst, Iraqi; then Aeroflot of the Soviet Union, Alia of Jordan, Union of Burma, JAT of Yugoslavia, Syrian Arab, Ariana of Afghanistan, Gulf Air and Bangladesh.

Singapore International was voted the best, followed in order by Japan Air Lines, Lufthansa, KLM, Swissair, Pan Am, Cathay Pacific (a Hong Kong-based British-owned carrier), British Airways, Qantas of Australia and All Nippon.

A survey of European and U.S. businessmen revealed Swissair to be their favorite long-haul airline. It was followed by Lufthansa, Pan Am, TWA and KLM. British Airways and Air France are ranked an equal sixth.

The most popular airlines within Europe were ranked as Lufthansa top, followed in order by Swissair, KLM, British Airways and SAS.

Airports themselves are not the subject of polls, presumably because they are considered unavoidable. I can offer a few random pieces of advice for those traveling abroad: we have already noted Seattle-Tacoma, Dulles and Tampa as the most favored U.S. airports.

Do not approach London Heathrow if there has been so much as a slurry of snow. The airport's proprietors, the British Airports Authority, who do much to tarnish the image of an otherwise great airport, are incapable of dealing with it and shut the place down. Like several other European airports, most notably Paris, Madrid, Rome and Milan, Heathrow is also very subject to strikes.

At Kinshasa, in Zaire, do not disembark unless you are leaving the flight there and never carry a camera. It is forbidden and the airport guards, if this phrase can be extended to such rabble, carry submachine guns with the safety catches off. The same applies to Entebbe, in Uganda.

At Lagos, it can cost up to $300 in extra "charges" just to get on a flight to the U.S. or Europe. This is known as *matabish* in Kinshasa, as *mukata* at Luanda airport and as a "donation" in Lusaka. But it all comes to the same thing: extract cash from pocket and give to Immigration officer, Customs man, policeman and baggage handler. In the Gulf and Pakistan it is known as a "contribution" and is paid to airline staff in order to get a seat. The fact that the seat may have been reserved months before does not affect the contribution.

The world's worst expensive food is to be found in Milan. It costs $19 for ammonia-flavored seafood salad, two slices of emaciated beef with congealed mushroom sauce, green salad and mineral water. Graffiti outside the restaurant accurately proclaim the manager to be an assassin. Why just the manager?

Beware the airport tax trap in Tripoli. It is not the tax that matters—no sane man begrudges a few dollars to leave the Libyan Arab Republic. But first the Libyans force the departing passenger to change his Libyan currency into dollars or pounds, a process that can take more than an hour. Then, slyly, they demand airport tax, to be paid in Libyan currency only. The Russians play the same game at Moscow Sheremetyevo. Thus, in Libya and Russia, a passenger should hang on to local currency until he has paid airport tax, despite the warnings that this is illegal.

Another airport ploy, Portuguese this time, is that refunds on air tickets bought in Lisbon must be claimed before leaving the country and will be paid in escudos only. Air tickets had blossomed into the equivalent of a currency racket. Portuguese would buy tickets in unwanted escudos and claim refunds abroad in French francs and dollars.

A fixer is vital at some airports, including Tripoli, Cairo, Lagos and Kuwait. For an investment of $20 or so, he speeds a passenger into the country and, more importantly, out. At Bogotá airport, on the other hand, a bodyguard might be of more use since it is perhaps the world's most violent airport. Bodyguards can be hired at Eldorado Airport for $25 a day.

Speaking of violence, one must mention Beirut, of course. A questionnaire on international route knowledge in a pilots' magazine read: "How do you find the Operations Room at Beirut Airport? One: in pieces. Two: in a shambles. Three: turn left up the second flight of stairs on the right, plus both of the above. Four: follow the incoming artillery fire. Answer: all of these."

Many passengers get very angry about so-called duty-free shops. One discovered that cameras from discount houses on 47th Street in New York were far cheaper than in the JFK duty-free stores. Locally bought bourbon also turned out to be less than duty-free.

There are major differences in price between different airports for the same item, despite the advertised lack of duty. Toronto is the cheapest airport in the world for cigarettes, with JFK and Amsterdam's Schiphol joint second, followed by Brussels, London, Geneva and, most expensive, Frankfurt. The cost of a carton varies from $4 at Toronto to $8 at Frankfurt.

Scotch has a slightly different order. A liter of Bell's is cheapest in Amsterdam, at $5.50. London comes next at $5.80 (1979 prices), and then Brussels at $6.40, Toronto at $6.70 and Paris at $6.90. JFK is up at $7.20, Frankfurt and Geneva at $8.30 and Copenhagen is a mighty $8.70.

Duty-free is a massive billion-dollar business. It has been estimated that if only half the passengers aboard a 747 take advantage of the U.S. Customs duty-free limit of about five quarts, they will bring one and a half tons of spirits on to the aircraft. It is a pity that there are so many passenger rip-offs, particularly in Germany and Scandinavia.

As for the wine served aloft, one brave outfit arranged a tasting on the ground. Masters of Wine tasted the economy-class wines of 20 international airlines for *Business Traveller*. Of the Americans, TWA and Pan Am both did relatively well: TWA's red and white both emerged as "agreeable" and the Pan Am red was classed as "clean and attractive, unusual nose." More than you could say for their cabin service.

Alitalia emerged as the best-wine airline, followed by Air Canada, Swissair and South African. Austrian Airlines' white was reckoned "aromatic, fine fruity nose, well balanced." KLM scored reasonably well with both red and white. It is safer to stick to white on British Airways—the red is "really hot, oxidized and awful." Likewise Kenya Airways, whose white is "delicately scented, of vin de table standard," but whose red has a "very hot nose, disastrous palate, sour smell, truly awful."

El Al's white is "quite atrocious" and the red "most unusual." Aer Lingus fared but slightly better of the ethnic airlines: the red has a "heavy, clapped-out nose and plastic taste," whereas the white is "too old and tired, syrupy palate." Even the Scots fared better—Caledonian's red rated a "small nose, pleasantly balanced."

The very worst wine flying the airlines is Thai International red. "Violent," reported one taster. "Must have been trodden yesterday afternoon as there appeared to be bits of toenail floating in it. If used in my car, would probably give me more miles to the gallon. Unspeakable."

Connoisseurs consider that Aeroflot's red wine may be equally bad, but the Russian airline refused to allow any to be sampled. Many travelers also consider it to be the world's worst airline, but again its secrecy makes this difficult to prove. It is the world's largest airline, by far, and its safety record and service leave a great deal to be desired.

This state-owned giant flies to 5,000 destinations in the Soviet Union and to more than 70 countries outside. It probably carries 100 million passengers a year, more than twice all the major Western European airlines combined. The actual figure is considered a military secret and is not revealed.

Neither are the accident statistics. Aeroflot suppresses all news of accidents unless foreigners are involved, in which case the news will leak out anyway. A midair collision in July 1979 was only revealed after correspondents noted that a team had disappeared from the listings in the First Division of Russian Soccer. The entire squad had been aboard.

A special panel had to be set up in 1976 to probe Aeroflot's operations after 17 crashes in 13 months. Its report said that flight safety was the airline's "most important task" and complained about inadequate training of crews and negligent checking of equipment.

Aeroflot has had two nightmare aircraft. The Tu-144 supersonic airliner, known as "Concordski," was withdrawn from its only passenger route between Moscow and Alma Ara after one of the series crashed on a test flight. The Il-86 was desperately needed to cope with passengers arriving for the 1980 Olympics. A 350-seater, it is Aeroflot's answer to the U.S. wide-bodied jets. But it has had serious problems with underpowered engines.

The service on Aeroflot is appalling, particularly on domestic routes. Overbooking is rampant. Moscow's Domadedoro airport is like a dormitory with hundreds of passengers waiting for aircraft for days on end. When an administrative error left all Aeroflot's Tu-144's at Khaborousk in the Soviet far east without fuel, several thousand passengers had to camp out in the forests surrounding Domadedoro.

First Class was introduced in 1978 on some routes to southern cities, thus making some comrades more equal than others. But meals are seldom served on flights lasting less than three hours. Aeroflot does have in-flight entertainment of a sort. A recent innovation on the long-haul flights from Moscow to Khaborousk has been the projection of color slides in the passenger cabin. The subject matter: Soviet engineering and agriculture.

Aeroflot is immune from retribution from its passengers: even a complaint, if pursued vigorously enough, can lead to imprisonment. No such restrictions exist in the West, where passengers have been attacking crew members in growing numbers. The FAA said that 75 passengers violated laws against interference with crew members in 1978, but cabin staff claim the true figure is much higher. Evans North, whose Washington-based law firm is handling more than 25 assault cases for cabin staff, says that the increase is alarming.

He cites cases where passengers have assaulted crew. Vacationers on a flight to Honolulu watched in dismay as a passenger choked a steward. The passenger had pinned a stewardess against the cabin wall and tried to kiss her. The steward had come to her aid.

On a transatlantic flight, a passenger grabbed a stewardess and was fined $100 for being drunk on an aircraft after the airliner landed in London.* A passenger on an Eastern Airlines flight from Atlanta to Hartford threw a cup of tea over a stewardess and she suffered first-degree burns on her stomach. A well-known baseball player became uncontrollable on an American Airlines flight between Boston and Detroit. He was fined $500 by the FAA after disrupting the flight. On a flight between Brazil and New York a

*Braniff International Airways. June 25, 1979.

drunken woman passenger was refused a drink and chased the cabin staff up and down the aisle, spitting in their faces and calling them pigs. She only calmed down after the copilot threatened to handcuff her to her seat.

The 22,000 members of the Association of Flight Attendants hired Evans North after it became clear that the amount of abuse from passengers had increased dramatically. North confirmed the already known fact that athletes from professional teams are the biggest behavior risks on a jetliner. But he also found that just as many sober passengers assault cabin staff as drunks, and that women passengers are as aggressive as men.

10

The Flying Zoo

More than a million and a half animals a year pass through JFK. Many of them are smuggled in—immigrants as illegal as any human. A Customs agent heard hiccups coming from a large crate that had arrived from Mexico. He opened the box, took out the false bottom, and came upon a flock of illegally imported parrots. They had been drugged with tequila.

They were part of a trade worth millions of dollars a year: animal smugglers, according to Kenneth Berlin of the Justice Department's Wildlife Enforcement Program, make profits "comparable to those that drug dealers make." The victims include macaws, buffleheads, pygmy and red-breasted geese, and African monkeys. The business is simple and can be hugely moneymaking.

Stashed away in a big room near JFK are racks of expensive fur coats, crates of Calcutta lizard-skin shoes, leopard skins and polished tortoise shells. A large moose head and a stuffed crocodile, in which furs have been smuggled, rest on a pile of elephant skins.

They have all been confiscated by the U.S. Fish and Wildlife Service. There are around 1 million* dollars worth of trophies and souvenirs in the Fish and Wildlife Service offices at 700

*The New York Times, October 3, 1976.

Rockaway Turnpike, near the airport. More than 200 pairs of crocodile-skin shoes and furs and skins are stored in Hangar 11, where the products from closed criminal cases are stored.

Individuals or companies who are found in violation of the wildlife laws can be fined up to $20,000 per unit of shipment and a year in prison.

Life has been hectic for the 20-man team of wildlife inspectors and agents. Examining a live snake, they found heroin stuffed down its throat in plastic bags, and the smuggler was arrested. They caught the exporter and middleman for an operation taking American alligators out of the country illegally, in shipments of $50,000 to $60,000 each.

The agents determine the legality of incoming wildlife and products, frequently confiscating $200 alligator purses and $10,000 leopard-skin coats from unwitting passengers. Under the Lacey Act, agents must also block the importing of species that may be dangerous to indigenous American species, like the red-whiskered bulbul bird, the Java rice sparrow and the multimammate mouse.

The JFK operation has been the pilot for the other seven airports through which all wildlife products must come—Miami, Chicago, San Francisco, Los Angeles, New Orleans, Seattle and Honolulu.

Two extremely rare spix macaws—they have not been seen in the wild since 1903—were shipped to JFK via London misrepresented as blue-headed macaws. They were sold for $12,000 the pair. Bird exporter Gordon Cooke admitted: "When this shipment of spix macaws arrived at London I told the Customs they were blue-headed macaws. The Customs men didn't know any different. They look very similar. These were little babies still being hand-fed.

"It was a mixed shipment from South America. I was acting for a Dutchman, looking after the shipping. We paid a thousand dollars to the man who gave us the name of the customer in the U.S. The American was willing to pay twelve thousand dollars; he had set his life on building a collection of rare birds.*

"His wife flew over from the States to Britain and flew them

*The Observer, January 14, 1978.

back as pets. They went out with her as blue-headed macaws."
Cooke says he has "no regrets about the deal, despite a bit of
collusion. I could not think of a better man to have them."

Cooke has had plenty of other U.S. business. He admits to
exporting red-headed geese. "They fetch seven hundred dollars a
pair. They are the most distinctive kind of geese, but the Customs
men still don't recognize them. I send them abroad simply marked
'geese.'"

Birth certificates were forged for two African monkeys of the
species *Diana roloway*. When a new private building was opened
at the Louisiana Purchase Gardens and Zoo in Monroe, Louisiana, zoo director Jake Yelverton, Jr., started a search for animals
to fill it.

Cooke came up with two monkeys. One was female, 15 months
old, and the other was a four-year-old male. The monkeys were
sold to Jake Yelverton for $600 and were shipped by air to New
Orleans. When the flight arrived at New Orleans' airport, Mr.
Yelverton was there to clear the animals through Customs. He was
disappointed.

The monkeys were seized by Fish and Wildlife officers and
placed in another zoo for their safety and health. There were no
proper importation documents. Yelverton wrote demanding either
a certificate saying the monkeys were born at a specific place and
date in Britain or an African export document.

Three weeks later, he had a document which falsely stated that
both the *Diana* monkeys had been born in the Wigstone Zoological Gardens in England. This satisfied the Fish and Wildlife
officers, who released the monkeys to Mr. Yelverton. They are still
thriving attractions at the Louisiana zoo.

The document was a forgery, although Cooke denies all
knowledge of it. Jake Yelverton was acquitted in a Louisiana court
in October 1978 of a charge of entering two monkeys into the U.S.
by means of a false statement. Although a British Customs officer
testified that no such place as Wigstone Zoological Gardens
existed, the prosecution was unable to prove positively that the
monkeys were not born in England.

A diseased parrot imported into the U.S. in 1971 caused an

outbreak of Newcastle disease that left 12 million chickens dead, slaughtered to control the deadly virus. Chicken farmers were paid $26 million in indemnities.

This illicit airport trade is not confined to birds and monkeys. In one month alone, February 1979, U.S. Customs officials seized $1.1 million worth of furs of endangered species from Mexico. The growing market for bobcat pelts, at $400 apiece, is savaging the populations of those small cats. Reptile skins, ivory and turtle oil have been seized from air cargo.

Money is at the root of it. Exotic macaws that sold for $30 to $40 in 1970 now sell for thousands in the U.S.: a particularly rare specimen fetched $30,000 in 1979. A Chicago businessman was convicted of trying to smuggle two peregrine falcons to the Middle East, as gifts for an oil sheik he wished to impress.

Animals smuggled into the U.S. through JFK include green tree pythons, Fiji iguana and Johnson's crocodiles. These sell for $750 and upward, the majority passing through the airport with false descriptions suggesting they are not endangered species.

The growing threat to wildlife from animal smugglers and their collector clients is clear. Many nations subscribe in theory to the Convention on International Trade in Endangered Species. Negotiated in 1973, the treaty divides endangered species into two main classes. It totally prohibits trade in some 400 animals registered as "endangered," and requires strict licenses for the import and export of species potentially threatened." More than 50 plants are also classified as endangered." Air shipments of cacti for foreign collectors are depleting many species of cacti in the U.S. and Mexico, and the once abundant growths of ginseng in the Appalachians have been denuded by people cashing in on the great demand for the supposed aphrodisiac in the Orient.

In practice, most countries are overwhelmed by the size and complexity of the trade—including the U.S., where importers bring in more than 90 million wildlife items a year. Customs men are often unable to distinguish between a rare and not so rare animal.

False descriptions and hidden compartments are used to get animals through U.S. airports, where the trade is heaviest at JFK, Los Angeles, Atlanta, Miami, and Dallas/Fort Worth. A large cage was consigned from Amsterdam. Traveling in noisy comfort up front were 400 budgies. Wrapped in sacking, drugged and hidden in a secret compartment at the back, were two king vultures.

Passengers have been caught at JFK with rare birds tucked in hair rollers with their beaks taped and strapped to their hind legs. Young gorillas are described as monkeys. Orangutans are dyed black.

JFK has a special Animalport, run by the ASPCA. It prides itself on providing "every type of food from live mealworms for foxes to bamboo roots for pandas, raw meat for lions and alfalfa for elephants."

It is a serious indictment of the airlines that the ASPCA should have to run the Animalport. The airlines, though happy to take animals to boost their cargo earnings, wash their hands of responsibility for the animals they carry. They leave crating to the shippers, who may well be smugglers with a callous disregard for their stock, and ground and transit operations to the ASPCA.

JFK is lucky to have an Animalport, which is equaled only by London Heathrow's RSPCA-run hostel, which has a fully equipped operating theater, and pools for dolphins and beavers. Most airports have no facilities at all despite the fact that many animals arrive half dead.

Temperatures and lighting are critical for hummingbirds, feed for marmosets, oxygen for tropical fish. They are often ignored.

The crates can be appalling. "There was a shipment of five gibbons packed face down in a box five inches high. A gibbon is thirty inches tall. They all died. Squirrels arrive wrapped in chicken wire to stop them eating through the box, starved to death. Coral fish are put in plastic bags. They cut the plastic with their spines, the water drains out and they die. Lions are put in cages with no through ventilation. If the animal turns, it blocks the air holes and suffocates," a volunteer recalls.

Cages have been opened to find live emerald doves as food for a leopard en route from India to the U.S., starlings to feed falcons and live parrots for eagles.

Other cages break in flight, and a British volunteer has had to capture two tigers loose in a 707.* "I put myself in the position the animals should have been in—in a cage. I shoved the cage along the aircraft to where they were sitting and shot tranquilizers into them," he says.

The American Air Line Pilots' Assocation has in its files the case of a 100-pound coon dog which broke loose on an airliner. The dog went berserk when the engines started up and ripped its way out of its wire cage. It attacked the cockpit door as the aircraft took off, trying to savage its way into the cockpit. The captain reported: "The crash axe was our only defense if he made it through. I have never been as concerned about the safety of a flight as I was about this one." He managed an emergency landing. The dog quieted when the engines shut down.

The Association wrote to the Federal Aviation Administration. The FAA replied: "This appears to be an isolated case since the last time we can recall a similar incident was many years ago when a panda broke loose in the cockpit of a DC-3." The aircraft almost crashed before the panda was overcome by the crew and trussed up.

Snakes escape, and volunteers are often asked by Customs to check a box of snakes, especially spitting cobras, that could contain smuggled goods. Finding cannabis in reptile boxes is not odd. "It's damn dangerous," says a volunteer, "but we do it."

Typically, the hostel will have upward of 50,000 finches. 1,000 monkeys, 40 elephants through in a month. It has even had a 10-foot manatee.

One volunteer complains that labeling is often totally insufficient. He points at a packing case in a corner labeled "Live Tropical Animals—Keep Warm." "It doesn't give even simple instructions on what to do if they get held up for three days in a fog or something," he says angrily. "It doesn't say what they are, and it has no viewing hole to find out. Could be snakes—they'd be fine for six weeks. But if it's alligators they would need heavy water

---

*Cargo pilots have a standard drill when animals run amok. They go on oxygen and then depressurize the aircraft. The animals breathe rarefied air and rapidly fall asleep.

sprinkling after forty-eight hours. We may know what to do, but hardly any other airport in the world would."

Animals are sent in whiskey cartons and tea chests. A falcon was strapped into a shoe box. More than 100 vervet monkeys and baboons died on a flight from East Africa: four animals at a time had been put in communal containers only 11 inches wide. It is often crucial to recharge the oxygen in water for fish, but no instructions are given.

The American Air Line Pilots' Association feels that "regulation is inevitable. It should behoove all involved to get with the program and correct the deficiencies in the system that permits live creatures to be tortured, maimed and killed during air travel."

There is a danger that the booming air trade in animals, as it escalates in value and rewards, may seriously endanger the fauna of Asian and African countries. The list of wildlife that goes through JFK includes myna birds, elephant parakeets, sea cows, bear cubs, Maribu storks.

A young lion en route from Karachi to Amsterdam was unloaded at London and found to be dead on arrival. Its metal container was found to be smaller than the overall size of the animal. The ventilation was totally inadequate. The autopsy showed the animal to have died from suffocation and heart failure due to overexertion and shock. Seven hundred out of nearly 4,000 wild Peking robins flown from Hong Kong died of pneumonia caused by climatic changes.

Volunteers moved into a corner of a warehouse used for animal shipments at Washington's National Airport. "We established this as an emergency measure," said the volunteers' director, Fay Brisk. "We just called for volunteers and went in with watering cans and buckets and food. We found dead animals. We found suffering animals. We found hunting dogs that were wild because they had been cooped up in their cages for two or three days."

Inadequate ventilation and extreme temperatures in baggage compartments are often cited. An American stewardess once placed a thermometer in the baggage compartment. It registered extremes of 104 degrees Fahrenheit on the ground and 0 degrees Fahrenheit in the air. Cages are flung in upside down and animals are left in warehouses without food.

Livestock transportation can be a terrible trade, with conditions more like a slave ship than an aircraft. Calves often die through overcrowding, which leads to heat exhaustion, heart failure through extreme distress, or simple suffocation. Sometimes the overcrowding can lead to the collapse of the cattle pens and the animals are literally crushed to death.

On one flight between Dublin and Athens, 450 ten- to twenty-day-old calves were loaded into an aircraft. It met violent turbulence approaching Greece. The upper tier of the pen collapsed, crushing and killing 20 calves in the pens below.

Some aircraft are so tightly packed that even their supplementary ventilation systems cannot prevent a lethal buildup of carbon dioxide from the animals' breath, and they become flying gas chambers. On one flight between Canada and the Middle East, 320 calves were dead out of 720 loaded when the aircraft touched down at Bordeaux, in France, for refueling. Livestock are flown south from Miami International to Central and South America on decaying Constellations and DC-6's.

Many airlines that pride themselves on the excellence of their service in the passenger cabins think nothing of letting animals die in the holds beneath them.

PART THREE

READY, STEADY, FLY

11

Maintenance

Maintenance is the most vital service at an airport. An "A" check is carried out on airliners every 60 hours. An engineer inspects the landing and anti-collision lights, landing gear, doors, tire pressures and oil level. The wings, fuselage and tail are checked for visible damage. The water system and the coffee makers are drained. Oxygen masks, fire extinguishers, life rafts and escape slides are examined.

The "B" check is much more thorough. It is done every 400 or so flying hours and lasts a night. Every system on an aircraft is examined, from passenger safety belts to the thrust reversers on the engines.

Full overhauls take up to a month. The frequency depends on the aircraft type and varies between 14,000 and 24,000 hours. This shows the basic simplicity and reliability of modern design. An airliner need only be taken to pieces after the equivalent of 1,000 days and nights of nonstop use.

Allowable deficiencies are the inoperative systems and faults an aircraft can be flown with. Pilots have "Go" and "No Go" items, generally drawn up by the manufacturer, though a great deal depends on the airline. No airline wants to ground a multimillion-dollar machine because of a minor fault, but some airlines push "AB's" much too far, flying with deficient windshield wipers, undercarriage solenoids and radio cooling fans. The pilot can get by on rain repellent, manual undercarriage and the standby radio: safety should be more than just getting by. The faults are not fixed but merely entered in the aircraft's "squawk book." After checking out, an aircraft is put through all checks by the "Run Gang." The inspections are very thorough. Any suspect part is put "into quarantine," stamped in red and to be used again only if an inspector signs for it.

There is little mechanical wear in jet engines. But the great heat at which they operate weakens them. Temperatures go up to 2,000 degrees Centigrade in the jet pipe and the finely engineered turbine blades can be exposed to 500 degrees Centigrade. A turbine has 130 blades or more, costing $1,000 each, on each stage.

Every component on the crucial turbines and compressors has a "life limit," which varies between 16,000 and 30,000 hours. Stones damage the blades. The engine starts burning too much fuel as it wears out. Eventually it is dumped. But where the scheduled airline sells it off for $3,000 for scrap, small charter operators in Latin America pay the scrap dealer five times that and use the engine as a "spare." All too often such spares get used.

Tires cost more than $2,000 each and are carefully logged. A card shows the history of each tire. The main tires last longer than the smaller nosewheels, even though they take more of an apparent pounding, with smoke pouring out as they touch down. On a twin-jet like a 111, 247 landings are possible on the main wheels and 202 on the nosewheel. A 707 takes 114 and 82.

Typically, an operator with 10 Boeing 707's has two "inflight shutdowns" (engines switched off in flight) in a month. He keeps six engines at his base. Elsewhere, he has a pool arrangement with other airlines. A big pool will keep spare engines at 160 airports around the world. A member pays a flat rate per hour into the pool for using an engine. TWA has $300 million tied up in spares.

A passenger on a long-haul route, say London to Los Angeles, an 11-hour distance, will be aboard a "spanker," as the engineers call a good plane. It means the engines are relatively new, operating at maximum economy. The "burners" go on the shorter hauls where fuel consumption is less crucial.

Special care has to be taken of aircraft operating to areas with high salt condensation, like North Africa, the Caribbean, the Gulf, the Bahamas, and the Red Sea. It corrodes aircraft badly and rapidly, and is present in the air up to 3,000 feet. The Caribbean also has coral sand in the atmosphere. Flying over deserts, where sand can reach above 15,000 feet, wears out engines.

Dirty atmospheres have an adverse effect on performance, the aircraft itself gets dirty and thus less streamlined. It costs $120 in extra fuel to send a dirty aircraft from New York to the Caribbean and back, which is why they are kept clean. The washing bays are just like car washes, with giant detergent sprays. Repainting a 747 costs $45,000 and the paint adds 1,000 pounds to the aircraft's weight. This is half a ton, which is why few airlines do a complete paint job on their aircraft.

The cabin also needs maintenance. A single seat may have 1,500 people sitting in it during a year. The carpets take an enormous pounding. Things are found in seat backs. "People dump things they have second thoughts about smuggling, like hash. On flights back from South America you get cartons of 200 cigarettes abandoned. They always seem to be State Express, still in the cellophane, but filled with drugs.

"Then you get blue magazines on the Mexican returns, and porno movies. They are a wretched nuisance because people fling them down the toilets and jam them," says a cleaner.

Air conditioning is a problem. People tend to smoke heavily on aircraft and nicotine jams the air filter valves. Passengers throw bottles into the toilets, and crew fill up galley sinks with tea bags. They get stuck in so tight that often the drainpipe has to be cut out.

Fuses are blown on ovens when stewardesses, trying to rush, overfill them. This can be expensive: the four galleys on a 707 cost $120,000, including the refrigerators, ovens, appliances, sinks and stowages. On a 747 the galleys cost more than $500,000.

The line (or ramp) maintenance man checks before departure and after arrival. He is also responsible for Customs bar seals, and for having the toilets drained and flushed. These have an electric flush, on a centrifugal basis, draining into a 30-gallon main tank. Washbasin and galley water goes straight out into the air under pressure, through a specially heated pipe to prevent freezing or icing up.

12

Turnaround

Aircraft can be serviced with astonishing speed. An international flight can be turned around in less than 90 minutes. It needs the same sort of cool urgency as a pit stop in an auto race.

The first warning comes when the plane is seven minutes out, as it comes off the stack. The men with the steps are warned. The caterers, cleaners, fuelers, engineers, apron controllers, Customs and Immigration get ready.

The aircraft is allocated a stand. A system of red and green lights guides the pilot to the correct position; red lights to right and left if he is off course, green if he is not. There are marker boards along the side of the pier to help him stop in the right place. When the name of his aircraft type is level with his shoulder, the pilot puts on the parking brake. Doors are in different positions with different aircraft so this is important.

The incoming aircraft is met by 15 vehicles and 30 people as it taxis to a stop. There is a ground power unit to run the lights and air conditioning while the plane is on the ground. Two pairs of mobile steps, two baggage cars and a truck are needed to take off the cargo. There are buses for the passengers and crew.

The ground engineers have a maintenance van. Three high-lift trucks carry fresh food, stores, cleaning equipment and commissary staff. Authority is represented by a Customs car and a supervisor's jeep.

As soon as the aircraft stops, it is berthed and chocks are put on the nosewheel. The auxiliary power unit is plugged in. The pilot cuts the engines, and the steps are driven up as the doors open.

Nobody can leave until Customs officers have cleared the plane. The captain tells the engineers of any faults that have developed.

The air freight, mail and baggage are cleared. The water cart arrives to pipe fresh water into the tanks, 99 gallons on a 707, 250 on a 747. The cleaners, called "groomers," and commissary attendants move into the aircraft. They change the pillowcases and blankets, check the seat backs for refuse, and clean the ashtrays, the galleys and the cockpit.

All the unused food is unloaded, and the ovens and containers and refrigerators are restocked with fresh meals. The surplus food, even smoked salmon and steaks, is thrown away. The groomers also change the spare oxygen cylinder, the medical kits, and the baby kits with their baby foods, evaporated milk, cornflakes, baby powder, diapers and pins, and toys. Three hundred cakes of soap, rolls of toilet paper, tubes of toothpaste, after shave are distributed around the toilets.

Red roses and a large basket of fruit are placed in the first-class cabin. Sweet trays, for handing around before takeoff, are laid out in the galleys. A van comes out with 300 newspapers: major international airports can supply same-day papers from 40 or more countries.

With 40 minutes to go, the maintenance men have finished their checks on tire pressure and treads, the undercarriage and the hydraulic system.

With 30 minutes to go, the sanitary servicing vehicle ("honey cart" to the crews) drains the waste from the toilet tanks and flushes and refills them. The pipes cannot be connected until an hour after landing because the valves freeze in flight.

The cabin maintenance man arrives to check seat lights, call lights, seat-reclining mechanisms, oxygen, refrigeration and air cooling. Seats that will not recline should be replaced from airline stocks. Often they are not.

It takes half an hour to check the radio, radar, electronics and instruments in the cockpit. The windshields are cleaned, and the wipers are checked.

Every window is cleaned. Fresh supplies of "seat literature" are put in the seat backs: maps, postcards, writing paper, envelopes, brochures, menu card, emergency instructions and sickbag. Special vacuum cleaners are used for the carpets.

The four galleys on a typical 707 flight will be loaded with 1,400 Lily cups, paper cups for water and fruit juice, 700 cocktail sticks and 400 swizzle sticks. There will be 140 packets of nuts, 16 pounds of sweets, 15 jars of onions, olives and cherries, 600 tea bags and 30 gallons' worth of coffee packs.

There will be 100 cans of fruit juice and 1,000 cans of bitter lemon, tonic water, ginger ale and soda. There are emergency cans of foods for the crew: luncheon meat, corned beef and tuna fish. They will eat this if there is a hijack or if the ordinary food turns out to be bad.

In reserve in the hold for use in countries where such things are unobtainable are 300 tea bags, six packets each of cornflakes, Rice Krispies and Sugar Puffs, 50 packets of Vita-Wheat, 36 tins of orange, grapefruit and tomato juice, ¼-pound each of Indian and China tea, 100 large and 100 small doilies, and six rolls of toilet paper.

Another emergency round of luncheon meat, corned beef and tuna fish is kept in the hold.

With half an hour to go, the second officer arrives to supervise the refueling. He also checks instruments, emergency oxygen cylinders, cabin oxygen pressure, emergency hatches and life rafts. A 707 has seven fuel tanks, and a pilot has to be on board to supervise the inflow from the two tankers. The aircraft can take 65 tons of fuel, and it is an important part of flying to keep it flowing from the right tanks to preserve trim.

Fifteen minutes from start-up, the crew bus drops off the cabin staff. They check that all food and stores are aboard. Loading of freight, mail and baggage starts. With ten minutes to go, the crew bus returns with the captain and flight crew. They have already had a briefing on the weather and have filed their flight plan.

The tankers go. As the passenger buses swing up with eight minutes to go, the air starter vehicle arrives. It supplies the compressed air that starts the engines by charging the compressors and blades. The doors close and are checked for pressure leaks. The captain radios for start-up clearance. The turnaround is completed.

13

Cabin Confidential

Like a hotel or a liner, an airliner has its own safes, its own secret recesses. On a 707, a special part of the freight hold is used for diplomatic mail. Valuables are stowed in a lockable container just behind and to the left of the cockpit door.

On a Jumbo, the diplomatic mail courier boards first class before anyone else. He sits unobtrusively in a front-row seat. In front of him is the "nose lowboy," a fitted table.

It looks unobtrusive enough, with magazine racks on it and a vase of flowers on the top. Indeed, at takeoff it may well have a child in a cot strapped onto it, since this is where infants are supposed to travel at takeoff and landing.

Inside, on the right-hand side, is a special locked and sealed compartment, the "dip-locker," for the world's diplomatic secrets, or drugs or duty-free whiskey or stolen blueprints or illicit love letters or whatever else still travels diplomatic, accompanied by the man in the front seat in the neat gray suit. The chief steward has the key if there is no courier.

At the back of the first class on many airlines there will be another man, whose jacket will remain on throughout the flight and who will show keen interest in his fellow passengers. He is the security guard.

Besides the "dip-locker," the Jumbos have a precious-cargo compartment, a simple cupboard next to the lavatory at the head of the stairs in the first-class lounge. The chief steward will take passengers' jewels and cash and place them in its rather flimsy care.

An aircraft can have up to 14 toilets, and each one will cost some $25,000. They will get well used. Studies show that more than 98 percent of all passengers on a flight of more than four hours will spend more than three minutes in a toilet, a figure only explicable by the fact that it is the only place to relax and get away from the claustrophobia of the cabin.

But toilets are not the sanctuaries they seem—they are designed to be easy to open. A British Airways manual for its well-bred stewardesses states firmly: "A locked toilet door can be opened easily from the outside by inserting a pencil, nail file or similar object into a slot in the occupied sign. Slide the sign diagonally to the left."

The toilets are expensive because they are fairly complex arrangements of plumbing. The power for heating the water has to be taken from a generator whirling at many thousands of revolutions per minute from the outer right (No. 4) engine. The flush has to be electric, since there is no gravity feed to help. The handbasin water is pumped in, but taken out under heavy suction and left to stream out of the aircraft's belly in a 580-mph stream of instantly iced spray—the only thing that deliberately leaves the aircraft in flight.

The toilet water system has three large pressurized tanks situated far away in the forward cargo compartment. Each tank holds 110 gallons of water, giving 300 usable gallons in all. This water is pumped to the galleys and ice-water fountains, as well as to the lavatories. Each washbasin has its own individual electric heater, thermostatically controlled to give a temperature of 125 degrees Fahrenheit.

Three hundred gallons of water would play havoc with the aircraft's electrical systems if it got loose. Should the shut-off valves in the galleys and lavatories not contain a flood, it is a serious enough emergency for the captain to be responsible, and not the chief steward. Through a special switch in the cockpit, he can depressurize the tanks and cut off the supply. Runaway toilets are part of a pilot's regular checklist.

Whereas water from the basins is sucked out of the aircraft, waste from the toilets is caught in tanks cleared on landing by the "honey carts." It is therefore quite safe to use the lavatories when the aircraft is stationary at an airport, unlike trains.

The aircraft holds such assorted necessities as seven gentlemen's wet razors, 20 electric razors, a dozen shoehorns, 300 "Do Not Disturb" labels, five packs of playing cards, 25 hand fans, 10 spare baby nipples. There is a special Baby Bar installation that will heat three bottles of milk at a time, with an automatic timer.

The heating is complex. Each oven—and there can be up to 15 ovens—heats 52 plates from frozen to a temperature of 120 degrees Fahrenheit in 45 minutes. Extractor fans remove cooking and lavatory smells along ducts and out of the aircraft. Hot plates boost temperatures to 200 degrees Fahrenheit in 45 to 60 minutes. Each galley has its own refrigerator, and bar carts have Dry Ice to keep drinks cool.

The lighting system is automatic. There are four phases on the light switch—SLP, TRANSIT, MOVIE and BRD. BRD, or Board, is full lighting. Transit and Movie cut it further and further until SLP, or Sleep, leaves only night illumination and the cross-over lights between cabin sections.

Passengers pushing the CALL button set off a faint blue light and a low-tone chime in the galley. When the flight crew want attention, however, the effect is a lot more urgent: the call light in the galley starts flashing furiously pink to the accompaniment of a high-tone chime. Passengers pulling CALL buttons in lavatories, in fairness, should also get prompt attention: a special amber light goes on together with the high-pitched chime.

The aircraft has a lot of a discotheque to it, with dimming and flashing lights. The cabin staff play taped music—the Zeppelins used to carry a piano and a pianist.

There is an internal telephone service so the crew can ring each other up on a special interphone with push numbers. The set has buttons with numbers from 1 to 5, and also the letter P for emergencies. To ring the chief steward, for example, the handset is lifted and 25 punched. For a nonurgent call to the pilot, his number is 31. But for urgent calls, punching P twice, PP, automatically cuts off any other conversations and gets straight through to the flight deck and captain. This is the "drunk funk" number in slang, Pilot Alert in officialese. (It is used mainly by stewardesses frightened of drunks; they want the captain and his four gold stripes to come down the aisle to impose discipline.)

Nowadays, the announcements that blushing real live girls used to give out in schoolgirl French or stammering English are often prerecorded in an impersonal studio. The Prerecorded Announcement System, bringing that old joke about "this is a fully automatic flight . . . this is a fully automatic flight . . ." closer home, is a complex piece of cassette-playing equipment. It has 12 punch buttons, each of which releases a different announcement. There is a "cancel" button and those who believe in live voices will be relieved to hear that "the activating of the cancel button will cancel the prerecorded announcement, and if necessary, allows an announcement to be made over the public address, using the handset."

So the lovely crew who welcome you aboard, with a prerecording of a girl who is not on the aircraft, can actually talk direct to you if they want, as long as they first remember to cancel the speaking equipment.

Buttons One and Two are red, and have guards over them so that they cannot be set off by mistake—not surprisingly, since Number One is the oxygen instruction (the one that is used when decompression has actually occurred), and this cassette should go on automatically when decompression happens.

Number Two is the ditching instruction. The reassuring voice that is saying "We are forced to make an emergency landing on water . . . The rescue services are aware of our intentions. . . ." was recorded months or years ago in a distant studio.

Then there are films, with four independent projectors. (Inflight movies are not new. British South American Airways had them in 1948.) The movies are started by pushing the MOVIE switch and keeping it depressed until the white light behind the

OFF switch changes to (aptly for the medium) blue. It turns itself off automatically when the film is over.

On Eastern and African routes, many passengers have never used a Western-style toilet before, with predictable results. Increasing numbers of illiterates fly, who cannot read safety leaflets. This is not restricted to the passengers. Much of the instruction given to cabin crews and ground fire-fighting teams from African airlines at the Beirut Flight Center has to be presented audiovisually, a chilling thought.

There is no need to panic if fellow passengers tug at the exit doors, thinking they lead to lavatories. The doors swing sideways and backwards initially, and the pressure difference at altitude would make it impossible to open them even if the handle could be twisted through its stop pin. It would be possible to open them at low level, but it would not matter much unless the muddled traveler stepped out.

Some aircraft cabins are very exotic. Hugh Hefner, the owner of *Playboy* magazine, had a long, black DC-9 called the *Big Bunny,* a temporary victim of an economy drive. The ordinary version carries 109 passengers. Hefner's carried just 33, in a series of chambers or caves. There was a boardroom with space for 10 directors, a disco and dance area, a master hi-fi system, a game room and a kitchen.

The focal point was the master bedroom. It was dominated by a huge elliptical bed six feet by eight. Sixty-eight raccoons gave their skins for the bedspread. By Hefner's fingertips was a complex of buttons. These controlled all the entertainment systems on board, enabled him to talk to the crew, darkened his polarized windows so he could watch a film, beamed in FM/AM shortwave radios and connected him by phone to whomever he wanted to talk to.

At the foot of the bed was a chair. It was motorized and could be rotated to face a typewriter ledge. Here Mr. Hefner wrote articles for the next issue of his magazine, or examined the color transparencies of his next Playmate of the Month on a light box. There was a shower.

The $5 million aircraft was designed by Dan Czubak. " 'Basically,' Mr. Hefner said, 'I want to take my mansion and put it in the aircraft.' Well, it's a big mansion, but he wanted the same sort of environment. He said he wanted first-class service all the way, and not airline first class. He wanted it the same as he had at home, at the mansion—bone china, cut glass, everything," said Mr. Czubak.

"So take the electronic gear he has on board. Seven color TV sets. Then we found a problem picking up interference flying from city to city, so we decided to have pretaped shows. We carry fifteen hours of TV tapes right there in the hi-fi cabin, along with the cartridge recorder, tape recorder, cassette recorder."

Hefner just beats Arab financier Adnan Khashoggi in the television stakes. Khashoggi's Boeing 727 has four sets. However, Khashoggi does have gold taps in his bathroom.

Mr. Hefner likes films. So the *Big Bunny* had a Cinema-Scope screen and storage for 10 films. Every seat had channel selectors so that guests could choose whichever of the many entertainments they wanted to listen to—and have a choice of headset, professional for purists, ordinary for others. Naturally Mr. Hefner had master control. He could preempt the entire entertainment system from the headboard by his bed.

Dan Czubak says: "Normally you get on an aircraft, turn on the overhead light and you have to hold your paper out two feet in front of you. On the *Playboy* jet, every individual seat has its own light position worked out. The operation in the lavatories is entirely electronic. Water, heat, everything is by button. There are no taps. The nozzle of the faucet is sculptured into the mirror so that the water appears to flow out of the glass."

The paneling was rosewood carved by German craftsmen. The seats are lined with Himalayan goat. And of course the *Big Bunny* was serviced by seven specially chosen Jet Bunnies.

Their uniform was a black knitted nylon ciré dress, with thigh-length boots in the same material and a long, white scarf with a black bunny on it. The aircraft had a large bar, but the Jet Bunnies stuck to nonalcoholic cocktails with names like Shirley Temple and Virgin Mary (a Bloody without the vodka).

Only two things disturbed Hugh Hefner as he jetted in his minimansion to the outposts of his empire in Chicago, Miami and Montreal. He tended to look slightly absurd strapped into his sybaritic bed when flying through turbulence; and his pilots, in their conventional jackets and caps, looked out of place in this flying dream.

The weather cannot be changed, and neither was he able to persuade the pilots to wear Buck Rogers spaceman-style coveralls in fluorescent colors.

King Khalid of Saudi Arabia has ordered a $42 million 747 executive jet. The plane will have a throne room and a hospital section with satellite communications to a hospital in Cleveland.

The Queen of England, by contrast, travels modestly. The first 30 rows of seats on a BA Super VC-10, normally the aircraft *Canopus*, are removed for her quarters. The entourage travels in the back. A lounge area, red-carpeted, with a settee and small dining table, is created in the converted first-class cabin. There are two dressing rooms with six-foot-high leather wardrobes for her and Prince Philip.

The royal cipher appears on the cigarette boxes, cutlery, wine decanters and silver trays which are specially kept for royal flights. But the beds, curtained off from the lounge area, are simple divans. Nor does the Queen have exotic tastes in food.

Her favorite is glazed duckling, with a little Nuits St. Georges. A stewardess often on royal flights says that "very often she'll settle for a ham sandwich and a coffee." The menus are sent over by Buckingham Palace well in advance, and it is quite common to find the Queen has asked for chicken when her equerries at the back have put down for oysters and champagne.

During flights she is briefed on her destination and the people who will receive her by an air vice marshal or equivalent. Lists of intelligent questions to put to locals, whose photographs will have been shown to her so that she can "recognize" them and ask after their families and affairs, are drawn up.

If she is flying out to join the royal yacht *Britannia,* 40 of her retinue travel in the back—personal secretaries, cooks, butlers. All ships at sea and other aircraft en route are informed of her royal progress. Only the President of the United States equals that, aboard his superbly equipped *Air Force One.*

14

HAUTE CUISINE
Or Cooking in the
Clouds

The dull crackle of meat on a spit competed with the whine of the jets. A succulent smoke filled the aircraft as the royal servants laid out gold plates with Lebanese hors d'oeuvres, hummus, shrimps, unleavened bread. Khazak carpets were laid in the eating area, so the King could lounge easily with his concubine of the moment, taking handfuls of the lamb and rice with dates and almonds.

Ibn Saud, King of Saudi Arabia and descendant of the Prophet, filled his lead crystal glass with his favorite Montrachet. With the Turkish sweetmeats and the jasmine-water ices came Taittinger champagne, and bitter black coffee was made on a brass stove in front of the King. When the King had finished, the spit revolved over the charcoal fire at 30,000 feet as the servants ate.

Such ostentation is no longer politically wise even for oil sheiks. Indeed, there was a plot to blow up Ibn Saud, gold plate, Comet airliner and all.

Mass travel has done away with the elegance of earlier days, when passengers ate in special dining rooms from a galley where food was cooked and not merely heated. They relaxed in the Smoking Cabin, or on the Promenade Deck, looking out of the extra-large windows with specially provided field glasses as the world slipped by at 80 mph.

Luxury in airships was even greater. Four times as long as a 747, they had mahogany and mother-of-pearl walls and ceilings, and wickerwork furniture. Each sleeping cabin had a sofa, table, stool, wardrobe and bed. There were Gramophones and baby grand pianos for dancing, and special smoking rooms sealed off from the inflammable hydrogen by air-lock doors.

The *Hindenburg* had a dining room 15 feet by 50 feet for its 70 passengers. The chef had five assistants, and he attended each meal. The classic *Hindenburg* lunch, served on the second and last day out over the Atlantic, was Indian swallows' nest soup, caviar and Rhine salmon, lobster, saddle of venison, crème Hindenburg, fruit and cheese. The wines were 1934 Graacher Himmelreich, 1934 Diedesheimer Kranzler Riesling, 1934 Piesporter Goldtropfcher and 1928 Feist Brut. The brandy was 1842 Meukow.

The only things that are cooked on aircraft now are the steaks in first class, and even they must have the surface browned and black grill marks burned on them before they come on board, since an aircraft oven cannot give this grill effect.

The size of airline catering is staggering. Every year, more than 350 million meals have to be preprepared, taken on board in the right numbers to the right aircraft, and served. Pan Am serves more than 16 million meals in flight, TWA 16 million, BA 20 million, United more than 30 million. Braniff gets through more than 320,000 chickens and 80,000 pounds of bacon a year.

On average, economy meals in the U.S. cost $10 each and first class $20. They may not taste that way. Richard Gordon summed up many passengers' disbelief that most economy meals taste the way they do, when airlines that charge for meals like Laker are so much better at only $3. He wrote to *The New York Times:* "The American airlines—and I refer particularly to Pan American, TWA, United and American—serve inedible meat, greasy and tasteless vegetables and desserts which appear to be almost entirely of chemical origin. Service of drinks is perfunctory at best. Recently I have had occasion to cross the Atlantic four times on Laker Airways and for $3 received meals that would be considered acceptable in a modestly priced New York restaurant."

The kitchens of a large airline are far bigger and more complex than those of any hotel and much more subject to strain. Because of the vagaries of fog and weather, there may be a sudden and unexpected quadrupling in demand. Aircraft that are going to remote airfields without adequate caterers must have meals specially packed in their holds on Dry Ice for return flights.

Even politics plays a part. Middle East Airlines found that it was carrying, quite unaccountably, Jaffa oranges on flights from London to sensitive Arab countries. After the embarrassing affair of the oranges stopped, something even worse started. The duty-free Marlboro cigarettes on flights into Cairo started appearing with "Specially packed for El Al Israeli Airlines" on them.

Airlines will go to great lengths to get the right ingredients. British Caledonian flies the long routes from South America to Europe. The airline's catering manager says: "There is no substitute for a British breakfast. Passengers are entitled to the real thing. So we fly British bacon and chipolatas out and store them specially in Buenos Aires and Rio. We do the same with smoked salmon and caviar and some liqueurs—you can't get them in South America.

"We've tried experimenting with local chipolatas there, and in West Africa. They just aren't up to it, so we fly out our own."

The same airline makes use of spare freight capacity to fly shellfish and crab from the Seychelles to send out to Los Angeles from London in fish dishes; mangoes, avocados, pineapples and limes are flown in on the African flights; coffee comes in the hold from Brazil, maté from Argentina, all to be sent out on other flights from London.

No aircraft leaves unless there is food for all aboard. With an aircraft on the ground costing a company about $2,500 an hour, with a crew that may go overtime, it's expensive to wait for food. It is a catering manager's nightmare, but it happens, despite the 20-minute-plus-five rule (putting on the food only 20 minutes before takeoff and allowing five spare meals above the number on the passenger manifest), and despite the "meals on wheels vans" that cruise permanently around to top up aircraft.

A strike by catering loaders is often the reason. Airlines are vulnerable to strikes by all the specialized groups they rely on, and pilots, cabin staff, engineers, maintenance men, refuelers, air traffic controllers and baggage handlers have all severely affected international flights in the past three years. Thus Pan Am always has enough food to last six weeks.

On a flight westbound across the Atlantic to Los Angeles, the aircraft will be taking off around 1 P.M., the peak period for the westbounds. Lunch will be served slightly west of Ireland. A typical first-class menu:

Smoked Scotch Salmon
or
Royal Game Pancakes in Madeira Sauce
Consommé Grande Duchesse
Grilled Fillet of Steak Aberdeen Angus
or
Sauté of Chicken Chasseur
or
Turbot in Shrimp Sauce
Green Salad—French or Italian Dressing
French Beans
Baby Carrots
Parsley Potatoes
Strawberry Chantilly
Cheeseboard, Fresh Fruit, Coffee—Brazilian

During the previous night, between midnight and dawn, the turbot and chicken will have been cooked, the shrimp sauce prepared and heated. The catering manager will have the manifest giving the numbers and names of first-class passengers, and will have made a subconcious decision on relative quantities. The plane cannot take off with 60 main courses for 20 first-class passengers—the economics would be mad.

It must be refined so that just one spare first-class entrée is carried for 20 passengers. And it must be right. "You can tell people at a first-class restaurant that something is not available and they take it without a murmur—even though you could go out and buy it," says a steward. "But if you tell somebody the fish is not available thirty-two thousand feet above the Atlantic, they go berserk—they'll say, 'I've paid eight hundred dollars for this meal.' And of course if they are traveling first they've got a point—they are paying much more for the pure transport, like the people back in economy are paying for, and they're in for a few hundred dollars for a better seat and better food."

Flight times are an important factor. A 1 P.M. takeoff means meat, but every hour before or after that means more fish. Names are examined. Women are more likely to choose chicken or fish; fish on Fridays will increase if there are people with Catholic-sounding names. Children almost always go for chicken; during the "lollipop flight" periods at the end-of-term times this is taken into account.

But for a normal London to Los Angeles run, the emphasis will be on steak, with the women listed for chicken, and two fish—one for a "rogue" who may order it, another as the reserve. The flight crew eat first class. They cannot eat shellfish, so the turbot in shrimp sauce is out. Steak is heavy. They are put down for chicken.

A flight to Africa would mean more chicken; to the Far East and Japan more fish. For the Middle East and West Africa, saddle of lamb would be on the menu—though for Japan, where lamb is not eaten, it would be rigorously avoided.

The manager makes sure there have been no mistakes regarding these regional rules, makes his guess on ordering patterns, and leaves a note for the chief steward with the amounts of each dish. Thirteen hours later, with the aircraft crusing, the chief steward will already have worked out what to strongly recommend to whom.

If the passengers prove awkward, the pilots and engineer will have to eat what is given to them—although the captain and the first officer should eat different dishes to avoid simultaneous food poisoning.

While the entrées are prepared, another chef makes the strawberry Chantilly. An urn is filled with consommé, and left to chill slightly.

The morning shift comes on at 6 A.M. and cuts the smoked

salmon and lemon wedges. At 10:15, with three hours before takeoff, as the passengers finish packing in their hotels, the chefs cook the royal game pancakes. These will be kept warm and go on board the aircraft warm.

Two hours before takeoff, the steaks are browned and seared. Some are partly cooked, and marked for well done with black foil. Others are left bloody, with red foil. On board the aircraft they will be heated and partially cooked. The green salad is carefully placed in bowls. Like bread, it is easily affected by pressurization and its crispness goes. Cream is also affected, quickly turning sour, which is why airlines use powdered milk packets.

Vegetables are taken out of the frozen-food stores. Twenty minutes before takeoff, the meals are taken out to the aircraft by van to be stowed in the first-class galley and packed in the ovens and refrigerators.

The economy menus were prepared and placed on trays during the night: 160 hors d'oeuvres, coq au vin with green beans and small roast potatoes, pineapple cheesecake, cheese and crackers.

Although a first-class menu can be as elaborate as the airline wishes, economy is strictly governed by IATA. The most that can be given is hors d'oeuvres, a main dish with no salad and only two vegetables, and dessert or fruit, not both. These rules are binding, but explain why almost every international airline gives so much salad with its hors d'oeuvres—it can't give it any other way.

The main food course is in wrapped foil containers inside ovens which are then plugged into the aircraft's electric system. The rest is laid out on trays in special containers. All the stewardess has to do is to heat the prefrozen main course, put it on the trays and serve.

Twenty minutes before takeoff, the galley closes. No more food will be taken on for late arrivals, but there are already five spare economy meals. If extra first-class passengers turn up, the crew must forfeit eating first class.

The bars are installed and sealed by Customs. A 707 on an intercontinental flight will carry 18,000 cigarettes, 900 cigars, 56 bottles of whiskey, 16 bottles of brandy, 8 bottles of gin, 200 miniatures of spirits, 200 quarter bottles of wine, and 5 bottles each, say, Château Latour-Camblanes 1967, Puligny Montrachet 1964 and champagne for first class.

Thirty minutes before serving the economy passengers, the ovens are switched on to 300 degrees Fahrenheit. These are electric ovens with a fan to give them even temperatures, since the trays are stacked in tight.

For first, the turbot gets 20 minutes at 350 degrees Fahrenheit, the chicken 25. The steaks get 10 minutes for rare, 13 minutes for medium, 20 minutes for well done. Turning on ovens should be in strict sequence, allowing each ovenload to be served before the next one is fully heated.

The routines are laid out to the smallest detail. Serving 434 passengers on a 747 is a military-style exercise, where all 10 cabin crew are taught meal service routine as per "diagrams" and "sequences."

The task of steward II in the aft galley of a 747 is thus: "Check progress of ovens, prepare meal carts 3 and 4. Position meals on carts 6, 7 and 8. Pass cart 6 to stewardess C, 7 to D, 8 to senior steward. Replace meals removed from oven 9 and oven 10 with 49 refrigerated meals for second cycle heating for meal service sequence 3."

There are the regulations for crew meals. Most airlines give the pilots normal first-class menus, except that they prohibit oysters and other mollusks (on medical ground to prevent food poisoning), and allow other shellfish provided it has come only from the U.S.A., U.K., Canada, South Africa and Japan and nowhere else. The crew are not allowed alcohol. Although insisting that "the chief steward shall see that full service is given in the control cabin," airlines draw the line at caviar for the crew on economic grounds.

Some airlines cling to tradition, still treating the crew as ships' officers from earlier and more gracious days. BA provides a white-coated steward on all-cargo flights to look after the crew. He serves their meals on a white cloth on the navigation table in the cockpit.

Such flamboyant touches apart, the food is predictable. Salmon, shrimp cocktail and trout travel well, keep their appearance, and so are common. Paté does not keep well; melon and green salads have a short life. Poultry and steaks are readily available, easy to prepare, acceptable and thus beat anything else.

There is a worldwide telex and computer code for people whose eating habits are dictated by religion, medicine or fashion. Airlines serve millions of "religious" meals each year. If KSML appears next to a passenger's name he will get a kosher meal, kept in a separate part of the galley from Gentile food, and presented to the passenger with the original seal intact. Most intercontinental aircraft have emergency kosher packs in the dry food stores, wrapped in plain brown paper for going through Arab countries.

On the other hand, a MOML will get a Moslem meal. The airline standard is lamb, goat or chicken with rice pilaff. HNML's, for Hindus, are the same as a VGML, or vegetarian—mushrooms in salad with diced potatoes and cauliflower—but with a curry seasoning.

There are BBMLs for babies with milk feeding bottles, seafood meals for slimmers, and WSML's, salt-free meals. Businessmen get DUML's, dietetic ulcer meals of grilled lean beef with little salt, boiled potatoes, boiled beans and fruit compote with fresh milk. All these meals can be produced to identical standards within a few hours at any major airport.

Airlines do get seriously victimized. One of America's largest wine producers was fined a quarter of a million dollars for successfully passing off cooking wine as first class.

But then it wouldn't be an airport business if there wasn't a racket in it somewhere.

PART FOUR

AIRBORNE

15

Flight

The theory of flight is simple. Drag and weight try to stop an aircraft; lift and thrust have to overcome them. Thrust in a jet aircraft comes from the engines, which push a "jet" of heated air through the exhaust pipes against the surrounding air. The push propels the aircraft forward. With a propeller plane, the thrust comes from accelerating the air through propellers.

Drag is the resistance of the air to the aircraft passing through it. Streamlining reduces the drag. The lift comes from the flow of air around the wings. Against this there is the weight of the aircraft and the force of gravity pulling it down.

Where thrust and lift are stronger than drag and weight, the aircraft can accelerate and climb. The wing develops lift because it is designed so that the airflow over it causes less air pressure on the top surface than on the bottom. The difference in air pressure causes a lift vertically upward.

The faster an aircraft goes the greater the lift. The higher the aircraft goes, the "thinner" the air becomes. Air is compressed by its own weight. One hundred cubic feet of air at sea level weighs about 8 pounds, but the same volume at 20,000 feet weighs only 4 pounds. Although there is less lift at high altitudes, there are also much less resistance and drag. This enables jets to fly high and fast without using so much fuel.

The air itself changes greatly with height, becoming colder, less dense, or "thinner," and with a steady reduction in barometric pressure. An International Standard Atmosphere is used to average out its qualities. At sea level, the ISA barometric pressure is taken as 1,013.2 millibars. Although the actual pressure may be different, every pilot at height sets the standard 1,013.2 millibars on his altimeter to give his height. If different pilots used different settings, collisions would result. The ISA temperature at sea level is assumed at 18 degrees Celsius, and relative density at 1.00.

By 10,000 feet, the temperature is already down to −5 degrees Celsius, the relative density 0.862. At 20,000 feet, it is −25 degrees Celsius, density 0.533 and the pressure has dropped to 466 millibars.

Just above the uppermost reaches of cloud, cruising at 35,000 feet, the air temperature outside the aircraft is −54 degrees Celsius. Barometer pressure is 239 millibars and the relative density 0.311. The jet is at home where the air is cold and very thin. Above this is the lower stratosphere where the temperature steadies but the density goes on dropping.

An aircraft has three basic instabilities that are used to control it (a totally stable aircarft would only be able to fly straight and level). Yaw is the name given to the swing of the nose to left or right. This is resisted by the large surface of the tail fin. A rudder set into the fin gives controlled yaw, so that the pilot can move the nose sideways through rudder pedals at his feet. The fin is large, 1,660 square feet on a Jumbo, which is as much as the total sail area of a racing yacht.

Pitch is the movement of the nose up or down. It is controlled by the horizontal stabilizer. Parts of the stabilizer are hinged and can be moved up or down by pushing the control column backward or forward. These are called the elevators. Sometimes the whole of the stabilizer moves: this is called an "all flying tail." Here, the bulk of the tail is used to get the plane in roughly the right attitude of climb or descent, and the elevators are used for sensitive trimming.

Roll is when one wing goes up or down relative to the other. The wings are inclined upward from the fuselage to prevent rolling. The angle of rise is called the dihedral: on a 747 it is 7 degrees. The wings are also swept back to delay the onset of high-speed shock waves, on a 747 by a full 37 degrees.

The wings have hinged surfaces on them called ailerons. They move in opposite directions: if the right aileron is up, the left one will be down. The aircraft will "bank" toward the aileron that is up—if the right aileron is up, the plane will roll to the right. The pilot controls the ailerons by turning the wheel on his control column to the left or right.

Engine power is controlled by pushing a hand throttle backward or forward.

That is the basis of control.

A modern jet airliner has a lot of hardware on it, though that does not change the basic rules. Take the wings. On a jet, they are designed for maximum performance at high speed and altitude. They must have low "drag" to pass cleanly through the air, so they are thin.

What is desirable at high speed is dangerous at low speed. Landing or taking off in a jet would have to be done at a very high and risky speed if the wing stayed the same shape as it is when the plane is cruising six miles high. So the wing has devices built into it which the pilot uses on takeoff and landing, but which are tucked away for the rest of the flight.

The most obvious devices are flaps. A simple flap is a section at the back of the wing which is rotated downward. On a modern aircraft it not only rotates downward, but it can also be pushed back, which enlarges the size of the wing. Some aircraft have a flap on the back of a flap, called a slotted flap. Other variations are zap flaps, Fowler flaps, blown flaps and split flaps, all of which are on the back of the wing for the same reason. They increase lift because they increase the size of the wing.

This means that the aircraft can stay in the sky at much lower speeds.

The flaps are normally fully down for landing, but only partially down for takeoff since they slow the plane's acceleration. Thus a high-speed cruise wing is converted into a high-lift, low-speed wing for landing.

More lift at low speeds can also be obtained from flaps on the front of the wing. They extend forward and down. An advantage is that, where flaps on the trailing edge pitch the nose down when they are extended, leading edge flaps counteract this by pitching the nose up. They are called droops, Kreuger flaps, variable camber flaps or slats.

Jet aircraft are so streamlined that it is very difficult to slow them down quickly. Flaps might do this, but they would tear the wings off at high speeds, and on most aircraft they are not safe to use at more than 250 mph.

So the wings are fitted with speed brakes, or "spoilers." These are panels on the top surface of the wings which can be raised to block the airflow. This cuts the speed very quickly, although it leads to buffeting and noise in the cabin. The spoilers also reduce lift and help the aircraft to lose height. Very powerful spoilers are called "lift dumpers."

The passenger's view of a wing while an aircraft is landing is impressive. On an aircraft like a Boeing 727, there are six devices used to convert the "cruising" wing into one that is safe for landing. From the cabin outward, there are: inboard spoilers, inboard flaps, inboard ailerons, outboard spoilers, outboard flaps, and outboard ailerons. On a 747, there are three Kreuger flaps and ten variable camber flaps on the front of the wing as well.

Hanging all this from the wing creates a lot of drag and wind resistance. The plane tends to descend very quickly, and to have what pilots call a "high sink rate." A number of airliners have hit the ground before they got to the runway because their pilots were used to earlier aircraft which were more gentle in their approach. The Russian Il-62 is so out of balance that it is thought to carry water ballast in the nose, and has a long, low approach pattern.

Another Soviet airliner, the Tupolev 104A, is unstable enough to have earned a reputation as the world's most dangerous jet. Since there is no way of avoiding Aeroflot Tu-104A's on the Moscow–Leningrad run, well-advised passengers take the train.

A jet has to use a lot of power on the landing approach. If the throttles were allowed to idle, it would take six seconds to get back to level flying from even a small rate of descent. So a lot of power is needed, for this and to overcome drag, on the approach.

There are often many changes of engine power and noise during an approach. This is partly because of the sinking effect of the flaps, and partly because if a jet is not set up for exactly the right descent, coarse power changes are needed to get it onto the runway.

The flaps themselves and the undercarriage make a noise when they do down. This worries passengers who have, up until then, been lulled by a near silent cruise and initial descent. It is, however, normal.

Jets have a number of handling problems. One is the high sink rate. Another drawback on the approach to landing is the absence of any propeller wash over the wings to give lift and reduce the stalling speed.

A jet is so streamlined that it can descend at 14,000 feet a minute, though the wings would probably fail if it attempted to pull out of such a dive. The normal descent rate on an approach to landing is only 700 feet a minute. The pilot must not let the plane drop too fast. Once it is allowed to do this, it is very difficult to stop it without losing a great deal of height.

All aircraft will stall. This happens when the air, instead of flowing smoothly over the wing and producing lift, breaks away and the wing loses its lift. Stalling on propeller aircraft is straightforward. It happens when the angle at which the plane is flying becomes too steep to maintain flight. The aircraft gives plenty of warning by buffeting and shaking. When it stalls, the nose drops straight down. The pilot increases power, or simply waits as speed builds up during descent, and then pulls the nose back to recover. Some height is lost. It is obviously a dangerous maneuver when close to the ground, but it is predictable and straightforward.

The early jets had the same good stalling characteristics. But most modern jets are capable of "super-stalling," or "deep stalling," and sometimes it is impossible to recover. Rear-engined, high-tailed jets are the type most at risk. The problem started on civil aircraft with the Caravelle. A stage comes with the nose lifted by about 35 degrees when the aircraft is as stable and immovable as a rock. The drag is so high that no amount of engine power is of any assistance. There is complete lateral control but the aircraft comes down like an elevator.

As this type of aircraft stalls, the nose pitches up. This puts the tail into the wash of the wings. The airflow has already stalled over the wings, and so both tail and wings are stalled. Because the tail is stalled the aircraft cannot be pitched nose down, even though only with the nose down can speed increase and the airplane recover. The wings are stalled, so the pilot cannot bank or roll the plane to an angle that will free the tail from the stalled wing wake.

The aircraft thus drops very rapidly. It will hit the ground slightly nose up, its wings dead level and with almost no forward speed. This is exactly how a British Airways Trident crashed at Staines on June 18, 1972, shortly after takeoff. The pilots withdrew the droops on the front edges of the wings at too low a speed, the nose went up, and the aircraft slammed into the ground with all the "locked-in" stability of a runaway elevator.

Aircraft like this would not be allowed to fly unless they had an advance warning system to make sure the pilot never gets into a stall. They stall without the buffeting that warned the pilots of earlier planes of imminent danger. This is largely because as wing design has improved, the air does not separate from the wing so easily, and the aircraft goes into the stall suddenly and without warning.

So the aircraft have "stick shakers" and bells* to warn the pilots of an impending stall. The angle which would induce a super-stall is calculated and if the angle is coming dangerously close, the column control automatically shakes. A motor starts up an

---

*Test pilot D. P. Davies, in *Handling the Big Jets*, published by the Air Registration Board, Redhill, Surrey, England, points out that tactile warnings are best in aircraft. Of the five senses, two (taste and smell) are useless in the air. Pilots respond best to touch, like the shaking control columns in their hands. Sound, the shouted warning, is also powerful. But visual warnings, such as flashing lights can easily be ignored. Thus visual warnings of real emergencies, such as fire, are often accompanied by bells and hooters.

out-of-balance weight on the control column, shaking it. Some types, such as the Trident, go even further. They have "stick pushers." When the aircraft is near a stall, the control column is automatically pushed forward to get the nose down. The pilot can, however, override the system.

Some jets are prone to "Dutch roll."* The nose yaws from left to right, and this starts the aircraft rolling as well. If the rolling gets bad, the plane will start to sideslip and go out of control.

This is countered by "yaw dampers" which automatically adjust the rudder to stop the nose swing. The pilot can deal with it himself by using his ailerons to check the roll, or he can lose height rapidly. Dutch roll is most dangerous at high altitude in thin air where there is less resistance to rolling.

Modern aircraft also suffer from "jet upsets." These are high-speed dives, often at a high angle of bank. A jet cruising at high speed is a delicately balanced machine. If it is upset, it will go out of control very rapidly.

This is normally caused by turbulent weather. It can also happen if an autopilot slips out, if there is a "runaway stabilizer," where the stabilizer starts moving of its own accord, or if the aircraft goes out of trim and stability. The nearer to the speed of sound, the more unstable some aircraft become. The rudders on all jetliners become less effective as the sound barrier approaches. On some the effect is reversed so that pushing right rudder yaws and rolls the plane to the left. Thus, no rudder is used when Concorde is flying supersonically.

Jets use huge amounts of fuel. As it is burned, the weight of the aircraft becomes less and the center of gravity alters. A pilot has to make sure that the aircraft does not creep out of balance as the flight progresses. A four-engine jet, like a 707 or a DC-8, can "lose" 60 tons of weight on a flight through fuel consumption and this has to be allowed for in trimming the aircraft. A 747 or a DC-10 can burn 140 tons of fuel. On Concorde the fuel is pumped around during flight to keep the plane in balance.

Speed is, of course, the essence of flight, the sole justification for

---

*This curious term has been inherited from the sea and is based on the walk of inebriated Dutch sailors.

jets and particularly the Concorde. The indicated airspeed the pilot sees on the clock in front of him has less and less relation with the airspeed as he climbs. The airspeed indicator, or ASI, like the altimeter, is affected by the density of the air. The higher the aircraft climbs, the lower the density of the air, and the more the airspeed indicator underreads. An aircraft with an indicated airspeed of 200 knots at 20,000 feet, for example, will have a true airspeed of some 275 knots.

This is important to the pilot in actually handling the aircraft. The forces of lift and stress on an aircraft also depend on the air density, and so the indicated airspeed is a reliable guide to how an aircraft can be maneuvered in terms of stall speed, flap limiting speeds and so forth. In other words, an aircraft behaves much the same at 275 knots at 20,000 feet as it does at 200 knots at sea level.

True airspeed must be known for navigation in order to work out the speed over the ground. To obtain it, the pilot feeds the indicated airspeed, and the height and air temperature, which affect the air pressure, into a mechanical computer which produces true airspeed.

Pilots talk and think in terms of indicated airspeed, and most of the speeds given here are IAS, not true. In general, the higher the altitude, the higher the true airspeed. On a normal day, when the world exactly corresponds in air density to the averaged-out International Standard Atmosphere, 160 knots IAS will be accurate at sea level, but will really be 220 knots at 19,000 feet and 323 knots at 37,000 feet.

Height also affects the speed of sound. Above 24,000 feet pilots fly more off the Machmeter than the airspeed indicator: the higher the aircraft flies, the closer it gets to the speed of sound, and this becomes more important than its simple airspeed. A Machmeter shows the speed the aircraft is flying at in relation to the speed of sound, the Mach number.*

The speed of sound, of "sound barrier," is important because of its relation to shock. An aircraft moving at less than the speed of

---

*Mach is named after the Austrian scientist Professor Ernst Mach, a nineteenth-century pioneer in observing shock waves.

sound sends out waves in front of it that warn of its coming. The airstreams then begin to divide to make way for it, and there is little change in the density of the air as it flows over the aircraft. The waves are similar to sound waves and they travel at the speed of sound.

If an aircraft flies at or near the speed of sound, no warning is sent out in front, and so the air hits the aircraft with a shock. Shock waves form over the aircraft and affect the wings and tail. Shock waves are accompanied by a sudden increase in the air density, a rise in temperature and a decrease in speed.

This causes a sudden and very large increase in drag, resulting in a loss of lift, and severe "buffeting." The aircraft's balance may be thrown off and lead to serious pitching of the nose. These symptoms are very like a stall and severe shock-wave effect is called a shock stall.

Shock stalls are highly unpleasant. There is a sudden change of trim, usually slamming the nose down, but sometimes leading to the nose pitching up and down. Very large forces are needed to move the controls. The aircraft will buffet, the ailerons will vibrate and the whole machine will start pitching and yawing oscillations which may go out of control. These may be "snaking," yawing from side to side, "porpoising" up and down, or roll and yaw combined in "Dutch roll."

The control problem can be very severe. If the elevator is in the turbulent air behind a shock wave on the stabilizer, the forces on it may be so great that it becomes almost immovable. To avoid this, an all-moving, power-operated tail must be used. (To guard against power failure, modern aircraft have several control surfaces. Concorde, for example, has two rudders, one above the other, and six elevons, combined elevator and ailerons.) Wings are fitted with vortex generators, small metal wedges projecting an inch above the wings and set in lines, which weaken the shock waves.

However, the only way to avoid shock stalls is to fly slowly enough to avoid them—or fast enough to get through the transonic difficulties of the sound barrier and into the less complicated supersonic world. Shock stalls can occur whenever any part of the aircraft is at the speed of sound. The airflow over certain parts of the aircraft, particularly the wings, can reach the speed of sound even though the aircraft itself is traveling well below this.

The speed at which this happens, with its inherent risk of an uncontrollable shock stall, is called the critical Mach number. Each aircraft has its critical Mach number, known by the diminutive of MCr. The simple stall is the critical speed below which the aircraft will go out of control: MCr is the same at the other end of the speed range.

The speed of sound varies with air temperature, and thus with height, and the Machmeter takes this into account. On the basis of the International Standard Atmosphere, in average conditions, the speed of sound is 661 knots at sea level, 640 knots at 10,000 feet, 614 knots at 20,000 feet, 589 knots at 30,000 feet and 573 knots at 40,000. The true speed at which a shock stall will occur on a large modern jet, with a typical MCr of Mach 0.9, is thus 595 knots at sea level, 552 knots at 20,000 feet and only 516 knots at 40,000.

Supersonic aircraft are designed to pass through the sound barrier and to minimize the effect of shock waves. Concorde does this so well that it is only by looking at the Machmeter that the pilots can tell they are going through the sound barrier.

The double curve, or "ogee," of Concorde's wings gives a very thin wing with low drag. The large wingspan also reduces drag, and the stalling angle is so large it cannot be reached in normal flight. The wings do not need the normal mass of flaps, spoilers and air brakes: the shape means they are good for speeds from 127 knots to 1,260 knots. Flaps are not needed because of the high lift of highly swept-back wings and the cushioning effect of a large delta wing when near the ground. The complex engineering required, however, made it necessary for Concorde to be tested for 5,800 hours before being granted a Certificate of Airworthiness. The subsonic 747 needed only 1,500.

A slim body and thin wings, together with limiting the top speed to just over Mach 2 (twice the speed of sound), have kept Concorde's temperature rise down. It has thus been possible to make most of it from aluminum alloys instead of heavier and more expensive stainless steel or titanium alloys. The relative lightness also reduces the sonic bangs, since these bangs—in fact, the shock wave as the sound barrier is broken, just as with a cracking whip or a bullet—increase in intensity with weight and volume.

Cosmic radiation increases with altitude and Concorde has a radiation meter to warn of high solar-glare conditions, although the radiation doses are substantially less than the limits for industrial workers.

16

Engines

A balloon will fly without power, apart from gas or hot air. Men first crossed the English Channel by air in a balloon in the eighteenth century. But an aircraft needs an engine.

The first engines used were piston engines developed for cars. The high-performance piston engine on aircraft makes Formula One racing-car engines look like power packs for mopeds.

The engines run up to 24 cylinders, set in four banks with six cylinders each. At 6,000 rpm they develop more than 3,500 horsepower. A single crankpin can have six pairs of connecting rods set on it. Six-throw, seven-bearing crankshafts have to be perfectly machined over months.

Fuel injection and superchargers are used to increase performance at altitude. Automatic controls sensitive to changes in pressure and height cut in the supercharger and prevent the pilot from pumping in too much fuel.

The propellers themselves are geared. At low forward speeds, when taking off or landing, the blades are most effective when they are full on to the airflow. They must force back as much air as possible over the wings to improve lift. Since the airflow is slow, the propellers meet little resistance from it. The full-on attitude is called "fine pitch."

As speed picks up, the blades are twisted to give less resistance to the air. The angle to the airflow is "coarsened" as the blades twist into it. On the most modern of the great piston engines, the pitch is automatically varied at different heights and airspeeds.

If an engine breaks down in flight, the propeller is twisted beyond the coarse position. Only the edge of the blade is into the airflow. This is called "feathering." An unfeathered propeller would windmill in the airflow and drag the aircraft off course as well as slowing it.

Beyond fine pitch, the blades can go into reverse. This spins the air forward and slows down the aircraft on landing. Most prop and propjet aircraft have "constant speed" propellers. They adjust automatically, twisting to coarse pitch as speed increases and back to fine as it drops off.

Piston engines are easily the most efficient engines at speeds below 300 mph. Over 400 mph, their efficiency tails off quickly. Jet engines bisect propeller engines at just over 400 mph on efficiency graphs.*

Getting more power means increasing the number of cylinders. Simply making larger cylinders is not possible, as they could not be cooled. Valves have to be cooled with molten sodium which splashes between the head and stem to transfer the heat. The pistons are cooled with oil; cooling the oil in radiators and large sumps is difficult.

More cylinders mean more oil. A typical piston aircraft, the DC-4, carries 20 gallons of oil for each engine, plus a 40-gallon reserve for topping up. Oil is a harsh master for piston-engine crews. Riding on no more than car engines beefed up to the ultimate, permanently going through extremes of temperature, vibration and stress, the crews spend nervous hours watching oil temperatures and oil reserves. A jet engine carries just over six gallons of oil—and crews worry if it burns two pints an hour.

Even the spark plugs are hammered hard. If they are large enough to withstand the pitting caused by sparking, they may not

---

*As a rule of thumb, a propeller engine is at peak efficiency at 300 knots, a jet at 1,100 knots and a rocket at 4,300 knots.

be hot enough to burn off oil when the engine is idling. If they are small and heat up quickly, they will explode the charge before sparking. The heat has to be conducted away from them.

Pilots call piston engines "hot engines." They are very prone to breakdown. They have reached the limits of design at 12,000 rpm. More power means more massive reduction gears to slow down the revolutions between crankshaft and propeller.

More height means less air for the blades to bite on. At 40,000 feet, where a jet comes into its own, a propeller can deliver only a quarter of the power it has at sea level.

Superchargers can compensate for only a fraction of the loss in rarefied air. Disks in casings on the engine drive air at increased speed into the engine or feed gases from the exhaust back into the engine. But the faster the propeller blades revolve, the less effective they are. The tips whirl faster than the speed of sound, and the air buffets off them without producing thrust.

Think of a car engine driving a propeller instead of wheels. On a typical flight, the outside temperature will vary from 70 degrees Fahrenheit to −40 degrees Fahrenheit. The altitude goes from sea level to 20,000 feet. The rpm reach 12,000; 6,000 is maximum on most cars. It is as if a car were regularly driven up a 20,000-foot mountain, went along a 1,500-mile plateau, and then down again. The propeller pitch is the gear lever, constantly changing. The accelerator has to be adjusted to the height to feed in rich or lean mixture.

Not surprisingly, a classic piston engine like the Wright Cyclone needs a major overhaul lasting six weeks every 2,000 hours. Because the ultimate is squeezed out of a basically crude power plant, the whole is far more complex than a jet.

Flight engineers are needed to nurse them along, playing with fuel mixtures, taking the strain off sick engines by altering oil flow and pitch, listening to the beat of the engines to pick up rough running before it becomes breakdown.

"You have to be a good listener on a piston plane," says a flight engineer now on Boeings. "The art is noise vibration, tuning like a mechanic in the pits at Monaco. In a jet you can't hear much, and if you feel any vibration it means the disaster has already happened."

The reliability of modern jet engines is shown vividly by the maintenance schedules. On a piston engine, 35 days in the air meant 42 days of overhaul on the ground. Turboprops need one day on the ground for every 166 in the air. With pure jets, major overhauls are only needed after 1,000 days in the air.

Piston engines are subject to complaints familiar on cars: piston wear, carburetor icing, crankshaft failures, broken push rods, scoured cylinders. Jets have very few moving parts to go wrong.

Simple turbojets suck air in at the front through a compressor which impels air in. This raises the pressure of the air three and a half times. This compressed air passes into a combustion chamber where fuel is poured in and ignited in a flame tube. As the hot air expands, it accelerates rapidly through a turbine and out of a propulsion nozzle. The turbine is linked by a shaft to the compressor blades at the front. This is the only major moving part.

The power comes from the rush of air through the propulsion nozzle at the back of the engine. This is, in fact, a "jet" of air pushing the aircraft along. The faster the aircraft is moving, the more air is forced in by ram effect, and the engine becomes more efficient—quite unlike the piston engine. It is best to give a small increase in velocity to a large amount of air: a large increase in velocity cannot be contained in thrust and is dissipated in the slipstream.

The jet comes in various forms. The "propjet" Viscounts, Electras, Friendships, seek to make the best of both propeller and jet worlds. They are very efficient at speeds under 425 mph, where the pure jet is still not at its best.

On a propjet, most of the power from the expanding air rushing through the turbine is fed to the propeller. Less goes out through the propulsion nozzles as thrust, although the aircraft is to some extent pushed forward by the jet of air as well as pulled forward by the propellers.

Simple turbojets do not use all the power that is available. "Bypass" engines are more efficient. Part of the air from the compressors goes through the turbines and combustion chambers as normal. But some bypasses this heating stage and pours into the combustion nozzles, where it mingles with the hot air to give additional thrust.

Rolls-Royce "fanjets" do not mix hot and cold air like the bypass engines. A large fan is made to work like a propeller at the front of the engine, where it is housed in a special duct. The fan blades are short enough not to break the sound barrier like the tips of ordinary propellers. But they increase the thrust. Also, because the jet velocity is reduced through having to spin them, they are quiet for the amount of power they produce. The DC-10 is only half as noisy as the DC-8.* They are also very economical.

Both bypass and fanjets can be called "turbofans," because they use the blades of the turbines like fans (or propellers) to increase the thrust of air from the propulsion nozzles, or "jet pipes."

Jet engines are small and light, for the power they produce. The control systems are also simple. Cold air is used to cool them, instead of oil and water. The quadrant at the front of the engine guides the air into the compressors, with their many blades. The speeded air is then partly ducted straight through to the jet pipes, and partly via the combustion chambers and turbines. The basic principle of the jet is that air that has been compressed and heated goes out faster than it came in. The air is accelerated and pushed back.

Heat and stress are the main enemies. The heat in the combustion chamber can reach 2,000 degrees Centigrade. Turbines spin at 20,000 rpm in heat of 500 degrees Centigrade. They can have 130 blades, all individually shaped and fixed, and all balanced so that they do not vibrate. Compressors come in 12 stages and more, with 20 blades all subjected to great centrifugal stress in each stage. Turbines and compressors do fail, although the engine housing should contain the disintegration.†

---

*Frank Tucker, of Ontario, Canada, took the most original action of the millions of householders affected by aircraft noise. He decided to frighten off aircraft flying over his house to nearby Buttonville Airport. He played a recording of antiaircraft gunfire through a loudspeaker and trained a searchlight on landing aircraft at night. Alas, Mr. Tucker's wit was not appreciated and he was found guilty on two counts of confusing and distracting the pilots of aircraft. *Globe and Mail,* July 9, 1977.

†Eighteen million man-hours of engineering safety checks went into the 747. Besides being able to contain engine explosions, it has 50 structurally independent control surfaces. It has two rudders, four independent hydraulic power systems and

"The real problem now isn't ordinary engine failure. The engines themselves rarely go wrong. It's the stuff that's hung on them to feed the plane—the hydraulic pumps, the heating systems, the thrust reversers, the dynamos and generators," says a senior engineer.

At $750,000 for a new 707 engine* and $2.5 million for 747 engines, they should be good. They are checked every 3,000 hours and have major overhauls only every 24,000 hours, or 12 million miles.

"Life limited" parts on the vital compressors and turbines have to be replaced at ages varying from 16,000 to 30,000 hours. This is a huge improvement over pistons.

But gradually engines do wear out, helped by stones, hail and birds damaging fans, and by dust grinding down the parts. They cope with water well, even though a single engine during a takeoff in monsoon rain will suck through water at the rate of an Olympic-sized swimming pool a minute.

Million-dollar engines have been lost to rags, stones, and jackets left by maintenance men. A single large bird can explode an engine, and a flock of birds can affect several engines.

Jet engines can be stalled, just as a wing can. If the airflow hits the compressor blades at the wrong angle, the air eddies and swirls about. This causes serious overheating so that the engine has to be closed down.

These flameouts are usually found only on start-up or when a sudden surge of acceleration is pushed into the engine. Several aircraft have crashed when pilots opened the throttles too suddenly in an overshoot.† Engine surges can be caused by flying

---

four separate ailerons and elevators. Even the undercarriage is designed to rip off in a crash landing without cutting into the fuel lines.

A 747 at San Francisco hit the approach lights on takeoff. This smashed two of the four main undercarriage bogies, knocked out three of the four hydraulic systems and cut through a stabilizer spar. Steel girders pierced the cabin, badly injuring two passengers as they sat in their seats. The aircraft landed safely.

*Prices in constant 1974 dollars.

†Autoreduction sometimes, but not always, prevents this. Safety valves open if sensing devices which observe the jet temperatures, compression pressure and speed show that the safe limits have been exceeded.

maneuvers. If a rear-engine aircraft climbs at too steep an angle, the airflow is blanketed from the engines by the wings. The engines overheat.

The positioning of engines is important, since there are pluses and minuses to all configurations. Burying the engines in the wing roots, like the Comet, means that the thrust is near the center line of the aircraft. If an engine fails, the aircraft will not swing much. The engines are also close to the center of gravity, so there is no need for a large stabilizer to counteract their weight.

Against this, the cabin is noisy, the fuselage can interfere with the airflow, and a disintegration in one engine can affect the one next to it.

Engines in underslung wing pods, as on the Boeing 707, 737, 747 and DC-8, leave a clear wing profile. They are easy to get at for maintenance and the airflow into them is not affected by the fuselage. But an engine failure will lead to yawing, as the plane swings toward the dead engine. Because the engines are slung low, the nose drops when power is reduced, and the engines are prone to swallowing stones from the runway. They are easily scraped if the aircraft lands with one wing low.

Three-engine aircraft have one engine built into the back of the fuselage, like the Boeing 727, DC-10, and L-1011. The other two engines can be mounted under the wings or also at the tail.

Other rear-engine aircraft are the twin-engine DC-9 and Caravelle and the four-engine VC-10.

Rear-engine jets have quiet cabins. There is little yaw if an engine fails. The wing is clear of engine mountings. However, passenger capacity is restricted since some of the rear fuselage is taken up with engines. The intakes can have their airflow interrupted by the fuselage and wings.

The aircraft is naturally tail-heavy, so the wings have to be set well back. This in turn leads to a large stabilizer which has to be put up high as a T-tail to be clear of the engines. And that gives the aircraft a natural tendency to deep-stall, which has to be overcome with automatic stall warning devices.

A jet engine rated to have 16,000 pounds of thrust produces only 42 horsepower when it is stationary before takeoff. But this soars with speed: one pound of thrust equals one horsepower at 375 mph and two horsepower at 750 mph.

So the horsepower of a typical engine varies between 42 on the ground and 25,000 horsepower when cruising at 580 mph. Fuel consumption goes from 738 gallons per hour during a descent to 4,500 gph on takeoff.

The higher and faster it goes the more efficient a jet engine becomes.* Speed itself helps by ramming air into the engine. All the air that goes through a jet when it is sitting on the ground has to be sucked in by the compressor, which labors to get it. As the aircraft speeds up, air is pushed into the compressor at a great rate. Thus an engine that is idling on the ground goes through three times as much fuel as one that is idle in flight.

Jets really need to suck in air at low speeds. Concorde has an auxiliary door underneath the normal intakes to let in additional air at low speeds. Supersonically, the ram effect of air being blown into the engines at 1,400 mph is so great that a special "dump door" lets out excess air from the intakes. The jet pipe, which can be narrowed to give maximum velocity to the exhaust as it rushes through, is opened wide. Methanol can be injected into the engine, which cools the air in the compressor and gives added thrust.

A Boeing 707 on a 1,000-mile trip at 18,000 feet will use 900 more gallons of fuel than one at 35,000 feet and take 45 minutes longer. Fuel is important: a 707 on a trip from London to Los Angeles will burn up 17,000 gallons.

Fuel management is a vital part of modern flying. Climbing too fast makes the fuel boil and evaporation losses of up to 10 percent have been known on climbs to 35,000 feet. A pilot who starts a descent 25 miles early on his engine/fuel optima chart will lose 225 kilos of fuel. If there are 20 other pilots like him, and they average 500 sectors each year, the airline will be wasting 616,000 gallons a year. If they put down the flaps too early as well, 2.5 million gallons could be, as the pilots put it, "pissed out the window."

---

*The maximum fuel efficiency of the propeller engines in the 1950's was 0.9 kg/kg/hr (or 0.9 kilograms of fuel per kilogram of engine thrust per hour). The first jets used only 0.8 kilograms of fuel for the same effect. Modern jets are below 0.6.

American pilots in particular are checked on their use of fuel. American Airlines saved two million gallons in one year by introducing more stringent taxiing rules.

Flying slowly wastes fuel. A 747 flying a 40-mile approach will use 200 gallons more if it approaches at 170 knots instead of 200 knots. A Concorde holding at 15,000 feet burns 65 gallons a minute at 200 knots, 52 gallons at 250 knots and only 50 gallons at 300 knots. (*Only* 50 gallons a minute? Well, in Concorde terms, yes.)

Aircraft are very thirsty. The average male passenger with his cabin luggage weighs 165 pounds. He consumes his own weight in fuel every 1,500 miles—every time he goes, say, from New York to San Antonio or Chicago to Phoenix—on a full plane. If he goes on a half-empty plane, he is going through twice his own weight, or some 41 gallons.

The typical fuel flow on a 707 shows the thirst. The "burn rate" in gallons per minute is 76 on takeoff, 32 on noise abatement after takeoff, 45 in the climb, 24 on the cruise, 12.3 on the descent, 32.8 on the approach and back up to 50 in reverse thrust on landing. With such changes in consumption, fuel management is a very important part of a pilot's job.

A 747 holds 47,000 gallons of fuel (177,294 liters for the metrically minded), enough for a good-sized swimming pool. It goes through 3,250 gallons an hour at its cruising speed of 580 mph. That is 0.18 miles per gallon, or five and a half gallons to the mile. The machine can weigh up to 366 tons, and carry a 90-ton payload (the rest is the weight of the craft and fuel). It will carry pipes up to 180 feet long with a diameter of 8 feet, or 73 VW Beetles, or up to 500 passengers.

The 747 is not that thirsty, either. When full, it can get more than 90 passenger-miles to the gallon. A BAC 111 gets only 60, and Concorde 42, which is worse than the old propeller Stratocruisers. Meantime, even a car gets 150 passenger-miles to the gallon, when full and driven at optimum speed. Diesel trains get 800.

Fuel management has one side effect, in letting passengers know how far they are from their destination. The pilots' rule of thumb for economical descent is that they need 300 feet of height for every mile to go. If the pilot has said that the cruising height is 30,000 feet, when you hear the power come off and the aircraft starts to descend, there will be 100 miles to go.

On a short flight the cruising height may be 24,000 feet. The power should be reduced then with 80 miles to go. The guide is to divide the height by 300, giving the miles to run.

On landing, and on some aircraft while still in the air, the engines are put into reverse thrust. A jet engine has two "clamshells" in the pipe at the back. These two are joined when the pilot lifts the throttles over a special gate into reverse, rather like a car gear lever. The jet pipe is now blocked and special ports open so that the thrust is pushed forward to brake the aircraft.

This saves brake and tire wear. Brakes are very efficient but they.tend to overheat tires and wear out the tread.

Turbine blades are the most checked part of an engine. On a transatlantic flight, each blade will have spun eight and a half million times, with great centrifugal force and under great heat. There is also a strong pressure loading as the hot air from the combustion chamber strikes them.

Checkers spend their working lives looking at individual blades for signs of cracks or wear. Isotopes and X rays are also used. Oil is examined on spectrometers, where the slightest trace of metal will be picked up, revealing wear.

Engineers have a nice phrase for engine breakdowns, an "unscheduled engine removal." (Flying is full of such expressions. For example, a nose dive is never called a nose dive. It is a "gross height excursion.")

It takes five hours to change an engine on a 707. Most jets can carry a spare fifth engine on a special pylon on its wing. Aircraft that break down in out-of-the-way places have to be "ferried" home—flown without passengers or payload on three engines.

When an engine fails in the air, the first action the crew take is to call out its number. As the nose swings toward the failed engine, the pilots have to put on rudder to keep straight. They also slap the knee that is pushing the rudder, as confirmation of whether the engine is on the left or right.

Aircraft have been lost after crew selected the wrong engine as failed, and the shouting and slapping is an effective if crude way of preventing this. A BAC 111 crashed at Milan* after the crew shut down the good engine by mistake. This, on a twin-engine aircraft, left them with no power at all.

The next action is to close the throttle. The essential power generator, which is normally run off the No. 3 engine, is transferred if necessary. Engine numbers run from left to right: the No. 2 is the left inboard engine on a four-engine aircraft, the central tail engine on a tri-jet and the right engine on a twin-jet. The essential power generator runs the radios and vital instruments.

The start lever is then cut off, the ignition and generator breakers are tripped, and the aircraft is trimmed to fly on the remaining engines. A modern twin- or tri-jet can maintain height on one engine alone. A landing is possible on only one engine on a four-engine jet, although extremely hazardous.

The odds of this happening on modern jets are virtually nil, apart from a human error, such as using the wrong type of fuel, or running out of it. As we shall see, this has happened.

---

*HMSO CAP 347. The British United Airways crew belly-landed the plane in a snow-covered field. It slid for 460 yards before stopping. The crew got the 20 passengers out safely.

17

The Weather

The sky is as varied in its currents and dangers as the sea, and it is charted in much the same way. Areas of severe turbulence and bad weather are plotted. The direction of airstreams are recorded so that pilots can use them or avoid them. These airstreams can go above 350 mph, faster than most propeller aircraft can fly. The charts show the pilot where he is likely to face icing, fog or sudden wind shears.

The most important winds are the powerful jet streams, found at cruising height from 25,000 feet to 35,000 feet. These winds have been recorded at 375 mph over the Pacific. Most of them are westerly, which means that they blow *from* west to east. This is why it can take up to two hours longer to fly from Europe to America than it does to go back.

Jet streams are rarely so aligned to a route that they blow exactly on the nose or tail. They will normally hit the aircraft at an angle, so that the effect is not exactly opposite on outward and return journeys. Nonetheless, some of the differences are considerable. Westbound flights across North America lose between 60 and 70 nautical miles every hour because of head winds. The wind gives them an extra 15 to 20 knots on their speed eastbound. Thus, New York to Los Angeles involves a reduction of speed due to head winds of 63 nautical miles an hour; Atlanta to San Francisco of 61;

Chicago to San Francisco of 58; Montreal to Vancouver of 56. The return flights gain 19, 14, 15, and 16 nautical miles respectively.

The same order of jet stream exists over the North Atlantic, adding an average of 62 nautical miles an hour to westbound flights and speeding those to Europe by some 14. The Pacific, however, is not so consistent. A westbound flight from Los Angeles to Honolulu loses a modest 35 knots and picks up 6 on the return. But a westbound flight from Tokyo to Hong Kong is set back 71 nautical miles an hour by winds at cruising levels, picking up 10 on the return.

Australia sees some of the biggest differences, with flights from Sydney to Perth penalized by 66 knots but picking up 24 when returning.

Surface winds are not as strong as these high jet streams. They are slowed to a third of their speed higher up by the friction of the land. But the winds bounce off obstacles, like hills, woods, even airport buildings, and are gusty and turbulent. The effect on aircraft, which are moving slowly as they take off or land, is greater than at altitude.

Differences in the heat of the earth also affect low-flying aircraft. Sandy and rocky areas and cities are hotter than grassland or lakes or sea. Hot air rises, cool air falls, and the result is severe bumping for the airliner. On sunny days, particularly when passing over coastlines from cool sea to hot land, the bumping from these thermal currents of air can be felt at a considerable height.

Flying at night and on overcast days is normally smoother, since there is less variation in temperature.

Sudden strong winds are a hazard, although the pilot will know when to expect them from his wind charts. The "foehn" can be a killer of aircraft. It is a warm, dry mountain wind that can spring from total calm to gale force in three minutes. It is normally a spring wind, which gusts down valleys on the lee side of mountains. It brings avalanches for skiers as well as trouble for aircraft.

It is most dangerous in the Alps, particularly at Innsbruck, although it also affects ranges as small as the Scottish Cairngorms. In the Rockies, it is called the "chinook"—ironically a helicopter is named after it.

"Funnel winds" are accelerated by being forced through valleys.

One of the most severe of these winds is the "mistral," which is intensified by passing through the Rhone Valley. It affects several Mediterranean airports.

"Ravine winds" are common in valleys that penetrate mountain ranges, and the tunnel effect makes them strong. The winds stay strong and gusty even in open country after leaving the valley mouth. A ravine wind affects Genoa, the "kosava" rips along the Danube close to Belgrade, the "vardar" can make landing at Salonika dangerous.

Fog is widespread in Europe, particularly in the spring and early summer. It is worst where an arid hinterland adjoins a coast. Southwest Africa, Chile, Morocco and California, the experienced pilot will know, are more of a hazard than ever was foggy London town.

Dust storms blot out visibility as brutally as fog. The dust soars up to 15,000 feet, wearing out engines like sandpaper. The danger areas are well marked: central and southwest Asia, the Sahara, southwest Africa and the Kalahari, northern Chile and central and southeastern Argentina, the central and southwestern United States, the interior and west of Australia. Pilots particularly fear the "haboobs" of the Sudan. These storms toss sand up to 10,000 feet with gusty winds within eight minutes of starting. Like all sandstorms, they are best avoided by flying at night when there is less wind.

Pilots steer clear of cumulonimbus clouds, the distinct anvil-shaped thunderclouds. The turbulence within these is vicious enough to tear an aircraft to pieces. The vertical speed of hot air rising can exceed 150 feet a second—going up at more than 100 mph, strong enough to stop the largest raindrop from touching the ground, and to whip a man in a parachute thousands of feet upward.

There are thunderstorms on *more* than 110 days a year in southern Mexico, Panama, central Brazil, central Africa and Madagascar. Java has 220 days a year with thunderstorms—the most in the world, and a graveyard of pilots and passengers.

Britain and northwest Europe in August, the southern Mediterranean in October, India during the monsoons, Hong Kong in September—these are times when pilots are on their guard.

Summer heat causes frequent storms in the central and eastern U.S. The crash of a jetliner in the summer of 1975 shows the dangers. An Eastern Airlines Boeing 727 crashed when it ran into a thunderstorm while approaching JFK Airport in New York, killing 113.* The National Transportation Safety Board found that the Eastern pilots had encountered a severe wind change, and that they did not immediately recognize that they were descending faster than normal.

The Board added a chilling rider: even if they had recognized the descent rate, "the adverse winds might have been too severe for a successful approach and landing."

Revolving storms are found in every tropical ocean except the South Atlantic. Cyclones in the Bay of Bengal and the Arabian Sea, hurricanes in the West Indies and South Indian Ocean, typhoons in the South China Seas, willy-willies in western Australia—the names differ, but turbulence and wind shifts are common to all.

Pilots know when to expect them, and where. From June to October they ravage the Northern Hemisphere, from December to April the Southern. They can be detected in the same way as thunderclouds, with weather radar. This reflects the water content of clouds, and an experienced pilot can distinguish thunderclouds, revolving storms, snow and hail.

Areas of "mountain waves" are charted. Hills and mountains cause the air to form waves on the lee side, the far side from where the wind is blowing. The wind accelerates and lifts as it passes over the top of the obstacle, but can then break downward in a welter of turbulence, like a sea wave as it breaks. Wave effects from mountain ranges like the Andes can be felt as high as 80,000 feet.

Both the updrafts on the windward and downdrafts on the lee side can be very strong. In the U.S., the powerful waves of the Sierra Nevada rise at 75 feet a second—10 times faster than most elevators, and faster than the plane itself can climb.

*ICAO Summary No. 7/75. About five minutes before the crash, a Flying Tiger DC-8 had warned of a wind shear on the runway, JFK's 22 Left. A Lockheed 1011 reported a wind shear two minutes before the crash. There were 11 survivors out of 124 aboard.

The waves should be smooth at height over mountains. Only the pilot would notice them through the change in his altimeter. But the waves can break.

When they do, they can have standing crests like a surf wave. In the area under it, called the "rotor zone," lurks extreme danger and turbulence. It was a rotor zone that hurled a Uruguayan airliner down 2,000 feet onto a snowfield in the Andes. The survivors were forced to eat the flesh of the crash victims to stay alive before being rescued.

There are "killer waves" which contain huge destructive power. They occur when the cross section of the mountain coincides with the natural pattern of the wind wave. This greatly exaggerates the effect, like a giant tuning fork. Mountains like the Alps, where air flows over a series of ridges, can build up confused wave patterns as one wave runs into another.

Clear Air Turbulence—CAT to flight crews—is found at cruising heights. It is a strong horizontal and vertical wind shear affecting a jet stream. CAT is probably caused by large temperature changes in the air at high altitude.

The temperatures move in horizontal bands, and CAT lurks where they meet. CAT is normally no more than a high-speed jarring, like driving fast over a cobbled road. But it can damage or destroy aircraft.

Pilots receive a stream of weather reports as they pass along their route. The International Weather Code, called SYNOP, gives them eight groups of information. It is detailed enough to keep them out of trouble. A typical message reads: 03772 60110 66022 09410 36202 03001 83830 86075.* It does not sound very inspiring. But this is what it reveals:

The airport is covered by six-eighths cloud. The wind is blowing from 010 degrees at 10 knots. The horizontal visibility is 16 kilometers. The cloud cover has not changed in the past half hour and more than half the sky is cloud covered.

The barometric pressure is 1,009.4 millibars, the temperature is

---

*Quoted in the *Handbook of Aviation Meteorology,* HMSO, London, 1971. This is the standard work on the subject.

10 degrees Centigrade, three-eighths of the sky is covered by (harmless) cirrocumulus cloud though some (bumpy) cumulus is present.

The lowest cloud base is between 3,000 and 5,000 feet. There is no medium-high cloud, although there is dense but harmless cirrus above 20,000 feet. The dew point is 3 degrees Centigrade. The barometric tendency during the past three hours has been to increase, decrease and increase again, although never by more than 0.1 millibars. There is three-eighths cumulus cloud at 3,000 feet and six-eighths cirrus cloud at 25,000 feet.

Which all means that there will be a couple of small bumps on the way down and that passengers will get a good view of the countryside. The high-flying jet streams are westerlies above 15,000 feet in both hemispheres regardless of what the surface winds are doing. It may, in fact, be blowing very hard from the east on the surface but it is still a westerly at height.

Things are more complicated in the tropics. Away from the equator, the surface trade winds, the easterlies, are replaced by westerly jet streams above 10,000 feet. But nearer the equator, an easterly jet stream stretches in a 1,100-mile belt from Africa to South America across the South Atlantic. It blows from the east at a steady 70 knots, attracting aircraft flying from Europe to South America, but sending those returning to Europe 1,000 miles farther north. In West Africa and in India, these easterly jet streams dominate the southwest monsoons above 10,000 feet.

Where the trade routes were laid out for the sailing clippers, the trunk routes for modern jetliners are also mapped and noted. The greatest trunk route is across the North Atlantic, with more than 400 aircraft plying it every day. In winter the jet streams above 20,000 feet are west southwest from the United States, becoming west as they near Europe. Winds are frequently 100 knots and sometimes more than 200 knots. They generally add an hour to a London–New York flight.

The weather is very changeable, and pilots have to use head wind/tail wind charts to compute a best course and height.

These are based on the frequency distribution of wind strength and direction at various heights along the route.* A pilot must work out a course that uses the wind to best advantage, and also maximizes fuel economy through the right height and speed. CAT is common on the North Atlantic and so is turbulence over the sea as unstable polar air drifts farther south in summer. It is very cloudy: average cloud cover is six-eighths. There is a danger of severe airframe icing in clouds, particularly at fronts. Fog is frequent on both American and European coasts.

Things improve a little in the summer. The Icelandic low of winter is replaced by weak low pressure over northeastern Canada. The Azores high-pressure system strengthens and moves five degrees north. There are fewer gales and the jet streams are not so strong. However, summer visibility over the Atlantic is actually worse than in winter.

There are predictable problems at airports on both sides of the Atlantic. Heathrow has frequent fog, aggravated by smoke when the wind is from the northeast to east southeast. Prestwick has good visibility. Keflavik suffers from gales seven days a month in the winter, with frequent drifting snow and drizzle. Montreal is snow-affected and often has a low cloud base. New York has poor visibility when a front is moving through. Bermuda has severe gales in winter and a hurricane season from August to November.

The subsidiary trunk route in the Atlantic runs on to the West Indies and South America. The West Indies have three hurricanes on average during the August to October season. Recife, in Brazil, has cloud and rain from March until August. Kingston reaches a thunderstorm high in September, Trinidad in August.

The second great trunk route is from northern Europe to Athens via Munich or Rome and on to Cairo and Beirut. Europe

---

*Weather hazards are dependent on height. Wind and temperature affect all aircraft, from 0 feet to 80,000 feet. Subsonic and transonic aircraft in the sea-level-to-40,000-foot belt meet heavy rain and icing. Transonic and supersonic aircraft can meet Clear Air Turbulence, wave motion and lee waves above 20,000 feet. Supersonic aircraft above 50,000 feet can be preyed on by horizontal temperature variation, cosmic radiation during solar flares and radioactive debris. Hail can be dangerous down to ground level: a Southern Airways DC-9 crashed at New Hope on April 4, 1977, after double engine failure in a hailstorm.

gradually changes from an oceanic to a continental system as the influence of the Atlantic slowly dies out inland. The westerly jet streams get stronger with height. Mean speeds of 100 mph at 30,000 feet are common. So too are icing, fog and low cloud. Cloud cover averages six-eighths in winter, only improving to five-eighths in summer.

The Mediterranean is warmer than the surrounding land in winter. Pilots have to watch out for squalls and showers, though the skies are generally clear. In the summer, with the sea now cooler than the land, light northerly winds set in, with quiet, cloudless weather.

There are only light jet streams in the western Mediterranean, although they pick up farther east, reaching 90 mph over Cyprus.

The Mediterranean has some savage local winds which can destroy aircraft. The mistral blows violently from the north and northwest in the Gulf of Lions and the Gulf of Genoa. Marseilles' airport is particularly troubled by it. A similar wind, the bora, lashes the eastern Adriatic. At Trieste, the bora can blow at 80 mph, with gusts of 115 mph putting aircraft landing or taking off at hazard.

The sirocco affects the western Mediterranean, with strong gusts and poor visibility. The khamsin, a southerly wind off the desert, brings sandstorms to Egypt.

The trunk route on to the Persian Gulf is liable to dust storms when the wind is in the south and southeast. The shamal, a northwesterly gale-strength wind, often kicks up vicious sandstorms over Iraq. The jet stream blows from the west at a steady 115 mph.

Conditions deteriorate farther on toward Calcutta. Severe turbulence rides with the southwest monsoon from mid-June to mid-September. Cyclonic storms lash the Bay of Bengal. The jet stream turns to the east, blowing back toward Europe.

Karachi is subject to dust storms, low cloud in summer and heavy rain in the southwest monsoon. Bombay has thunderstorms and squalls in June. Calcutta is hit by 60-mph squalls in the evenings during the hot season.

The easterly jet stream remains onward to Rangoon and Singapore. During the northeast monsoon, from December to

February, aircraft hug the west coast of Malaya. The east coast is subjected to severe thunderstorms and wild turbulence as the northeast monsoon drives in from the South China Sea. But when the southwest monsoon blows, in the summer, the east coast is the best-protected.

Flying conditions are often difficult in this region. Huge thunderstorms rage, particularly in the afternoons. At night "Sumatras," violent squalls, drive across the Malacca Straits. Singapore suffers from low cloud and strong gusts one day in two throughout the year.

The equatorial rainy climate continues from Djakarta most of the way to Darwin, in northern Australia. Cloud, thunderstorms and heavy rain cover the islands, and tropical cyclones veer across the Timor Sea from January to March. In Darwin itself, dust haze cuts visibility to less than 100 yards.

The westerly jet streams start up again between Darwin and Sydney and Melbourne. Severe dust storms are blown in with hot, dry air from the interior of Australia. Cold fronts bring "southerly busters"—cold, strong and violent winds—to New South Wales. Sydney also has the aptly named "black northeasters" sweeping in with low cloud. Dust storms are driven in front of northwesterlies. By contrast, peaceful Melbourne suffers from nothing more than light fog.

From Singapore to Hong Kong and Japan, the "crachin" predominates from January to April on the long haul from Cape Cambodia to Shanghai. Siberian air mixes with the warm sea air and produces a low cloud, drizzle and mist like Scottish mist for long periods. Storms in western Japan can be severe.

The westerly jet stream is at its strongest here. One stream reaches from Tibet to southern Japan. Its *average* speed in winter over Yokohama is 175 mph. It can go above 225 mph, bringing severe CAT.

The China Seas are liable to typhoons from May to November. Many curve and move over Japan. Occasionally, one slips the other way into the Gulf of Thailand. The hot, sticky weather brings thunderstorms. Twenty typhoons a season rage through the area.

Conditions on the long polar route back to Europe from Japan are surprisingly good. Although ice-fog is a hazard when fog particles freeze, icing itself is not severe. It is mostly too cold for moisture to develop. The visibility, especially in winter, is excellent.

Icing is not much of a problem on jets. The friction of the speed through the air generates enough heat on the airframe to keep ice away. Jet engines produce large amounts of hot air which can be piped to danger points. The air at the cruising heights of jets is so cold that it is dry and cannot hold much moisture. (Indeed, it is so cold that an early problem with jets was that the kerosene fuel turned to wax. Research came up with a kerosene that only froze at −50 degrees Centigrade.)

Icing is a more serious problem on propeller aircraft. Alcohol is sprayed onto the propellers to keep ice away. There are rubber tubes on the leading edges of the wings which continuously inflate and deflate, splintering the ice away. Hot air from the exhausts is piped into the carburetors. But the main defense is to climb, as the ice is slung off the propellers and bangs against the cabin, and the controls wallow and the speed drops off, to climb, seeking cold and dry air, and move out of the ice belt.

Some of the smoothest flying in the world is to be had over the wastes of the Arctic. Some of the most dangerous is said to be in the "Bermuda Triangle." It is worth taking a look at this claim, and the similar reports of flying saucers and other Unidentified Flying Objects.

The Bermuda Triangle spans an area of the western Atlantic bounded by Florida, Puerto Rico and Bermuda, where aircraft and ships are said to vanish without trace. Legend has it that they are snatched away by an inexplicable force, possibly from space. Last messages from the doomed crew members are said to tell of Unidentified Flying Objects, spinning compasses, strange surges of power.

It might seem to take a special brand of courage by pilots and passengers to fly in this area. However, the facts are rather different. The air safety record in the Traingle is actually better than it is in the continental U.S. as a whole. Where Charles Berlitz in his book *The Bermuda Triangle* has two KC-135 jet Stratotankers disappearing "in strange circumstances" in 1963 with wreckage from each being found hundreds of miles apart, the actual accident report shows that wreckage from both planes was found at one spot. A midair collision in turbulent conditions was given as the cause of the crash: the aircraft were flying in close formation at the time.

Again, Triangle enthusiasts say that a Navy flight, Flight 19, disappeared in daylight in clear weather in December 1945. But U.S. Navy records show that the five Avenger bombers with 27 crew disappeared after dark in stormy conditions after the flight leader, Lieutenant Charles Taylor, had totally mistaken his position. He thought he was flying over islands off southern Florida, when in fact they were off the Bahamas. Navigational error, and not the strange faces of the unknown, was responsible for the flight running out of fuel and crashing into the rough Atlantic.

A plane with 13 aboard took off on a rescue mission and is said to have also disappeared, a victim of the Triangle. But a nearby ship saw it explode. It was known as the "flying gas tank" because of the amount of fuel it carried.

In another incident, an Eastern Airlines jet flying to Miami is said to have been lost on radar for 10 minutes. Full emergency services were called out for its landing. But the puzzled crew had no idea anything was wrong—until they checked their watches. All the crew and passengers found that their watches were 10 minutes slow.

This would be a tremendous tale, except no date, time or flight number is given for the incident and neither Miami Airport nor Eastern Airlines has any record of it.

If the Triangle is slight and suspect, a mass of sightings of Unidentified Flying Objects has been made by pilots and passengers. The term "flying saucers" itself comes from a pilot, Kenneth Arnold. A 32-year-old businessman, piloting his own plane, he was near Mount Rainier, in the state of Washington, when he saw a chain of nine "saucerlike" objects flying from north to south. That was on June 24, 1947, and there have been many thousands of sightings since.

These were taken seriously enough for the U.S. Air Force to set up a series of investigations beginning in 1948 as Project Sign and followed by Projects Grudge and Blue Book. A contract was also awarded to the Rand Corporation for an independent study of flying saucers. Alas for the saucer enthusiast, all the studies concluded that the saucers were all misinterpretations or inventions and not from space.

The Arnold sighting was put down to temperature inversion, where "mirages of moisture" can appear in the sky. An apparently sensational case, where an Air Force captain was killed while climbing to intercept a reported UFO over Kentucky, had a similarly mundane solution. The UFO was either the planet Venus or a U.S. Navy balloon. The pilot died because he blacked out through lack of oxygen in the climb and the aircraft went into an uncontrollable spin.

It is thought that at least 90 percent of sightings are in fact of natural or man-made objects, commonly aircraft, satellites, meteors and stars and planets. The crew of a BA jet on a flight in 1977 to Faro, in Portugal, saw "UFO's" on the outward and return sectors. These were established to be meteorological balloons. The remaining 10 percent are fraudulent, notably from people who claim to have been abducted by UFO occupants. Thus two U.S. shipyard workers who claim to have been seized by visitors from space with lobsterlike claws had their lie detector tests, the sole evidence for their story, conducted by an unqualified operator in uncontrolled conditions.

Although pilots and passengers will continue to see UFO's, it is very unlikely that any of them will collect the huge reward offered to the first person who proves that UFO's are from outer space and not natural phenomena. The *National Enquirer* is so confident of the impossibility of this that it has upped its reward from $100,000 to $1 million. Vapor trails, clouds, balloons and planets do not count.

18

Flight Deck

There is a stately progress to a flight. The pilots check in 90 minutes before takeoff. The first call is the duty room. The pilots start collecting paper work: airways maps of the route to be flown, flight manual for the aircraft, emergency checklists, forms for the number of passengers and cargo weight.

The meteorological office supplies weather maps and reports from airports along the route. A weatherman gives a brisk briefing on wind, cloud, temperature, pressure and any special difficulties expected.

The papers are in rows of boxes. The pilots go around picking up the sheets they need like guests at a buffet lunch. One set of papers covers most of the major airports. It shows, for example, runway repairs in progress at Atlanta, a new terminal under construction at Boston, navigational equipment out of service at Cleveland.

A map on the wall divides the world into sectors. Red flags with numbers are pinned on it. The numbers refer to sheets in other boxes: a glider competition over the Catskills, military target practice in West Texas, naval gunnery off San Diego. It is important that the pilot keeps clear of the military. A French Caravelle flying from Corsica to France was shot down by an accidentally fired missile over the Mediterranean.

The aircraft itself needs documents, its certificates of registration, radio, insurance and of airworthiness, and its log of all past flights.

The paper work disappears into the battered leather attaché cases that most aircrew carry. Flying involves a great deal of form-filling. The most important is the flight plan. The captain fills in his expected time of departure and arrival and the route he wants to take. The details are sent to air traffic controllers down the route.

The pilots wait in a lounge for a crew bus to take them out to the aircraft. The flight crews introduce each other. The pilots must be "airfield qualified" and know the airports en route. This can be simply a film of the approach for easy airports. For difficult ones like Hong Kong, the pilots must have flown it with a route captain before tackling it on their own.

Once everyone knows who's who, they set off for the aircraft. The captain walks around it, looking for any external damage, checking tire pressures on the undercarriage, or "gear." The cockpit (the "flight deck" or "office" as the crew call it) is small. It is crowded with more than 20 square feet of knobs, buttons, levers and lights.

The captain's first check is to see that all switches are off. Aircraft switches are down for off and up for on. He looks for the emergency kit, an axe, walk-around oxygen, CO_2 extinguisher, first-aid kit, rain repellent, asbestos gloves and goggles in case of fire.

The captain then reads the logbook, in which previous pilots will have noted any of the plane's faults and snags, from faulty warning lights to torn pillowcases in the passenger cabin.

Slowly and methodically, the captain and first officer go through the checklist of controls and instruments. There are 59 preflight checks on a 707. Most of this goes by without any noticeable event, but the checks for the stall warning are spectacular. A light flashes on and off, a hooter grunts, and the stick shaker shakes the control column.

Fire bells clang, and a strident bell rings from the undercarriage lock control. The cacophony can be intense. Some aircraft have so many audible warnings that they have to use a tape-recorded voice to shout out what is happening. A bell rings, and a voice shouts "Fire, fire." When the height warning device goes off, the voice shouts "Pull up! Pull up!"

The chief steward tells the captain the number of passengers. He confirms when they are "all strapped in and calm." If they are not all calm, but noisy and boisterous, the captain will go back and talk to them. Any fighting drunk or hysteric who might endanger the flight is taken off at the captain's discretion.

From now on, the pilot will refer to "people" if he means only the passengers. If he means the total, passengers and crew, he refers to "souls." So a flight can have 150 people and 10 crew, or 160 souls. Nobody quite knows why.

The captain now computes his takeoff speed: the weight of the aircraft should be accurate to the nearest passenger.*

Takeoff speed is computed by taking aircraft weight, air temperature, altitude of the airport and wind speed. These are plotted on graphs, which show the speed at which the aircraft will fly, and also the correct throttle settings to get enough engine power. The worst combination is a heavy aircraft, in thin, hot air, at a high altitude, with no wind to take off into. The carrying capacity of a 707 is halved at an airport at 7,000 feet compared with one at sea level.

Temperature and altitude are crucial. Concorde can take 90 passengers from London to Bahrein. But it can only bring 60 back: its takeoff performance in the hot air of Bahrein is much inferior to that in London. Planes using airports that are both high and hot are very restricted in their loads. Addis Ababa, Nairobi, Bogotá and Mexico City are examples.

One knot is added for every quarter degree of upslope on the runway, or subtracted for downslope. One knot is also added for every 18 knots of head wind, to extend decision time. A knot is subtracted for every three and a half knots of tail wind, which should never exceed 10 knots.

The captain writes the power settings he has calculated onto a

---

*Airlines work on the assumption that women average 130 pounds and men 155. The pilot adds 10 pounds for footballers and the like, who tend to be heavy. About 20 pounds are added for merchant seamen, who carry a lot of gear.

card. Three speeds are written down. There is V1, the decision speed beyond which the pilot must continue to take off even if he loses an engine. Vr is the speed at which he rotates the aircraft by pulling the nosewheel off the ground. V2 is the safe takeoff and climb-out speed and also the speed at which the aircraft can fly safely with one engine out.

Speed is calculated in knots, a nautical mile per hour, up to 24,000 feet. One nautical mile is 1.1515 miles, so 100 knots is 115 miles an hour. Above 24,000 feet, the aircraft speed is calculated by the Mach number, its speed relative to the speed of sound.

The speeds are set on the plane's airspeed indicator with white "bugs," or movable pointers. The copilot will shout them off as the speed needle passes each bug.

The speed qualities of his aircraft are vital to the pilot. He must remember them continuously, even though they alter as fuel weight is reduced. Those figures must be engraved in his mind: Vms, minimum stalling speed; Vmca, minimum control speed in the air; Vmcl, minimum control speed on landing. If he gets these far wrong, he will crash.

Vc is the cruise speed (Mc if the speed is in Mach terms). Vra is the rough air, or turbulence, speed. Vne is the never exceed speed and Vmo the maximum operating speed. Exceed these and the aircraft could break up. On landing, he must check the Vle, Vf and Vt—landing gear extended, flaps down and target on threshold speeds.

Permission to start engines comes from the control tower. The crew work through 11 prestart checks. The engines are spun with compressed air, and fuel is pumped in and lit. A tug appears at the nose and pulls the plane into position. Taxi clearance, permission to move off to the runway, is given.

The pilot needs a lot of power to start the plane moving. The weight of plane and fuel is near the maximum, and he must never taxi at more than 30 mph. Turning corners, using the steerable nosewheel controlled by a steering wheel in the cockpit, he slows down to 15 mph. A further 11 check items are performed during the taxi: window heat, probe heat on the airspeed indicator, flaps selected, yaw damper, flaps down correctly, radar sweep, attitude stall warning, departure clearance, radios, takeoff speeds bugged.

The aircraft has ordinary brakes on its wheels, like a car, with brake pedals at the pilot's feet, but they overheat if used too much. There is an emergency hydraulic system with 10 brake applications in it if the brakes fail.

If a pilot swings off the narrow taxiways while turning, he will almost certainly bog down in the grass. The main wheels can be 100 feet behind the cockpit, so there is a tendency to try to cut corners. Fuel, freight and passengers must be removed before tractors try to drag the plane free.

Takeoff speed on a laden jet on a hot day can be more than 200 mph, which is the normal top speed for tires. There are special high-speed tires, good up to 225 mph, with fusible plugs that will deflate the tire before it explodes.

Overheated and burst tires can set a plane on fire when they are retracted into the wheel wells after takeoff. Most of the inhabitants of a Swiss village died like that when their chartered jet caught fire.

The jet is held at the end of the runway while the final nine checks are done. The parking brake is checked "off"—a big DC-8 jet crashed when it tried to take off with the brakes jammed on at Anchorage, Alaska, November 27, 1970. The ice-covered runway was slippery enough for the jet to reach 120 mph even with the brakes on. Forty-six of the 210 passengers on the crowded plane died in the ensuing fire.

All engine instruments must be in the green sector, not red. All controls should be free: aircraft have gust locks put in the controls to stop the surfaces flapping in high winds when they are parked. Airliners have crashed after trying to take off with the locks still in. Indeed, a Canadian DC-8 crashed at Heathrow after the captain, who had 21,428 hours of flying time, throttled back after taking off. He mistakenly thought the gust locks were still in.

The flaps are partly down, at 14 degrees. Takeoff trim must be selected, the aircraft correctly balanced. Fuel must be sufficient and flowing. The "squawk," a transponder that will identify the aircraft on the controller's radar is set.

Takeoff clearance is radioed from the tower. The pilots check visually that there is no other aircraft in the way. They cannot, however, look backward to see if another plane is trying to land on top of them.

The pilot now concentrates on his seven basic instruments. The airspeed indicator gives his speed through the air in nautical miles an hour, or knots. He must make sure that the pitot tube on the outside of the plane which measures the thrust of air does not ice up. If it does, the indicated speed will drop and he will put the nose down and increase power in the mistaken belief that he is going too slowly. Eighteen passengers literally hit the roof on a German flight when the pilot pushed the nose down after failing to switch on the pitot head heater switch. A Northwest 727 stalled at 24,800 feet and crashed 12 minutes out from JFK. The pitot head heaters were not on, and the pilots stalled the aircraft through reacting to false indicated airspeeds. The left stabilizer was torn off in the stall at 3,400 feet and the three-man crew was killed as the plane slammed into the ground near Stony Point, New York.*

The artificial horizon shows the aircraft's attitude relative to the horizon. It uses a silhouette of a plane. If the model plane is below the horizon line on the instrument, it is nose down; if above, it is climbing. If the horizon tilts to the left, the plane is banked to left, and the same for the right. Without an artificial horizon, most pilots lose control of an aircraft in cloud in 45 seconds. Unlike birds, man must have a horizon to orient himself in space. A British Airways Comet crashed at night in Ankara because a small screw in the artificial horizon worked loose and jammed it. On takeoff, the captain could not get the right angle of climb on the horizon and continued pulling back on the controls until the aircraft was pointing almost vertically up. It then stalled and crashed, killing 27.

The rate-of-climb indicator shows quickly how fast the plane is going up or down. It reads in hundreds of feet per minute.

The altimeter shows height. It can be set to height above sea level, or height above an airport. It depends on knowing barometric pressure for its accuracy, which must be radioed to the pilot from the ground.

*NTSB-AAR-75-13.

There is a gyro compass, and a special radio compass which points toward radio beacons.

The Instrument Landing System, the ILS, has two needles, one showing if the airplane is to right or left of the runway and another showing if it is too high or low. When they are centered, the plane is on course to land.

The initial roll is slow as the throttle settings are pushed forward toward their targets. The movement is coarse and bumpy as the speed builds up, and the rudder comes in to replace the nose-wheel steering at 80 mph. Fairly hard heaves are needed on the rudder to keep the nose straight at low speed.

A warning horn at this stage of takeoff means that the aircraft is not safe to take off: the speed brakes are not locked away, the stabilizer trim is not in the green, or the flaps are not at the correct takeoff angle. A Lufthansa 747 crashed at Nairobi killing 59 because a wrong flap selection was not noticed during the takeoff roll.

Passing through 90 mph, the acceleration builds up much faster. The needle on the airspeed indicator winds up rapidly toward the first white bug, the decision speed. At 30 seconds, well into the roll, with the speed more than 110 mph, the rudder is much more sensitive. Kicking it too hard can put a wing down and start a cartwheel crash.

If an engine is lost at this stage, only just enough rudder must be pushed on to counteract the swing. The decision must be made quickly. An average decision speed for jets is 150 mph. To stop, the power comes off, wheel and speed brakes go on, and reverse thrust is applied. The problem is keeping straight.

The runway is blurring now, and the nose has to be kept on it by firm forward pressure on the stick. The thousand-feet-to-go boards flash past, and the runway bumps jar less as the wings begin to take some of the weight. V1 is shouted as the needle passes the first bug. Very shortly afterward comes Vr. The control column is palmed rather than pulled back, although it needs firm movements at these low speeds. The nose lifts and the tire marks on the runway beneath drop away.

At V2, a steady pull back on the stick and the nose comes up farther. Tugging too hard scrapes the tail along the ground: 747's can do this. A last slight bump from the undercarriage and the aircraft flies.

Once airborne, typically 50 seconds after brakes off, the full power of a jet is felt. The landing gear retracts, the airspeed indicator winds around and the altitude builds up. This phase is called the "climb-out." There is a sinking feeling as the flaps come up in stages, but after edging the nose forward for a few seconds the speed and rate of climb pick up again.

Noise abatement is awkward. After a quick initial climb to put the aircraft and the noise as high as possible, power is reduced when it crosses housing. The aircraft is often in a turn, under air traffic control and in cloud. The rhythm of the flight is not yet established.

The flight engineer leans forward and eases the throttles back. The steady increase in values—height, speed, crew coordination— is immediately diminished.

As the power comes off, the nose drops, and the pilot flicks the stabilizer to retrim with a loud clatter of noise. The momentary lack of trim at low height and low speed is unpleasant, and the controls, which have been improving steadily in feel, appear to get mushier again.

The pilot has to think ahead. The values of jet flying are high, in speed, height and weight. The factors multiply very rapidly. The aircraft should be in a nicely trimmed climb at 1,000 feet but the pilot must already concentrate ahead on cutting the power for noise abatement.

Otherwise he will be through 2,000 feet before he knows it. He will have to heave forward on the control column, cut back power, perhaps be forced to bring in flaps and then re-extend them, while worrying about height. Erosion of concentration on a modern jet is severely dealt with: a new 1011 of Eastern Airlines crashed into the Everglade swamps in Florida while the crew, unaware of their high rate of descent, chatted about a faulty warning light.*

Once noise abatement is over, the throttles move forward again

*NTSB-AAR-73-14.

and the flaps come fully in. The aircraft settles into the climb. The main stabilizer keeps the aircraft in the right attitude for the climb, and the pilot gets the precise angle with the column. Its rattle keeps the radio company as it clatters on to new frequencies for the different air traffic controllers.

Best climbing speed is normally 280 knots. The rate of climb depends greatly on the aircraft's load and the local temperatures. A lightly loaded jet could get to 30,000 feet in 15 minutes. It could take 40 minutes if it is hot and heavy.

The autopilot is switched on. There is an occasional rattle from the stabilizer as it counters passengers moving about in the cabin: one person going to the toilet makes enough difference in trim for "George," as pilots call the faithful autopilot, to counteract it.

The cockpit heats up as the sun splashes off the glareshield. The engines seem remote and quiet, the gauges the only proof of their existence. The crew drink coffee: in the thin pressurized air, they should take liquids every 20 minutes.

At the top of the climb, at cruising altitude, the crew come alive again. A knob on the autopilot is turned to "hold altitude." The autopilot obeys the instruction by gently pushing the control column forward. As the nose sinks, the throttles come back. The stabilizer clatters again as the aircraft is trimmed for the cruise.

The speed builds up on the Machmeter. The pilot is noticeably gentle with the controls. The aircraft is eased along. The air outside is very thin at this height—if the cabin decompressed so that the crew had to breathe the outside air, they would be unconscious in half a minute.

There is little air resistance at this height, so it takes time to change the aircraft's altitude. But once the effect starts, there is less to slow it down and a slight change can be greatly exaggerated.

Pulling back on the controls is easy because the thin air makes it easy. But once the nose starts coming up, it will quickly rear too much if the pilot is not gentle, causing a "jet upset" after the sudden climb.

The sense of isolation and beauty is at its height in the cockpit. Apart from the throbbing of air on the windshield it is very silent. The earth is too far below to matter. The plane is part of the sky, a new world of white cloud and the deepest blue. From the passenger cabin, looking out the side windows, you see the sky go past. In the cockpit, you are hurled forward into it—you are in the nose of a great projectile that is penetrating the sky.

The slight sway of the aircraft as it cuts through the air penetrates the soles of the feet, but no farther. The feet feel movement, but the rest of the body does not. The eyes run in constant checks over the instruments—altitude, speed, engine settings, temperatures. They are the only proof to the mind that there is movement—they, and the contrail of another jet, the cloud of frozen water it leaves in its engine wake.*

This idyllic scene is ruined in a millisecond if the aircraft hits severe turbulence with a harsh jarring that must be countered at once by a reduced speed.

The descent is heralded by the clatter of radio circuits as the pilot gets clearance to go down. The throttles are pulled back and the engine whine drops away. The altimeter starts unwinding and a degree of concentration that can almost be touched comes into the cockpit, as sharp and fresh as the smell of lemon.

The initial descent speed could be the Mmo: the maximum Mach speed. But the pilot would normally stay 10 knots below this so that he does not edge over it when talking to ATC or otherwise busy. If he does exceed it, alarm bells are set off.

The aircraft seems to stop and hang in the air when the speed brakes go out. It lurches and buffets, and a push on the control column puts the nose down to counter the sharp reduction in speed.

The descent is regulated in steps, the pilot getting permission to descend a certain number of thousand feet at a time. One thousand feet before the height he has been cleared to, where he

---

*A jet contrail is made of fine ice crystals and not smoke. Kerosene gives off water droplets in the engine exhaust and this freezes at altitude to give the smokelike contrail. There are other optical illusions in the cockpit. St. Elmo's fire is a dancing light of static electricity that glitters on the nose and wings. Electric rain is charged drops of rain that hit the windshield like phosphorescent beams. A lightning strike is a sudden explosion of light and noise. And on the transatlantic there is the aurora borealis, the northern lights that dance on the horizon like a glowing halo of snow.

must level off, he pushes the throttles forward and the plane slowly levels out. Unexpectedly speed is regulated through putting the nose up or down, and the rate of descent is controlled by the throttle, and not the other way around.

The crew check fuel reserves, altimeters, radar, landing lights, flaps, speed brakes, gear, antiskid on the wheels. Throttle settings are worked out in case the landing is aborted and the aircraft has to go around again.

There is a clatter and a sinking feeling as the stages of flap are unrolled. The undercarriage locks with a bump. The speed drops and the undercarriage warning lights between the two pilots turn from red to green. The pilot banks and turns the plane onto the approach path; as he turns he gives it a burst of power, since stalling speed is higher in the turn.

A typical approach would see 18 degrees flap at 230 knots, undercarriage, or "gear," down at 220 knots, flaps 20 at 190 knots, flaps 45 at 180 knots with a flare-out and touchdown between 118 and 138 knots.

The navigational instruments flick into life as the plane connects with the ILS glide path, the path of radio beams leading down onto the runway.

The runway appears. The approach speed is calculated like takeoff speeds, from graphs. The tower gives the pilot wind speed and temperature. He adds weight—now considerably less than on takeoff since tons of fuel will have been burned—and computes the safe speed, putting it on the airspeed indicator with a bug.

The Vref, or keep above speed, on a 707 weighing 100,000 kilos is 129 knots, but if the pilot has lost the use of his flaps this shoots up to 189 knots. If there is a gusty wind, the pilot will add up to 23 mph to his speed to insure maximum control in the gusts. The pilot uses occasional rudder to keep straight, controlling his height with the throttles and his speed by raising or lowering the nose.

As he passes the start of the runway, he throttles back and begins the landing "flare"—putting the nose up so that the plane sinks onto the runway instead of flying onto it. He will angle the plane into any crosswind to stop himself drifting away from the runway.

As he pulls the nose back, he kicks the rudder so that the airplane is facing down the runway and not at an angle that would strain the undercarriage.

As the main wheels touch, he pulls the throttles out of the gate and into reverse thrust. The lift dampers flip up to kill the lift on the wings. The wheel brakes must be used smoothly. The pilot pushes the control column slowly forward to get the nosewheel firmly on the ground. He is still moving at 120 mph.

The aircraft slows down through 100 mph. It is kept straight with the rudder. There is a temptation to relax. A final burst of reverse thrust and the plane is slowed enough to go to nosewheel steering.

As he turns off the runway, the pilot brings the flaps in to save them from damage by stones. The ground controller or a "Follow Me" van brings him to the right taxi stand. The pilot cuts his engines. The gyros on the instruments spin slowly to a halt. Needles sink back to zero.

He enters the flight in his logbook and notes any deficiencies in the aircraft's log. Another few hours in the air.

19

Getting from A to B

Jets very rarely get lost nowadays. Navigation is so straightforward that most aircraft no longer carry a navigator. Most twin-jets and some three-engine jets fly stages of 1,500 miles and more with two pilots as the only crew.

It was quite exceptional when a Korean Air Lines 707 drifted hundreds of miles off course on a flight from Paris to Seoul over the North Pole. The pilots blamed their poor navigation, which put them deep inside Russian airspace, on a failed gyrocompass. Exceptional, too, was the captain's skill in landing on a frozen lake after Soviet Su-15 fighters shot down the airliner.

The captain sits in the left-hand seat, the traditional seat of aerial power. He looks to the handling side of the aircraft, monitoring the autopilot, checking the basic settings of the altimeter to insure the correct height, heading the aircraft on the right course.

The navigation log work and the setting of radio aids is done by the copilot. He checks each aid and identifies the beacons he has tuned to the captain.

The captain has overall responsibility for the flight. If a ground controller gives him an instruction which he thinks is dangerous, he will override it. This is very rare, and most of the navigation is really done by the ground controller and the copilot.

The major airports of the world are linked by systems of airways 10 miles wide and extending from a base of 5,000 feet up to 25,000 feet; above 25,000 feet the whole of the sky is controlled, not just the airways.

English is the international language of air control. This has led to near disaster. A Brazilian pilot on an approach to a European airport was told: "Set altimeter to 997." He took this as "2997" and set his altimeter at 29.97 inches of mercury instead of the 997 millibars meant by the controller. The altimeter thus showed the aircraft to be 500 feet higher than it actually was. Fortunately, visibility was good or the pilot could have flown into the ground.

The airways are very like the block system on a railroad, where no train can enter a block until the one in front has cleared it. A system of navigational beacons, transmitting on VHF, radiates a series of bearings. These are picked up on the aircraft's radio compass, which points toward them.

The beacons are normally 60 or 70 miles apart. Every time the aircraft crosses a beacon, the copilot reports the time it was crossed, his height and the estimated time for crossing the next beacon. The controller who is sequencing the airplanes from the ground will not let the next airplane cross that beacon until 10 minutes after the previous one has left, if it is at the same height.

There is a separation of 1,000 feet between levels, and there are alternate eastings and westings, or north and south. Imagine a series of layers on which aircraft go about their business, crisscrossing each other. That is what you see from the cockpit. Aircraft from the opposite direction pass 1,000 feet below, those on the same course 2,000 feet below.

The aircraft makes its way flying from beacon to beacon. Controllers on the ground watch it as a small white blip on their radar screens and check its progress against the flight plan filed by the pilot. As the aircraft leaves one sector, the controller simply passes it on down the line.

The controller has to make sure that the aircraft sticks to the airway and that it does not conflict with other planes. This can happen when several aircraft converge on a beacon. An airway has only a given capacity. The airways also converge on to beacons, and the controller has to coordinate several airways flowing into one beacon. The result is sometimes aerial traffic jams, with aircraft having to "hold," circling around in oval patterns.

The amount of sky that can be used is limited. Huge chunks are reserved for military use.

The copilot can tell when he is over a beacon because the pointer on the radio compass swings around and he has an audible warning in his earphones. He simply changes radio frequencies for the next beacon and homes in on that.

The controller also has to get the aircraft from the airways system to its terminal airport. A transcontinental jet inbound for New York will start its descent from its cruising height of 33,000 feet or so over Bethlehem, about 100 miles out. The controllers look for clear enough airspace to bring it down through the lower levels of the airways.

If he has an outbound at 20,000 feet, he will clear the inbound to 21,000 feet, asking the copilot to "call passing 25,000 feet" to check on how fast he is coming down. The controller waits for the blocking aircraft at 20,000 feet to get clear: he can see its height and position on a secondary radar screen.

When it is out of the way, he reclears the inbound jet to carry on down. He wants to get it to an "entry point" where it can join the flow of landing aircraft. There are two entry points to JFK from the west. The controller juggles his traffic to get an even flow of inbound traffic over the two entry beacons.

The aircraft may be cleared at once right through to land. But if there is any hang-up at lower levels on the run-in—as there usually is at busy airports—the aircraft has to circle over the beacon. This is called the "holding stack," where aircraft wait until they become the bottom plane of the stack and are cleared to land.

Aircraft fly a racetrack pattern, or oval, around the beacon while they are stacked up. It takes four minutes to get around, and there are 1,000-foot intervals between each aircraft. As each plane is cleared off the bottom of the stack, the ones above all move down 1,000 feet.

A different controller takes over as the plane leaves the stack. His aim is to put it about 12 miles from the runway and four miles behind the previous plane.

The approach radar shows a line of dots moving at four-mile intervals.

When he lines up with 12 miles to go, the pilot should be at about 3,500 feet. He prepares for an ILS approach, using the Instrument Landing System. Radio signals are sent by a beacon beside the runway to the ILS instruments in the cockpit. The instruments tell the pilot to fly right or left, or up or down, to maintain a smooth glide path onto the runway.

The ILS gives the pilot visual guidance. By keeping both the height needle and direction needle in the middle of the dial, he brings the aircraft down in line with the runway and at a steady three degrees of slope.

The ILS is sufficiently accurate to give most of the information for a plane to land automatically. The ILS, coupled with the autopilot, takes over with a mile to go and the height at 250 feet. Some sophisticated systems enable a totally automatic landing to be made in thick fog, but there are still very few aircraft or airports which have been fitted with the equipment.

A passenger jet of a major airline landing at a big airport will probably adhere to the "Category 2" weather minima. To land, the pilot must break out of the cloud base at not less than 100 feet and must be able to see at least 800 meters in front of him. Otherwise he must go around again or divert to another airport. A handful of aircraft at only the biggest airports are cleared to "Category 3A," where the equipment is so good that the pilot can land if he has a mere 270 meters forward vision at an altitude of only 12 feet.

Taking off is the same system in reverse. Aircraft take off and land into the wind, to cut back on ground speed, so the choice of runways is dictated by the weather. Major airports have parallel runways, one for takeoff and one for landing.

To regulate takeoffs there is an international system of Standard Instruments Departures, known as SID's. These are printed diagrams showing the route the pilot should take after takeoff.

In essence, there are three types of control. Airport control is situated on the top floor of the control tower. Its controllers regulate aircraft on takeoff and landing, and give permission to start engines. They also control taxiing and pier allocation, and check runway surfaces and lighting systems.

Approach controllers order the safe positioning of inbound aircraft in the right sequence, and separate inbound, outbound and transit traffic in the airport zone. They also work in the control tower although from behind darkened windows, since they work off radar and have no need to look at the outside world.

Air Traffic Control Centers, or ATC's, are so remote from the takeoff and landing of aircraft that very often they are not even situated at an airport. They control the airways, where the high-flying jets are a spot in the sky and on their radarscopes. They have to separate aircraft in the airways and keep in touch with the pilots as they progress along them.

Control is a high-pressure job. Controllers have to cope with aircraft speed differentials, where a turboprop may be dawdling along at 270 knots with a jet at 500 knots behind it; with aerial snarl-ups; with safe separations. Occasionally, they blow it, steering two aircraft together. Controllers need personal stability and the gift of coping under tension, as well as good hearing, good eyesight and a good education. To make sure they understand the pilots' problems they may be trained to obtain a private pilot's license, and also "fly" on jet simulators.

The control sequence starts when the pilot files his flight plan 30 minutes before takeoff. This is a statement of his intentions—where he is going and the speed, height and route he would like to take.

The control tower passes on the flight plan to the outbound controller at the Air Traffic Control Center. He sets up a route for the aircraft to follow, specifies which beacons it must cross and at what height, and the airway the aircraft must follow after leaving the terminal area.

He also allocates a height (or "flight level") to the aircraft and gives the time and place at which the aircraft should start climbing to this height. The aircraft's expected speed and route are fed into a computer which works out the time at which the aircraft will be over the beacons.

The outbound controller then gives the aircraft its basic airways clearance, say: "Flight One is cleared to Los Angeles via Airway Red One, to cross Beacon One at 3,000 feet, Beacon Two at 4,000 feet and Beacon Three at 4,000 feet and then climb to flight level 300." (Height is given in hundreds of feet, so flight level 300 is 30,000 feet.)

The airport controller then clears the aircraft to start engines and to taxi to the holding point on the takeoff runway. If there is already a line waiting to take off, the aircraft will not be cleared to start engines until the snarl-up has eased.

The pilot gets the airways clearance at the holding point. The airport controller gives him takeoff clearance after checking with the outbound controller that the skies are clear.

Once the aircraft is airborne, the outbound controller correlates the time with the computed speed and route. He writes the times and height that the aircraft is expected over the beacons en route on flight progress strips.

The airways controller at the ATC center now checks the aircraft down the beacons, altering the progress strips if the aircraft does not run to schedule. He passes the aircraft over to the next ATC center as it passes out of his zone.

When landing, the ATC inbound controller starts the aircraft descent and then hands it over to the approach controller. Once the aircraft is well established on the approach and is closing on the runway, it is passed over to the airport controller, who gives it landing clearance and then controls it along the taxiways to the terminal pier.

Controllers also try to cut down on noise annoyance by routing aircraft around towns. Video maps show towns and cities and the controllers keep noisy aircraft, like Concorde and 707's, away from them for as long as possible.

The controllers deal with emergencies. A typical JFK emergency: an aircraft with a hydraulic fault on a flight from St. Louis. Landing may be difficult. The plane is given an immediate "straight in clearance." The controller rearranges the other aircraft waiting to land.

Then the pilot reports that he is on half power. The alert status changes to a 3:3. Eight fire engines roar out of their bays toward the runway. The plane is 11 miles out.

Local fire brigades and ambulances are informed. The runway is cleared. There are fire engines at the point of touchdown, more halfway along the runway and another group at the end of the runway.

The controller relays weather conditions, temperature, pressure and wind to the plane. The undercarriage is lowered, and the aircraft comes in rather fast and a little unsteady, because the hydraulic fault has robbed it of full flap. It uses a lot of runway but stops.

The fire engines return to their bays, the ambulances depart, the airport chaplain relaxes, and the 3:3 is canceled. The controllers settle down to unblock the jam of circling aircraft that has built up. At JFK, they average two emergencies like this a day in summer.

It is the great accuracy of navigation, and control on the approach and landing, that has made flying so much safer.

Navigational aids that plot an aircraft's position from its own movement are available. LORAN has a receiver and indicator accurate to a millionth of a second to measure the difference between ground stations. This gives a number readout, which is transmitted onto a map print-out in the cockpit, showing exactly where the aircraft is as it moves.

Inertial Navigation Systems, INS, are precision-based on gyros. An inertial platform is equipped with two accelerometers, one exactly north–south and the other east–west. The pilot punches in his original position on the departure airport before takeoff, remembering that it can take 40 minutes for the gyros to spin up to the required degree of accuracy. Every acceleration as the plane moves from its taxi stand is recorded and mapped.

INS is accurate to one mile times the hours flown. After 10 hours it will be good to at least 10 miles. It is highly accurate westbound, giving a biggest error of only five miles on westbound transcontinental flights in the U.S. The counterrotation of the earth affects it eastbound, and that five miles could become ten. During its introduction, however, the maximum recorded error was 27 miles on a nine-hour flight from Seattle to England. Besides position, INS gives the track, the course the aircraft is making and ground speed.

Three INS are normally carried on a big jet like a 747 or DC-10, and two on a 707—the third ones on the bigger planes are "hot spares." INS is sophisticated—positions can be updated in flight by feeding in VOR and DME from beacons—but also simple enough to insure its general acceptance everywhere.

The first instrument landing was made in 1928. The equipment used by James H. Doolittle (later the first man to bomb Tokyo) is still the basis of finding a runway. A simple radio beam guided him toward the runway, and radio markers on the approach told him how far he had to go.

The simple radio beacon is still the most common landing aid. It works on exactly the same lines as an ordinary radio station. The pilot tunes his radio receiver to the right frequency for the beacon he wants. He can tell when he has got it because it plays an identifying Morse Code signal through his earphones. A needle on his instrument panel then points toward the beacon.

But these systems are badly affected by static and thunderstorms. They can be used only as a homing beacon, and not as a reference for other courses. VOR, very high frequency omnidirectional range transmitters, get around some of these problems. Being VHF, they are not affected by static. Together with DME, the bearing can be fed into a small computer which will give an instantaneous position on a map.

It is easy to tell when the aircraft is passing over a VOR station: a small pointer on the cockpit instrument changes from flying "to" the VOR to "from."

Some VOR transmitters also have Distance Measuring Equipment. The pilot reads off the exact distance he is from the station on an instrument.

This combination can be used for landing as well as en route navigation. The VOR needle shows the correct heading for the runway, the altimeter shows his height, and the DME shows the distance to go from the runway. This makes it simple to work out the correct angle of descent. With five miles to go he should be at 1,500 feet, three miles out at 900 and so on: the rule of thumb is 300 feet for every mile.

Take a VOR/DME approach at Tokyo's Haneda Airport, on runway 33 Left. (JFK's main runways are on the more sophisticated ILS.) The aircraft begins its descent 120 miles out over the Pacific. The VOR is tuned into the Kisarazu beacon, across the deep bay from Haneda. The pilot keeps well to the south to avoid the Kawasaki refinery: as with most oil refineries, overflying is prohibited. The DME shows the distance to Kisarazu ticking off.

As the aircraft passes over Kisarazu, the "to" slides over to "from" on the instrument and there is a clattering on the headphones. The copilot now sets his VOR to the transmitter on runway 33 Left. The crew know from their airways map that it is 10.3 nautical miles from the Kisarazu beacon to the runway threshold. The map also tells them that at their ground speed of 150 knots it will take them four minutes and seven seconds to the threshold. They start a stopwatch.

As the distance to go diminishes on the DME equipment, the crew check the altitude. They are at 2,500 feet at the beacon.

The VOR needle has to be kept centered. It if drifts left, it means the aircraft is easing away from the airport toward the refinery. Right, and it is off towards the heavy-industry plants at Shinagawa. Centered, it is heading straight down the runway.

As the DME shows two miles to run, the pilot looks out of the windows for the runway lights. The copilot scans the instruments, particularly altitude against distance to go. He must insure that they do not get too low, because a jet engine takes time to correct errors.

The captain is helped by the runway approach lights. They will show red if he is too low, and be invisible if he is too high. He must keep on the white lights. When he has all white lights and the runway well in sight, he goes on to land visually.

The VOR/DME system is the most commonly used at airports. But it gives only heading and distance to go. It does not give any height indication, and so can only be used in fair visibility.

Runways with ILS can be used in everything but the worst conditions. Yet only 12 percent of the runways used by commercial jets in Europe are equipped with it. In North America the figure is 10 percent, and for the rest of the world 6 percent.

ILS tells the pilot a great deal more than VOR, and it does it in much simpler form. It has four essential ingredients. The "localizer" is a radio transmitter placed at the far end of the runway. Its beam is picked up by a needle in the cockpit, which shows the pilot where to head the aircraft. By keeping the needle centered, he will stay on the right heading.

ILS also gives him "glide path" information. This tells him whether he is descending at an angle that will bring him down gently onto the beginning of the runway.

It consists of another transmitter, about 1,000 feet down the runway, which sends out a beam that indicates a three-degree slope in the air. The pilot can tell from his instruments whether he is above, below or on this ideal slope.

The "Outer Marker" is a beacon which tells the pilot how far out from the runway he is. It is normally six miles from the beginning of the runway. As the airliner flies over it, a blue light flashes in the cockpit and there is a buzzing in the pilot's earphones.

The "Middle Marker" is 3,500 feet from the start of the runway. An amber light flashes in the cockpit as it is crossed. The pilot should now be at the right angle of descent, distance and speed to touch down 1,000 feet along the runway. Landings can be made even when the cloud base is under 200 feet and the visibility less than half a mile.

The ILS system is also used with precision approach radar. This reads an aircraft's height so accurately that the ground controller can warn the pilot if he strays as little as five feet below the glide path.

Most of the smaller airports, including many of the busy holiday airports around the Mediterranean, are not even equipped with VOR on all their runways. The American Air Line Pilots' Association has found that deaths at airports lacking precision approach aids are 10 times higher than at airports with fuller control aids.

Control is not infallible. In a typical year, 1968, 2,230 near misses were reported in the U.S. alone, with 38 mid-air hits. Since most near misses take place in cloud, where the pilots could be unaware of them, the true figure is perhaps double this. The official definition of a "near miss" is when two aircraft are close enough to be in danger of colliding. Some pilots say they should be rechristened "near hits."

Air misses in the U.S. have become so serious that the FAA was forced to ask Congress to raise the maximum penalty for civil flying violations from $1,000 to $25,000 and to get criminal penalties for the worst offenders. The FAA's Administrator, Langhorne Bond, also proposed a new rule to make it easier to "track down the shadowy figures who hide behind multiple leases and sham corporations." He said that regulations would help the FAA to expose "cockroach corners—those unsavory operations conducted at Miami International Airport and elsewhere."

The FAA move was prompted partly by the fatal crash between a Pacific Southwest Airlines 727 and a private plane over San Diego in September 1978. The airliner was approaching to land at San Diego's Lindbergh Field and the Cessna pilots were practicing instrument flying from nearby Montgomery airport.

A conflict-alert alarm, a warning that two aircraft are close, sounded in approach control but the controllers were not over-worried since the alarm sounded eight to ten times a day when there was no real danger.

The cockpit recording shows how easy it is to lose track of a light aircraft.

"Are we clear of that Cessna?" asked the PSA first officer.

The flight engineer responded: "Supposed to be."

The PSA captain: "I guess." Sounds of laughter.

Another PSA captain, one of two riding as passengers in the cockpit: "I hope."

The PSA captain: "Oh, yeah. Before we turned downwind. I saw him about one o'clock, probably behind us now."

About 10 seconds later, the first officer added: "There is one underneath."

"What have we got here?" the captain asked.

"It's bad," replied the first officer. "We're hit, man. We are hit."

In all, 165 lives were lost in the air and on the ground.

Langhorne Bond said the FAA would change an aviation safety reporting program which provides immunity to pilots and control-lers who report violations of safety rules. "No longer will a violator be able to draw a cloak of immunity around himself by simply turning himself in—even if the violation was witnessed and subsequently reported by others."

Bond noted that, in Spokane, Washington, "a DC-9 on a missed approach almost hit a DC-10 taking off from the same runway at the same time. Both the DC-9 pilot and the controller were in serious error—and we all knew about a near miss as soon as it occurred."

But both men filled in a report on the incident with NASA, thus blocking the FAA from taking any action against them. NASA is the clearinghouse for the immunity reports.

"The guarantee of immunity, I'm afraid, can be too easily corrupted into a license to endanger hundreds of lives with no fear of punishment," said Bond. Under the modifications, "airmen will no longer be able to claim immunity for violations—witnessed by others—of safety regulations. And controllers will no longer be able to shield themselves behind a claim of immunity if they direct an aircraft into another's airspace, runway or taxiway, or if they give an accept on inaccurate briefing when changing control positions."

The American Air Line Pilots' Association said modification of the immunity policy "will without question substantially reduce the number of reported air traffic system errors." Clearly, the near-miss position in the U.S. is dangerously lax. The primary cause of an unnerving series of near disasters in a three-week period early in 1979 was air-controller error.

The frequency of close calls around New York is due to the absence of altitude information on controllers' radar sets, the heavy volume of traffic at La Guardia because of its nearness to downtown, and work load on controllers.

The first incident involved an Empire commuter service and an American Airlines 727. The commuter plane, a twin turboprop, had taken off from JFK's runway 31 and was headed northwest on 310. The crew had clearance to turn east after takeoff. It was on a flight to Utica in upstate New York.

Meanwhile, the American 727, inbound to La Guardia, was cleared to turn right into La Guardia's runway 31. JFK and La Guardia runways are parallel. According to the FAA, the Empire turboprop did not turn east after takeoff, but continued north, penetrating the buffer zone between the two airports. The JFK controller eventually saw on radar the Empire blip closing on the American blip, although he had no altitude information. He warned the commuter crew.

They missed by an estimated 300 feet horizontally and just 50 feet vertically.

Then an airport controller error brought two 747's, a cargo plane inbound to Kennedy and a passenger aircraft outbound to Europe, within 500 to 700 feet horizontally and 300 to 500 feet vertically.

Not long after, an American 727 had just landed on La Guardia's runway 4 when a controller radioed: "Traffic rolling on runway 31. Looks like he's going through the intersection." The traffic on 31 was a Delta 727 that had been cleared for takeoff and later was to hear about the incident when the conflict was discovered.

The American crew was able to stop before the intersection, but a disaster had been close.

At the same time, in Chicago, a Flying Tiger Line 747 cargo jet that had just landed at O'Hare swerved off the runway to avoid hitting a Delta 727 that had been cleared to cross the strip. The issue was how the Delta jet had been cleared across the runway on which the 747 was landing.

And in Memphis, a Falcon business jet operated by Federal Express was in its landing roll when its right wing smashed into the left wing of a Beechcraft taxiing across the airstrip. Again, controllers appeared to have given conflicting instructions.

Some parts of the sky are grossly overcrowded by civil and military aircraft. At any time in daylight, there are 5,000 aircraft in the Chicago, Washington and New York triangle. Pilots still call the Ruhr "fighter alley" because of the number of Dutch, American, British and German fighters roaming the area on NATO business. West Germany recorded a massive 216 near misses in 1976, of which 88 presented an "immediate danger."

Pilots fault the Sudan for "vastly inadequate communications coverage." The poor quality of controllers in Iraq has been noted by IFALPA. In Turkey, there is "inadequate and unreliable VHF with Ankara control when approaching from east or south. Dense traffic flow and occupied flight levels compound the situation."

Iran has "poor quality of controllers," something it shares with Egypt and Indonesia, though improvement is noted for all these.

Military aircraft are a particular danger. Coordination between military and civil controllers can break down. An Italian fighter has brought down a British Airways Viscount.* Another Viscount crashed in Maryland after being hit by a jet fighter trainer, and all the passengers died.† A U.S. Air Force F-100 fighter hit a United Airlines transcontinental flight near Las Vegas, and 49 died.‡

A U.S. Marine Phantom fighter-bomber took off in California on June 6, 1971. The air traffic controller who was supervising an Air West DC-9 that was climbing over Duarte, California, could not warn the flight of the nearness of the Phantom. The Marine pilot was flying visually with no responsibility to inform the controller of his plans, and the transponder which would have shown his position on radar was not working.

As he reached 15,000 feet, the fighter pilot rolled the Phantom. His radar observer in the rear seat saw the left wing and fuselage of the airliner appear. Before he could shout, the pilot rolled to the left again and 18 tons of fighter slammed into the DC-9. Only the radar observer lived out of the 51 involved.

Sergeant Yoshimi Ichikawa was on a training flight over Japan with his instructor in another fighter close to him.§ The instructor shouted, too late: "Climb and turn right!" Ichikawa's Super Sabre crashed into an All Nippon Airways Boeing 727 and 162 died in a second.

Light aircraft, often flying visually near airports and not under a controller's orders, have crashed into airliners with deadly regularity. Pilots call the area around 1,000 feet, where the light aircraft fly, "Indian territory" after the Piper range of small planes—Comanches, Apaches and Navahos. There are some 200,000 private aircraft in the U.S. In one brief period a Caravelle hit a Beechcraft over Bangkok, a DC-9 hit a Cessna at St. Louis, and a

*CAA 19/58.
†CAA 10/58.
‡CAA 8/58.
§CAA 16/71.

Convair 580 hit a Cessna at Milwaukee. A student on a cross-country flight from Indianapolis filed a Visual Flight Rules flight plan. This is used only if the pilot becomes overdue, so a search of his route can be made. It is not passed on to air traffic controllers.

The pilot, who had only 30 hours' flying experience, became overdue. The controllers knew instantly. He hit an Allegheny Airlines DC-9, which disappeared from their radar as it crashed and 82 died.*

Another DC-9 of Eastern Airlines hit a light Cessna and carried the little plane and its two occupants wrapped around its undercarriage, like a bird of prey with a mouse. The Cessna eventually fell off, killing the pilot and his passenger, and the DC-9 survived.†

In Europe, two Spanish airliners collided at 30,000 feet over western France. One made a miraculous landing; the other crashed, killing 68. French air traffic controllers were on strike, and the airliners were under French Military Control. Strikes by air traffic controllers have spread in Europe and lethal chaos has resulted. The summer-long dispute of Spanish controllers in 1976 brought congestion over Europe well above the danger level. Also that summer, Yugoslav controllers at Zagreb brought a British Airways Trident en route to Istanbul into a fatal crash at 30,000 feet with a Germany-bound charter airliner full of vacationers. One hundred and seventy-six died.

The pilots of jets are very dependent on controllers to avoid collisions. Speeds are so high that it is very difficult to see other aircraft, even in perfect, clear conditions. Another airliner cannot be seen until it is within five miles. Slim-winged fighters are invisible until 2.3 miles. A pilot flying at 600 mph uses 300 yards while his brain registers whether the object is a plane, a cloud or a smudge on the windshield. Decision time to climb or dive takes another 1,000 yards and 1,900 yards are burned up before the plane responds to controls.

The margins are in the splits of split seconds. FAA psychological tests have shown that controllers undergo more stress than combat

*NTSB AAR 70-15.
†NTSB AAR 72-13.

pilots. At Chicago's O'Hare, the nation's and the world's busiest airport, controllers are allowed to work for only 90 minutes at a stretch during peak hours. They have to land an aircraft every two minutes while keeping track of half a dozen more.

About one-third of O'Hare's controllers suffer from peptic ulcers; another third have gastric or emotional problems.* The Chicago branch of the Professional Air Traffic Controllers Organization has sued the FAA, claiming that the O'Hare unit is understaffed, that backup equipment is lacking and that the training programs are ineffective.

Charles Cacace, a JFK controller, says: "You don't look at an airplane as if it were carrying three hundred people. It would affect the way you do your job. Makes you nervous. You look at it as though it were a piece of tin needing to be put someplace, but in the back of your mind you always hope you don't get involved in some mess."

A pilot, Captain Power-Waters, interviewed a controller for his book *Safety Last.*†

"Have you ever seen a man panic in the position?"

"There is one vivid experience I will never forget. A man froze on the mike. His eyes rolled back in his head and he broke out in a cold sweat. He keyed his microphone continuously but said nothing. A nervous breakdown right on duty."

"What happens when the radar or radio goes out?"

"Chaos. I have seen radar fail in two or three sectors at one time. This means that approximately one hundred planes are in danger of colliding.

"The only course that the pilots have to take is to try and separate themselves. It's a frightening situation. About all I can do in a case like this is pray the Great Controller will do his job."

"Who is the Great Controller?"

"God."

Time, April 11, 1977.
†*Safety Last,* by Captain Brian Power-Waters, Millington, London, 1974.

PART FIVE

EMERGENCY

20

Hijack

Passengers are more likely to be involved in a hijack than a crash. The takeover of flights by armed men has soared over the hundred mark in some years. The scheduled flights of major West European airlines are the most popular targets.

These strange odysseys by exhausted crews and passengers, forced over the globe at gunpoint or by threat of explosives by a mentally or politically disturbed person, seem a very modern phenomenon. The word "hijack" itself was first used to mean the seizure of an aircraft in *The Times* on February 19, 1958. Before that it meant the stealing of liquor in transit during American Prohibition.

The first aircraft to be hijacked was a Ford Tri-Motor during a Peruvian revolution in 1930. Six years later, the film *Lost Horizon* jammed the box offices and made Ronald Colman a superstar. The hero was a Tibetan called Talu who wished to repopulate the isolated valley of the Blue Moon beneath Shangri-La. An aircraft was the only way to get there. So Talu learned to fly, knocked out the English pilot of an airliner and abducted the passengers to a crash landing near Shangri-La.

Talu would be called a hijacker today. Millions of dollars are spent every year trying to combat his descendants.

Many ideas have been dreamed up. When Havana was the most common destination, it was thought of building a replica of the airport near Miami. During a hijack by Japanese students to North Korea, an airport at Seoul, in South Korea, was disguised to look like Pyongyang, in the North. The students almost fell for the ruse.

There was a suggestion to build a trapdoor just behind the cockpit out of which the hapless hijackers would fall. This would decompress the aircraft, however. Nerve gas has been proposed to put hijackers quietly asleep. A drawback is that they could well pull triggers or drop grenades while nodding off.

The FAA developed a high frequency ray system to stun hijackers. Labeled "Operation Zeke," the system consisted of two "ray boxes" near the cockpit door. Anyone passing through the rays would be knocked unconscious. But the FAA decided that it was too risky to use on commercial aircraft: there might be more than one hijacker.

Doped food and drink worked until hijackers started insisting that crew or passengers sample everything first. Police dressed as mechanics had a short-lived success. Afraid of concealed weapons, some hijackers will not let people near the aircraft unless they are wearing swimming trunks.

A crash course for skymarshals was developed in the U.S. in 1970. A special firing range was built. It was a mock-up of the interior of a passenger jet. The marshals had to be able to fire 12 bullets in 25 seconds, at a range of 45 feet (about 12 rows of seats away), to hit a profile of a hijacker in the aisle.

Marshals carry .38 revolvers, adapted for use inside an aircraft. A normal .38 carries for up to a mile. A 707 has an interior main cabin of just 111 feet and a normal bullet would penetrate through several layers of seats.

The airline version uses a special slug that has a lethal range of only 50 feet. Beyond that it slows down rapidly and will not carry beyond 170 feet. The "bullet" is a flat canvas bag filled with lead shot, tightly rolled to fit in the chamber.

It comes out of the barrel at 1,000 feet per second, and as it spins, the bag opens flat. This slows it down so rapidly that at 100 feet, roughly at the end of the cabin, its speed is down to a dawdling 190 feet per second.

The energy necessary to kill someone depends on the shape of the bullet and the place where it hits, normally between 30 and 90 foot-pounds of force. When it leaves the muzzle, the "pancake" exerts 125 foot-pounds, well above that needed to kill. But at 100 feet it is 6 foot-pounds, well below. This means that if the shot misses the hijacker but hits someone farther down the cabin, he will survive.

A normal bullet passes through objects leaving holes little larger than itself. The pancake, or "airline special," delivers all its energy into the first thing it hits, and because it is pliable and not solid it makes a very large and ugly hole.

At short range, it is more likely to kill than an ordinary bullet that can pass straight through a man. The danger of ricochet is very small because the pancake loses power so quickly, and because they are pliable, the new projectiles will not penetrate the airframe.

The main danger of piercing the airframe is not, as most people think, depressurization. A bullet hole is much too small to suck anyone out, and the cabin compressors will more than compensate for the outflow of air. All it will do is make an unpleasant, high-pitched shrieking noise as air escapes. The danger is that the bullet may sever a control line or puncture a fuel tank.

The skymarshal's job is not a romantic one. The best-paid get only $12,000 a year—considerably less than a young stewardess. The routine is a month on duty at an airport, then two months' flying.

Not that the flying is glamorous. The skymarshal cannot sleep, drink alcohol, watch the in-flight movie, or reveal his identity. Each one is given a separate cover story to use if he gets into conversation with a passenger. He is known only to the crew, and comes under the captain's command, although he can act independently if he feels that he can defuse a situation on his own.

The only known characteristics of a skymarshal are that he will be male and aged between 21 and 50. Although his main function is to monitor passengers' behavior continuously, he should be trained to conceal this. On a few airlines, however, the skymarshals stick out like very sore thumbs. On Ethiopian Airlines, four young men board the aircraft at Addis Ababa after everyone else is on board. They wear, despite the heat, identical trench coats with identical bulges under the arms, and blink out at the passengers through one-way silvered dark glasses.

The airline provides them with identical Samsonite attaché cases with their initials on them. Their cover story is that they are businessmen.

The easiest way to stop hijacks is to stop hijackers boarding the aircraft. This is done partly by machine. Magnetometers can isolate solid masses of metal, like a gun or a knife. There are various types of metal scanner, whose sensitivity can be set to pick up a pair of keys but is normally set to record at the density of a .22 pistol. One system has poles that the passenger walks between. If metal is detected a light on an alarm box will flash on. This is watched by a security guard some way away so that the man actually working the magnetometer will not be overpowered or shot by the passenger, as he might be if he was the person to discover that the passenger was armed.

This system costs around $1,000. For $32,000 airlines can buy a system that picks up pistols, whiskey bottles, gelignite sticks and even heroin stuffed inside plastic dolls. Through sensitive X rays it shows the outlines of forbidden articles on a screen. But it is too expensive, the airlines say, and slow to operate. Other devices are too sensitive, even picking out women wearing contraceptive coils.

The "electric truncheon" is another way of searching passengers without having to touch them. The "truncheon," which looks like a flashlight with a metal loop on the end, has a dial which registers when it gets close to a metal mass. This costs only $100. And, to be more discreet, there is a system at $250 where the detector is hidden in the searcher's sleeve, giving off a bleep to a "hearing aid" in his ear.

A new type of lie detector measures psychological stress through changes in voice patterns. A lie alters heartbeats and pace of breathing and upsets the nervous system. Where an honest voice pattern comes out as a straight line on the machine's graph, a lie comes out as rectangular shape. However, lie detectors rely on a series of questions, rather than a simple "Are you going to hijack this aircraft?" So the time needed by this Dekto Counter-Intelligence and Security System is considerable.

Physical searching, "frisking," is often done in addition to checking by machine. It can be highly effective. Not only did British Airways relieve Prince Kalifa bin Ali Al'tani, brother of the ruler of Qatar, of his gold-plated Walther PPK, but another brother, this time of Jordan's King Hussein, was in trouble with the same airline within a week. His luggage, on a flight to sunny Bermuda, was found to contain three submachine guns, several pistols and dozens of ammunition clips.

Carrying weapons is not restricted to those of blue blood. In three months at London, BA passengers alone were relieved of 19 revolvers, several shotguns, 300 rounds of ammunition, 800 pellets, 160 antique and replica firearms, and 400 knives. There was also a motley collection of axes, bayonets, cutthroat razors and the Peruvian naval attaché's dress sword.

Americans are easily the most common weapon carriers, and security men soon get a feel for what other nationalities carry in their pockets and in their hand luggage. "For flights to the Far East you almost start getting worried if they aren't laden down with chocolate, Alka-Seltzer, masses of Tampax—all the things they can't get in India, or Pakistan. They go in for carving sets, too, so you don't panic if you find an Indian with a great carving knife. It's quite common.

"But you would not expect knives with an Arab. Their things are electric razors, transistor radios and pullovers. Israelis go for suet puddings and cornflakes."

There is a well-taught pattern to the "frisk." Using the standard international method, perfected by American detectives and British troops in Cyprus, Aden and Ulster, it should be possible for six men and two girls to check out a Jumbo load of 340 passengers in less than an hour. (Using machines alone would take 30 minutes.)

The searching hands slide in an unbroken pattern down the body. They start around the back of the neck, feeling for anything concealed in the jacket collar. The lapels are lifted slightly so that the hands can feel the weight of the jacket and sense if anything heavy like a gun is in it. Parting the jacket the hands brush the wallet pockets and under the arms, and then run down the back as the eyes check the exposed shirtfront.

At the waist, the hands come around the belt, feeling for a weapon. Experience has shown that guns are seldom concealed in shoulder holsters. People who want to conceal guns normally strap them to the small of their backs or to their thighs. Shoulder holsters are too obvious, although the security men keep them there for quick reaction. A police sergeant said: "Look at that Aeroflot flight engineer," as the Russian airline crewman stood by his aircraft during a turnaround to Moscow. "He's got a very developed left breast and any normal engineer would either be in the crew room or working on an engine. He wouldn't be standing around in the cold."

The trouser pockets are checked, and the hands slide to the crotch and down the inside and the outside of the legs as the eyes check whether the heels are built up enough to have a secret compartment. At no stage should the hands have left the body or slowed down the rhythm of search.

But things go wrong. If the passengers are all wearing overcoats or raincoats it can almost double the time. All the coats should be taken off and searched individually. It is very difficult to search through both an overcoat and a jacket. There is too much bulk for sensitive feeling of weight or bulges. So flights on cold or rainy days pose more problems than most. Throw in a charter holiday flight, with passengers laden down with presents and souvenirs as well as raincoats, and the supervisors who have to monitor the flow of passengers for frisking will more than double the time estimate over a similar load of businessmen in good weather. Hence the choice of a holiday charter flight by the Palestinians who hijacked the Lufthansa Boeing from Majorca to Mogadishu in October 1977.

Despite magnetometers and frisking, some hijackers have gotten through. The great majority were never searched at all. The number of hijacks in the U.S. dwindled as soon as searching became compulsory.

Some people feel the U.S. may have gone too far with a regulation that blind persons surrender their canes before boarding airliners. After United Airlines upset them by refusing to carry six blind passengers with their white sticks from Minneapolis to Baltimore in 1978, a thousand blind people demonstrated at the Transportation Department in Washington. The U.S. has, however, been more successful than many nations in combating hijacks.

Searching is not compulsory in Europe. The favorite hijacking method is to board a nonsensitive airline at a nonsensitive airport and to board the target aircraft as a transfer passenger. Thus a hijacker might join his target flight from Paris to the Middle East after being transferred to it from a nonsensitive Manchester–Paris flight.

A few airlines insist that joining passengers at transit stops should be searched more thoroughly than anyone else. El Al has done this with such success that attacks on it became limited to random machine-gunning of passengers in airports, rather than actual attempts to board their aircraft.

Hijackers have gotten past security with extraordinary ease.* Two Palestinians were refused tickets by El Al during the great 1970 desert hijack operation, when three aircraft were taken to a desert airfield in Jordan. El Al had fairly good grounds for suspicion. The men could give no satisfactory reason for being in Europe, let alone wanting to fly to South America via New York on El Al when a direct flight was available. They offered to pay cash. Despite their scruffy clothes, they insisted on first-class tickets.

---

*The Rand Corporation, ever diligent, worked out the probabilities of risk and success for hijackers as of 1977. They had an 87 percent probability of actually seizing hostages. There was a 79 percent chance that all the members of the terrorist team would escape punishment or death, whether they successfully seized hostages or not. They had a 40 percent chance of obtaining all or some of their demands when they wanted more than just safe passage or exit. The odds of full compliance with such demands were 29 percent. When safe passage or exit for the terrorists themselves or for others was the only demand, the chance of success was 83 percent. If concessions were rejected, there was a 67 percent chance that all or virtually all the terrorists could still escape alive by going underground, accepting safe passage in place of their original demands or by surrendering to a sympathetic government.

They thus showed four distinct peculiarities. Normal passengers want direct flights. If they take a roundabout route, they almost invariably want a stopover on the way. They know why they are in the country. If they appear to be poor they rarely travel first, particularly on a 10,000-mile flight. And airline passengers very rarely pay cash.

El Al refused to fly them on their target flight from Amsterdam to New York. (Two others, the notorious girl hijacker Leila Khaled and an Argentinian who sympathized with the Palestinians, did board it and attempted to hijack it. The Argentinian was shot dead by an Israeli security guard and Miss Khaled was captured almost without a struggle.)

The Palestinians booked onto a Pan Am Jumbo instead. The pilot was so suspicious of them that, despite their elevated status in the first-class compartment, he insisted on personally searching them before takeoff. He neglected to check their hand luggage under their seats. Ten hours later, after failing to land in the desert because of the Jumbo's size, they blew up the plane at Cairo.

In America, a ramp agent demanded proof of identity from a suspicious-looking passenger. The man indicated that he was deaf and dumb. Pressed further, he produced a quite valid commercial pilot's license. He was allowed on board and hijacked the plane. Nobody on the airline staff had asked how a deaf-and-dumb person could get a pilot's license. Richard C. Bland was another eccentric. He tried to hijack a 737 from Richmond, Virginia, to Newark, New Jersey. The crew escaped through the cockpit windows. Mr. Bland was 15 years old at the time.

"Positive frisking," as the airlines put it, varies greatly. It can involve a highly complex scanning machine or it can be the captain of a Gulf Aviation turboprop refusing to fly the bodyguards of the Sultan of Oman, with their Lee Enfields and daggers, from Muscat to the other side of the Empty Quarter at Salala. (A compromise was made. The men kept their rifles. The pilot took the bolts and firing pins.)

The airlines have another, more secret check, the "mind frisk." It is just as efficient. A study of hijackers shows that they behave differently from normal passengers. So a "behavioral profile" of *normal* passengers was worked out. The profile does not point at the guilty or the suspicious: it simply clears the innocent.

The 10-factor profile has been found to clear 99.5 percent of all passengers. The remainder (and that is 2,500 a *day* in the U.S., with 500,000 passengers moving daily by air), are checked out with special interviews and with physical frisks.

The profile, for obvious reasons, remains secret. But every time a passenger boards an aircraft of a security-minded airline he will be "mind-frisked" by the check-in girl, by the airline security personnel and the plainclothesmen who always patrol terminals, and by watchers from behind the concealed two-way mirrors that exist in most departure lounges. If he passes the 10 very simple requirements, he is considered normal.

What can be revealed is the reverse, the rough I.D. of the hijacker. Research has come up with a fair picture of the "Havana riders," as the airline staff call them. Texas psychiatrist David Hubbard interviewed a considerable cross section of hijackers and found there was much in common.*

The hijacker is likely to be very shy and soft-spoken. So shy, indeed, that the famous parachuting hijacker, Richard McCoy, had to use pre-typed notes to take over the aircraft.

He will probably be small, unathletic and have very poor coordination—one hijacker had difficulty in tying his shoelaces, another in reversing his car.

He turns up at the ticket counter with all the signs of being a regular flier. His briefcase is plastered with stickers from recent trips; he has a general air of knowing his way around, and is not at all the lost and puzzled wild man you might think.

His clothing is often absurdly unsuitable for the destination. A hijacker on a Toronto-bound flight from Kansas City in January wore a sports shirt and slacks, but then he knew the flight was going to Cuba and not Toronto. Hijackers very rarely bother to bring luggage with them. "It's like prostitutes and hotel doormen," says a check-in clerk who foiled a hijack attempt on this basis. "If

The Skyjacker, by David G. Hubbard, The Macmillan Company, New York; Collier Macmillan, London.

a man has no luggage on an airplane flight, he's like a girl with no luggage at the Waldorf. The sort of customer you think about twice."

Though both experienced and shy, the potential hijacker asks a lot of questions. The favorites are: the number of intermediate stops en route, the number of passengers, cruising height, location of the engines, distances to cities not on the route. He is probably unsure of the advertised time of arrival, unusual for a passenger.

His general behavior in the terminal will be odd, even by the standards of the mentally unstable who are attracted to airports. Most of those like the size and transient nature of the buildings, where they can loiter anonymous and free in the big open spaces. But the hijacker feels trapped and stays close to walls and pillars.

He takes devious routes to cover short distances; he constantly moves around the shops, newsstands, bars, telephone booths, lavatories, without using any of them.

For many hijackers, travel and particularly flying is their only enjoyment, the only way to cope with upsets and crises. One man who had inherited $350,000 traveled 200,000 miles in two years before turning hijacker. This schedule was getting close to what actual aircrew might do. But the man never stayed at any airport he flew to. He simply turned around and flew back.

Another man used to drive the long round trip from New Orleans to Houston to Los Angeles and Colorado and back to New Orleans whenever a family row loomed. He took to flying it, and eventually went to Cuba.

Almost all of the hijackers Hubbard interviewed were unemployed at the time of their crime.

"Mind frisking" these people is not difficult, but it can break down. Richard McCoy hijacked a United Airlines 727 on a flight from Denver. He was the last to board the aircraft, but had left a large manila envelope behind in the staging area in his nervous panic. This was his only luggage.

As soon as the envelope—which contained all his hijack plans and pre-typed notes—was obligingly rushed out to him by a United employee, McCoy went straight to the lavatory.

The aircraft's second officer was sent back to ask him to leave the lavatory so that the aircraft could take off. McCoy came out of the lavatory wearing a black curly wig, a false mustache, a large blue tie, a blue suit with red stripes, blue shoes and reflector silvered dark glasses.

Also on the aircraft was a recaptured convict, William Coggin, who was being flown back to prison in California by a prison officer. Coggin noticed that McCoy's hair and mustache had changed color while he was in the lavatory. He saw him putting on gloves. When he told the prison officer that McCoy was acting strangely, he was told to forget it.

So even the most obvious hijacker can be successful, although McCoy was later captured after parachuting out of the aircraft with $500,000. He was arrested shortly afterward, having had time to spend only $30.

Picking up the "politicals," who hijack aircraft for ideological reasons, is much more difficult. There are no obvious traits to give them away. Even ethnic signs help little—there are plenty of blond, blue-eyed Palestinians.

Their passports are often diplomatic, forged Jordanian or Lebanese, or genuine Libyan, Algerian and Yemeni. Holders of diplomatic passports can object to themselves and their luggage being searched, even though it is known that arms and explosives for Palestinian hijackers have been smuggled into Europe by Libyan diplomats. When searches are made, diplomats often get very upset. A Saudi diplomat in London kept an intercontinental jet waiting for five hours and got an official apology after he had refused to be searched.

The U.S. is no longer a haven for hijackers. Special hijack "command rooms" deal with incidents. They monitor world air traffic and can call up fighter chase planes and special radar surveillance. They are in contact with the Pentagon, the United States Air Force, and the White House. Presidents since Kennedy have all taken a personal interest in hijacks. Kennedy himself ordered the tires of a Delta jet to be shot out by the FBI to prevent it taking off for Cuba. Resident coordinators, routing experts and psychiatrists are used.

Europe has nothing to compare with this, which makes it all the easier for the hijackers.

The German Ministry of the Interior ordered a report on security at foreign airports following the hijack of a Lufthansa jet to Mogadishu. A leak of its confidential report revealed a list of 13 dangerously lax airports. Bombay, Dakar, Istanbul and Tripoli were classified as "very unsafe." Accra, Algiers, Baghdad, Barcelona, Jeddah, Karachi, Lagos, Palma de Majorca and Toronto were considered "unsafe." Security measures were described as "inadequate" at a further 37 airports.

Pilots react extremely well to hijacks. There have been almost no flying incidents connected with hijacking despite the pressure of flying with a gun in the back for long periods to unfamiliar airports. Three big jets crammed with passengers made flawless landings on an unmarked desert strip in Jordan.

Captain Isaac Risseeue, a fit 53-year-old, was senior pilot of KLM's Flight KL-861 as it took off from Amsterdam's Schiphol airport at 12:10 one Sunday morning. The giant Jumbo was named *Mississippi*. (All KLM's big planes are named after rivers or composers, as National uses girls' names, Tammy and Sue, Sabena the towns of Belgium, Air France the great châteaux.)

The flight was routed to Tokyo via Beirut, Delhi and Bangkok. Three Palestinians seized it after it had reached its cruising altitude of 32,000 feet. Captain Risseeue was forced to make an unscheduled landing at Damascus. The Syrians refused to refuel the aircraft, and he flew to Cyprus and then on to Tripoli, Libya.

The hijackers expected a heroes' welcome. But the Libyans ordered them to give themselves up. They refused and ordered Risseeue to take off again. The 247 passengers were ordered into the rear of the plane, and grenades were held above their heads.

The Libyan army started moving tanks and vehicles onto the runways to prevent a takeoff. One hijacker pressed a gun into the captain's neck. "Take off, or everyone dies."

Risseeue had by now already flown 2,600 miles and made three difficult landings under great strain. But he calmly opened the engines wide and swung the Jumbo toward an unused runway that still had sand smeared across it. There was a tank on it, and Risseeue swerved his plane around it, almost into the sand, before taking off.

He was ordered to land in Malta, the first Jumbo to land there.
As the wheels touched down on the lip of the runway, full brakes
and reverse thrust were piled on.

Risseeue convinced the hijackers that he could not take off again
with any passengers aboard. The weight would be too great, with
additional fuel. So he got all his passengers released, and took on
27,000 gallons of fuel.

A relief KLM pilot came aboard. Risseeue declined to hand
over control of *Mississippi*—"This is my aircraft," he said.

At dawn on Monday the Jumbo was cleared for takeoff and
started the long haul eastward into the sun. Airports closed as
Mississippi approached over the Mediterranean—first Istanbul,
then Ankara, then Beirut, then Damascus wanted nothing to do
with it. Baghdad's airport was sealed. Far down across the desert,
in the Gulf, Kuwait and Bahrein also closed.

By now the 27,000 gallons were almost gone. Risseeue radioed
to the tiny gulf sheikdom of Dubai: "My tanks are almost empty. I
need immediate permission to land." Reluctantly Dubai agreed.
But three hours after landing and being refueled, *Mississippi* took
off again, this time flying through the gathering dusk of Monday
night across Arabia's Empty Quarter to Aden.

Aden's airport was closed. The Jumbo circled above it in the
darkness for three hours while the hijackers pleaded with the
ground. Risseeue had now been flying the plane for 43 hours. The
dawn of Tuesday broke. Aden remained closed.

Mississippi started the long haul back to Dubai. It landed softly,
although the tires were burned almost bare. The hijackers were
given 30,000 more gallons of fuel. But Risseeue warned them that
the tires were now too stripped to be safe. Another takeoff might
be possible. But there would be no safe landing. The hijackers
surrendered.

Captain Risseeue had been in command of *Mississippi* for 69
hours and had flown 6,950 miles.

Performances like this, on a hijack that broke the previous
record, held by a TWA crew that flew from the U.S. West Coast to
Rome, have become commonplace. "It is curious," says one pilot.
"You will never be able to stop pilots from reading instruments

wrongly and killing people from time to time. But they take hijacks in their stride."

A major reason is that pilots can play it by ear.

Only in Russia are pilots ordered to resist hijacks at all costs. The results of this policy slip out in small news items. "Soviet police shot dead two hijackers who attempted to take over an Aeroflot Yak-40 flying between Bryansk and Moscow." "More than one hundred passengers on an Aeroflot flight in Siberia are reported to have died after their Ilyushin aircraft crashed during shooting in a hijack attempt." These are two examples.

All American and European crews are advised by their airlines to accede to the hijackers' wishes. They are not ordered to do so, and there have been some cases in the U.S. where pilots have disarmed hijackers, in two cases at the cost of the copilots' lives.

The norm is to go along with anything the hijacker wants, as long as it won't jeopardize the safety of the aircraft. Some airlines now have printed hijack emergency sheets, exactly as a pilot carries instructions for engine failure or radio breakdown.

The first action is to quiet the hijacker. The second is to punch the emergency hijack transponder that most aircraft carry. This automatically blips the radar image of the plane on the air traffic controllers' sets. Without the hijacker's being aware of it, his presence is known on the ground within seconds as the radar image fades and re-forms, unlike the constant echoes of other aircraft.

The pilot next tunes one radio set in to his company frequency. This is normally used for informing the airline of a late arrival, of special requirements needed on landing, such as wheelchairs, or relaying VIP's messages. During hijacks, using this frequency means that the pilot will not have to wait while other aircraft talk to ground controllers and that he will probably not be picked up on the ground by radio hams who could alert news and television networks to the drama.*

---

*An Israeli radio ham picked up messages from German Air Force planes carrying the squad that stormed the Lufthansa Boeing at Mogadishu in October 1977. He passed this on to Israeli papers and the news was soon transmitted worldwide despite German attempts to suppress it. Fortunately the hijackers did not hear it. If they had, the Mogadishu operation would not have been so successful.

The fourth priority is to make sure the hijacker understands the fuel gauges, the altimeters and has some idea of navigation. "If you're going to do what the guy wants you to do anyway," says a TWA pilot who has been hijacked, "you want to make sure he knows you're helping. Fuel is always vital. If you explain things right off, they'll trust you later when a decision has to be made. With mine, we started running short of fuel and couldn't make the destination the man wanted. But he knew we weren't tricking him."

A reassured hijacker is a safe hijacker, and if he knows the height and rough position as well, he will get a glowing, if unjustified, feeling of power and knowledge.

The pilot next decides whether to inform the passengers or not. With most "political" hijacks, this is done by the hijackers themselves at considerable length, as they expound the always complex and often boring motives for their act. But with psychotics, passengers can go through a flight without even being aware of it having been hijacked. "Passengers do tend to believe anything that comes from the captain. If you say you're diverting from Chicago to Miami on a cloudless day because of 'bad weather conditions,' it is amazing how many people will just accept it without question," says a pilot.

Finally, the captain insures that there are no misunderstandings about routes and destinations. He attempts to keep talking to the hijacker. In many cases, pilots have talked men into handing over their guns without argument in the cockpit.

The hijack drill should be as effortless as an engine failure, reassuringly well inside the safety limits.

Passengers do not react so well to prolonged hijacking. They tend to become servile toward the hijackers and start having bitter fights among themselves. When passengers are released after fairly short flights, they are often amused by it.

Japanese passengers on a KLM flight insisted that the hijackers autograph their airline brochures before they left the plane. An Englishman who found himself hijacked from Rome to Beirut said: "I wouldn't have missed it for the world. It was a splendid show."

But those who survived the long desert hijacks came out of their ordeal shattered and exhausted, their physical and mental health deteriorated. Airlines have incorporated some of the findings from the TWA aircraft into the training of their cabin crews—interestingly, the passengers on the British Airways and Swissair aircraft showed much less stress.

There is a pattern of reaction to hijack.

The first real concern sets in at the time when the plane should have been landing at the original destination. Before then, there is a sense of excitement and adventure. But when people realize the aircraft is overdue at the airport they should be going to, and that anxious friends and relatives will be waiting for them, the truth seeps in.

People start swapping notes and addresses with guarantees that survivors will pass them on to the families of those "who may not make it." This tension exists during the flying part of the hijack.

Once the aircraft lands, and the passengers are held as helpless hostages, they start going for one another. The hijackers in the desert demanded all passports, and immediately split the passengers by nationality. Some had dual nationality, Israeli and American. They automatically formed a group and protested bitterly when the baggage hold was opened to get medicines for the sick: they were afraid their Israeli second passports would be found in their baggage. By the end of the first day, the sweltering cabin had split into permanent camps along lines of common age and nationality.

Next day food became the focus of rows. The plane's food and water gave out, and only small amounts were brought in by the hijackers. This was rationed. But several passengers immediately started hoarding food and water in plastic cups. When this was discovered, they were accused of stealing.

On the third day, irritation ran right through the plane. Young children were annoying people and were snapped at for playing or laughing.

Their mothers became aggressively protective and formed a powerful subgroup of their own. Any passenger found chatting with others of a different nationality was accused of "fraternizing with the enemy" and was disowned by his fellow countrymen. The hijackers were no longer considered the common foe—each group competed for their favors.

Belated attempts by passengers and cabin crew to establish order never got under way. Most people simply sneered, "Who gave *you* any special rights?" Arguments became more commonplace, and self-discipline started to slide. Some people began to crack up, sobbing without reason.

The health of young children and men of military age was markedly low. The children had less natural resilience than girls and boys above ten. The older men and women accepted the situation better than younger men, who may have felt guilty at doing nothing.

By the time the passengers were taken from the aircraft, shortly before it was blown up, paranoia had set in. Every move by the hijackers was seen as the prelude to being blown up. And each group, Europeans against Americans, old against young, mothers against everyone, thought that the others were trying to make a deal at the expense of their own lives.

Typical passengers appear to have breakdowns after four days. Where a group has a lot in common, this can be extended enormously. But where there is no such family feeling, people split into small groups and fear persists. And it does not apply to airline passengers alone. Immediately after the desert hijackings, and as a direct result of them, 100 or so reporters were trapped in a hotel in Amman as a battle between troops and guerrillas who supported the hijackers raged outside and occasionally inside.

All were journalists or television men with war-reporting experience. Many of us knew one another from previous stories around the world. Yet we reacted in almost exactly the same way as the TWA passengers. There was an instant split by nationality. English and French journalists, as befits their countries' history, were exchanging insults within two days and punches in three. Hoarders were common and created ill-feeling—one French TV crew was found to have a bathtub full of bottled beer stolen from the Americans.

Every time a photographer was seen by the troops taking pictures, long volleys of machine-gun fire were poured into the hotel. So we journalists split from our photographers, and rumors went around that particular cameramen were trying to get everyone killed for "political reasons" to outrage world opinion.

After five days, with the hotel a bullet-pocked mess, a serious breakdown was narrowly averted when an elected committee enforced POW-camp-style rules and regulations. By this time there had been a complete nationality breakdown. The English and Americans automatically combined against the French and Italians; the Germans sided with the British. The Scandinavians kept neutral, to the contempt of the other two sides. There was only one non-European, a Japanese, and his welfare was totally ignored by all. King Hussein personally intervened for the French, sending armored cars to get them out of Amman. The King was afraid that his troops would turn on them. In fact their "colleagues" were on the point of doing so.

That complete strangers, of different professions, ages, nationalities and sex, should break down in the far smaller confines of an airplane seems inevitable, by comparison.

Some airlines give training on hijacks. Stewards are taught how to identify the subgroups, the little knots of like-minded travelers which will inevitably form. They are told to make sure that none of them is left out of any arrangements or consultations. The PA system is used to prevent the cabin becoming a rumor factory. Food and water must never be hoarded. And if passengers can be told that there is a known pattern of how they are expected to deteriorate, and that it is quite natural if they do, the edge of their fear and hostility toward others will be blunted.

Captain W. H. Davidson of CP Air, a Canadian Air Line Pilot's Association security member, has published* a detailed study of terrorism. He is worried by the spread of high-technology equipment. Terrorists have obtained RPG-7's—highly portable antitank grenade launchers. The Russian-built fin-stabilized grenades were used in an abortive attack on a taxiing El Al jet at Paris, Orly. The terrorists missed the El Al but hit a parked JAL, causing severe damage.

Intelligence officers estimate that there are 200 sophisticated

*Pilot, CALPA, 1978.

SA-7's in terrorists hands. Code-named GRAIL by NATO, this is a Russian portable heat-seeking missile with a passive infrared homing guidance system and an HE warhead. It has range of 2-1/4 miles at heights between 150 and 5,000 feet. It is particularly dangerous on approach and takeoff. It is supersonic and so can be fired after the target passes. In 1973 two SA-7's and a launcher were found in an Ostia apartment close to the departure flight path from Rome's Fiumicino.

Captain Davidson gives a profile of terrorists. Age: 22 to 25 and decreasing. Sex: male, but female increasing and often violent. Marital status: single. Life-style: urban, middle to upper class. Education: student/professional. Recruitment: university. Politics: anarchist/Marxist. Philosophy: nihilist. Davidson accuses these countries of providing assistance to terrorists: Libya, Cuba, U.S.S.R., China, North Korea, Algeria, South Yemen, Tanzania, Congo, Zaire, Egypt, Syria, Iraq and Lebanon.

He lists points that pilots should consider if they are hijacked or held hostage: Comply quickly and without protest to orders and directions. Express serious noncontentious interest in your captors' political beliefs. Attempt, whenever possible, to persuade your captors that alternative means exist for achieving their aim. Avoid conveying information that could be useful in identifying your captors. Where other hostages are involved, meet whenever safe to discuss your own strength, sicknesses and capacity for self-help and your impressions of the captors' characters and susceptibilities.

When troops or police come to the rescue, continued Davidson, take cover and do not engage your captors unless you have to for your own safety. It is likely that some passengers at some stage will show the "Stockholm syndrome," named after a Swedish bank hostage incident where captives identified with the captors and sided with them against the authorities. Davidson stresses that pilots should be prepared for this and should realize that a passenger could easily give them away to the captors.

Practical advice for passengers* starts before boarding. Go to the toilet before boarding if possible: hijackers normally forbid

*Payne and Dobson, *Business Traveller*, Summer 1978.

movement in the cabin until they have arrived at their destination or have the passengers well covered. Dress in casual, comfortable clothes: it does not label you a capitalist pig and makes sense anyway in terms of relaxation. Always take lots of paperbacks, crossword puzzles, packs of cards to pass the time. Like soldiering, hijack can be long periods of boredom interspersed with short periods of fear. And anyway, a long delay at the airport is always a likelihood.

Advice during a hijack is much the same for passengers as for pilots: Do nothing. No heroics. Stay calm, mentally and physically.* If you have to listen to political harangues, do so. Try to establish a rapport. If you have to move, make sure you ask permission first. No precipitate moves. If the authorities attack and they warn you to get down on the floor, do so. Get on the floor and stay there. Don't get up, shout, try to tackle a terrorist—in short, don't do anything that might make a commando think you are a terrorist, *or* vice versa.

Hijacking, like so much else in flying, is largely a matter of fashion. It snowballed so rapidly in the U.S. that one man seized a United Airlines plane and ordered the pilot to fly to Detroit. The aircraft was on a scheduled flight already to Detroit.

Postwar hijacking started with refugees from Eastern Europe forcing aircraft to the West. On a single day in 1950, three airliners were hijacked from Czechoslovakia to West Germany, something that was not to be repeated until the height of Arab hijacking in 1970. The hijackers, former Czech RAF pilots, were treated as heroes in the West and few thought more about it.

But with the arrival of Castro in Cuba, hijacking entered a semipermanent relationship with flying. During the fighting against Batista, guerrillas of the famous "Column Six" hacked an

---

*Physicians at Harvard Medical School have devised a simple relaxative technique. Breathe in. Breathe out again. Before reinhaling, inwardly say to yourself "One." Breathe in again. Breathe out. Inwardly say "One." Continue for 20 minutes. If you find your mind wandering from the word "one," particularly in a way you find uncongenial, refocus it. The results are claimed to be similar to transcendental meditation. Again, this technique will help you keep cool during a terminal delay or a long stack just as effectively as getting you through a hijack.

airstrip out of the jungle and hijacked two DC-3's of the national airline Cubana to it.

Once Castro was in power, Cubans used his old methods to escape, this time hijacking Cuban aircraft to get to Miami. Castro was the first political leader to have to enforce rigorous security checks at airports. Then Cubana pilots themselves started absconding with their aircraft. Castro was forced to put armed guards aboard to watch over the pilots—the first skymarshals.

The traffic soon started going the other way. On May 1, 1961, a man checked onto a National Airlines flight from Miami to Key West. He gave his name as Elpirata Cofrisi. The pirate Cofrisi had scourged the Caribbean in the eighteenth century but the airline missed the joke. Cofrisi pulled a knife on the captain and a gun on the copilot and told them to fly him to Cuba.

The pilots agreed, and the first hijack of an American aircraft began. It lasted just 45 minutes before the Convair airliner landed in Cuba. Cofrisi was arrested, and the aircraft and passengers were safely on their way back to Key West before anyone in America knew what was happening.

Since then hijacking has blossomed almost into an industry. Two-thirds of the world's hijackings have taken place in the U.S. But they reflect troubled politics elsewhere. Palestinians have been using hijacking as a political weapon since July 1968, when they had their first and only successful attempt to seize an El Al 707. The Israelis promptly put highly effective guards on their planes, and since then Palestinians have only succeeded in hijacking and destroying the planes of other nations. The list of victims is bewildering—British, American, German, Japanese, Dutch, Greek, Swiss, Belgian, Turkish, French and Jordanian aircraft or airports or both have been attacked.

Other, more private but equally bizarre hijacking wars go on. An SAS aircraft was hijacked in Sweden by extremist Croatians, who also hijacked a jet in the U.S. and flew it to Europe to drop leaflets on London and Paris. Ethiopian aircraft became battlegrounds for citizens opposed to the Addis Ababa regime. In one gun battle, fought 30,000 feet above Madrid in a 707, one would-be hijacker was shot ten times by a skymarshal, and the plane's skin was pierced six times. Extreme right- and left-wing Japanese students seize their country's aircraft; the same happens in Argentina.

Nations themselves indulge in hijacking. A British Airways VC-10 was forced down by Libyan Air Force fighters over Libya, and two Sudanese were removed. The Israeli Air Force diverted a Middle East Airlines Caravelle. They thought that Georges Habash, a prominent Palestinian hijacker himself, was aboard. He had canceled his flight that morning.

Money has gradually become as important a motive for hijack as politics, or simple mental instability on behalf of the hijackers. The first man to attempt to steal an aircraft for money was a former Nationalist Chinese pilot called Chio Tok. He was tempted by the Catalina flying boats that flew daily between Hong Kong and Macao.

They carried rich British bankers, dealers from Hong Kong, and gold for the smugglers in Macao: a promising mixture of ransom and precious metal. Chio Tok planned to take over the Catalina, the *Miss Macao*, and land it in a hidden part of the estuary of the Pearl River, safe from the police and the pirates who still infested the area in 1948.

With a gang of four, Chio Tok tried to hijack the plane immediately after takeoff from Macao. The pilots resisted, and the captain was shot in the back. His weight was forced forward onto the controls and the plane went into a fatal dive into the South China Sea. Chio Tok died, together with passengers and crew. He had been unlucky. Half a million dollars was found on the body of one bullion-dealer passenger.

Twenty-three years later, in the state of Washington, another, almost certainly also an ex-pilot, planned his own updated version of Chio Tok's bungled effort. Nobody yet knows whether or not he was successful, although he has become a folk hero:

> *With your pleasant smile*
> *And your dropout style,*
> *D. B. Cooper, where did you go?**

*Copyright © Fremont West Music.

Like Chio Tok, D. B. Cooper knew aircraft. But he did not plan to hijack it to a ground destination. He planned to jump out of it, with a ransom of $200,000. He chose a Boeing 727—like the DC-9, BAC 111 and Caravelle, it has an exit downstairs in the tail, perfect for jumping clear of the engines and tail of the plane. He bought his ticket in the name of D. B. Cooper, had apparently no disguise apart from dark glasses, and was so quiet that none of the other passengers knew the plane had been hijacked when they left it in Seattle, Washington, after an apparently normal flight from Portland.

He hijacked the plane simply by giving the stewardess a note and showing her some cylinders connected by wire. His note demanded four parachutes and $200,000 in $20 bills. The money went into a manageable parcel for a parachutist, two feet long and only eight inches thick. The money was picked up at Seattle.

He ordered the pilot to fly at 7,000 feet, with 15 percent flaps and the gear down and the rear stairs extended. He jumped at night into the wooded Cascade Mountains half an hour after leaving Seattle on a course for Reno. No body or parachute has been found but neither has any of the numbered money been spent.

The fashion spread. Shortly afterward, five other Americans jumped out of airliners with more than $1.5 million. All were caught, but $303,000 is still missing. Extortion hijacks have been most common on Fridays because hijackers thought it easier to get large sums of money at the end of the week.

One sprained an ankle on landing, another dropped half a million dollars into the slipstream as he jumped, another was picked up after a perfect night jump into the Nevada desert because he had left his car waiting for him—and the police had been keeping an eye on it as a suspicious vehicle. Another virtually hitchhiked home; he jumped only five miles from his house.

Today radio bleepers devised for locating shot-down pilots in Vietnam are placed in the parachutes, chase planes follow close behind, and crews can tell from a slight jolt back on the control column when and where the hijacker jumps.

Extortion is out of fashion, but the threat of political hijacks remains. The odds of a passenger being injured during an attempt are low—out of 15,000 hijacked up to 1974, 12 were killed or injured.

But the fear and helplessness of a political hijack, and the difficulty of arranging deals for prisoners to be released instead of just collecting money, come out vividly in this transcript:

The pilot of a Lufthansa Boeing 737, hijacked from Rome after five Palestinian gunmen had killed 32 people on the ground with phosphorus grenades, said to Athens control tower: "For God's sake, do something. These people are not joking. They have already killed. Get someone there who speaks Arabic."

Control: "We are doing our best. We are getting the Syrian ambassador."

Pilot: "Rush him there."

At 5:44 P.M. a shot is heard over the radio. An Italian policeman, seized as a hostage in Rome, is reported shot dead. There is another shot 51 minutes later.

Hijacker, in Arabic: "We will wait half an hour. That's the end. We've waited too long already."

At 7:26 P.M., Lufthansa reported a third hostage shot.

Pilot: "We are already past the deadline. They've already killed four and they're not joking. Now they've got three women outside and their guns are pointed at them."

Control: "All right, hold on a minute, take it easy . . ."

Pilot: "Come on. Bring their Palestinian friends to them. They're getting very nervous."

Control: "Hold on, we have technical problems."

Pilot: "Stop fooling around with them. Get those Arabs on the line. I can't hold off these Arabs any longer. They don't believe me anymore. They've gone out to get the women."

By midnight, the plane was still parked in a dark corner of Athens' Hellinikon Airport. Greek troops were preparing to storm it, when the pilot again came through on the radio in desperation.

Pilot, above the noise of shots: "Jesus, there's shooting going on back there."

Hijacker, in broken English: "Where are the two men? Stop all talking. No further talk is necessary."

At 3 A.M., with the Greek authorities still refusing to hand over two hijackers held in Greek jails, a hijacker came over the radio again.

Hijacker: "Can you hear? This woman will die. Scream!"

Control tower reported hearing female screams over the Boeing's radio.

Hijacker: "If our demands are not met, we will kill all, keeping the pilot and copilot for last. Listen to them."

A woman was forced to the microphone. She pleaded to the control tower in English: "Come please. Come. Help me. Help me."

Control: "Please be patient."

Copilot: "Christ, they are going to shoot me . . ."

Hijacker: "If I don't have an answer within a minute, I'm going to kill the copilot."

A shot came over the radio.

Hijacker to tower: "I'll kill two more within half an hour."

At 4:50 A.M., with the sun coming up, the jet suddenly rumbled down the runway and took off toward Kuwait. A body was found on the runway as the jet hauled past on takeoff. A seriously wounded hostage lay nearby. The others, and the crew, were released in Kuwait. The hijackers were never brought to trial.

A new form of hijacking has started. In a classic "man bites dog" incident, a Filipino pilot attempted to hijack his passengers. The DC-3 plane was carrying workers and cash to an oil field, and the pilot planned to abduct the aircraft to a small island. From there he would make off with the money by boat. It was a Swiftair service to Sanga Sanga in the Philippines.

The flight was on March 31, 1977. He tried to force his copilot to alter course for the island by holding an automatic rifle to his head. The copilot refused and the passengers tried to rush the cockpit. The pilot opened fire to keep them back, killing four and wounding three before being overpowered. He was sentenced to life imprisonment for murder and attempted piracy.

21

Turbulence

The most noticeable emergency is turbulence. One pilot reports
it:

"We encountered the most violent jolt I have ever experienced
in over 20,000 hours of flying. It was like sitting on the end of a
huge tuning fork that had been struck violently. Not an instrument
on any panel was readable to their full scale but appeared as white
blurs against their dark background. From that point on, we had
no idea of attitude, altitude, airspeed or heading. Violent buffeting, ripping, tearing, rending crashing sounds. Briefcases, manuals, ashtrays, suitcases, pencils, cigarettes flying about like un-
guided missiles. It sounded and felt as if the engine pods were leaving and the structure disintegrating. As my briefcase was on the
ceiling, I looked up through the overhead window and felt I was
looking down on the top of a cloud deck. We applied as much force
as we could to roll aileron control to the left. The horizon bar
started to stabilize and showed us coming back through 90 degrees
vertical to level . . ."

Captain Stephen Parkinson was flying a DC-8. He was climbing
between two thunderstorms on a flight from Dulles International
in Virginia. The aircraft finally rolled right side up and was
brought under control 1,400 feet above the ground.

The pilot had no idea how long the condition lasted. But during it, the 120-ton aircraft and its 109 passengers had rolled completely upside down. Extreme turbulence like this can either pull an aircraft to pieces in midair or it can force the pilot past the limits of his skill, so that he loses control and the aircraft stalls or spins into the ground.

An Eastern Airlines DC-8 dropped 13,000 feet in severe turbulence over Texas and had an engine torn off before the crew made an emergency landing. It also had been climbing between thunderstorm cells. The copilot on this flight was later killed when his DC-8 and its 51 passengers crashed into Lake Pontchartrain, Louisiana, after hitting turbulence.

As Donald Davies, the chief test pilot of the United Kingdom Airworthiness Authority, a man not given to overstatement, has baldly written in his classic book *Handling the Big Jets,** in turbulence "you must fly the airplane properly in order to survive."

Few passengers will ever have come across this degree of turbulence—after all, it took the pilot quoted at the start of this chapter 20,000 hours, or more than two years permanently in the air, to meet up with it. When it does come, it is unmistakable. It's not the sort of nasty bumping that may spill coffee or spray it over the ceiling. Nor is it the kind that will throw standing passengers around. It is when coffee floats in midair as the cabin revolves around it.

The most common cause is a storm, particularly of cumulonimbus clouds. These towering, anvil-shaped clouds can soar to 40,000 feet in U.S. and temperate climates. In the tropics, they can get to 60,000 feet. A jet cannot get above them at that height, but it makes little difference since flying over them is as dangerous as flying through them.

They have enormous energy. Air currents can be rising and falling at 5,000 feet a minute very close to each other. Between them, in the "mixing area," are extremely violent sharp-edged gusts which can destroy an aircraft. Particles of moisture can be

*Published by the Air Registration Board, Reedhill, Surrey, England.

hurled down from 30,000 feet to 10,000 feet, then be shot up again in a rising current, getting larger and larger until they freeze, become too heavy to stay in the cloud and fall as hail.

Each cloud can be 30 miles wide. They can appear, grow to 40,000 feet, produce five-inch hail on the ground, and then decay, within 15 minutes. At the base, there is heavy rain and hail up to five inches in diameter. Sleet, rain and hail go up to 30,000 feet, and above that there are snow and ice crystals.

The friction between the air currents as they rise and fall whips up static electricity as the whole cloud mass is charged and lightning flashes to earth, to another cloud or flickers inside the same cloud. The storm systems are often large, and line squalls can stretch for several hundred miles. Gusts of 100 mph have been recorded, but since they strike the aircraft as it is also being thrown up and down at high speed, this is far more serious than a hurricane at ground level.

It is frightening in the cockpit. "St. Elmo's fire starts dancing around the windshield. The static builds up so most of your radios and direction finders go on the blink, and your communications. There's so much interference you can't talk to the ground anymore," says a pilot who flew through a severe storm in the South China Sea. "Lightning strikes give a great flash, bang and a burning smell. The compasses go off. You get shocks from the controls, static again. And all the time there's the noise of the hail, battering on the windshields to get in."

But the roughness is the worst. "The whole aircraft is thrown around so much you feel it is going to slide out of control. The instruments seem to go mad. The airspeed indicator and the vertical speed indicator keep going up and down like Yo-Yos. You think you are about to stall, and you heave on the power and the next thing is that you're rapidly approaching the maximum dive speed and you get the engines back to idle."

Storms can be picked up by weather radar. A black center with a white line around the cloud cells spells danger, although the radar cannot distinguish between rain and hail, and a storm can be hidden by great areas of moist but innocent cloud. When a water concentration comes up on the radar, the rule is to reduce airspeed and avoid it by 15 miles, or 20 miles if flying above 30,000 feet. A typical turbulent, or "rough," airspeed on a 707 is 280 knots or .80 Mach.

No pilot should ever fly into a storm, or try to work his way through on radar. There can be severe gusts between clouds, and large, dry hail, which will not show on the moisture-seeking radar. A cloud can develop in a previously clear bit of sky, to a height of more than 30,000 feet, in two minutes. As the pilot slips between clouds, he may come to a dead end as the gaps fill in.

Severe storms must be avoided if possible. No takeoff should be attempted in the area of a thunderstorm. These are the rules. They are sometimes broken.

Heavy thunderstorms were approaching an airfield. The captain of a Martin 404 airliner decided to take off.* Not only that, but he ordered his first officer to fly, and from the captain's normal seat, the left-hand one. Hail, heavy rain and winds gusting to 50 mph had already hit the airport as the aircraft taxied.

The copilot took off into a wall of heavy rain, shifting winds and hail. The left wing dropped, and the aircraft was severely buffeted by turbulence. The right wing dropped, followed by the left. The airliner hit the ground, cartwheeled and caught fire.

The inquiry found that the captain's "attempt to take off into a severe thunderstorm raised serious doubts as to his judgment."

The pilot of an American Airlines 707 over Texas ran into severe hail at 26,000 feet. It ripped off the radome section of the nose, severely dented the airframe sections, finely cracked the cockpit windshields to complete opaqueness and damaged the wings so severely the flaps could not be used. In the flapless landing at 240 mph, the pilot slammed the nose forward because he couldn't see through the windshield properly, and the nosewheel collapsed.

Yet a tornado had been forecast in this section from Dallas to Los Angeles. A Severe Weather Forecast had been made and the pilot turned down a suggestion from ATC of the smoothest ride in preference to a more direct route.

Clear Air Turbulence is another killer. CAT is unseen and

*CAA 12/63.

cannot be picked up on radar. It is normally a by-product of the jet streams, the currents of fast-moving air at high altitude. CAT is the turbulence where two different streams meet. Flying through CAT is normally like shooting the rapids. There is a series of hard shocks and bumps, frightening to the passenger since it comes out of a cloudless sky, but not worrying to the pilot. The aircraft is not being thrown around, merely bumping over an uneven surface, and the pilot can easily descend to get out of it.

But when CAT combines with the turbulent waves thrown up by great mountain ranges, the results are more savage. A high chain lying broadside to strong winds, and particularly to jet streams, will throw up a wave on its windward side to very high altitudes, 40,000 feet and more.

Aircraft can be severely buffeted by these killer waves, particularly if they are in the downdraft area on the lee side. An Egyptair 707 on a night flight from Cairo to London was flying over the Alps at 31,000 feet at more than 500 mph. It hit a rapidly descending pocket "like a brick wall."

The aircraft dropped vertically for 200 feet. Fortunately, 124 passengers were strapped in, as glasses and bottles shattered on the cabin roof. But one man was out of his seat, coming back from the toilet. He was hurled around the cabin and died later of multiple injuries.

Turbulence is worst in the tail. It is furthest from the aircraft's center of gravity and can buck more. Most injuries in turbulence are thus to stewardesses in the rear galleys, and to passengers waiting to use the rear lavatories.

Killer waves can rip a big jet to pieces. A British Airways 707 took off on a flight from Tokyo to Hong Kong in 1966 with 124 passengers, mostly Americans on a package vacation, and crew.* Visibility was excellent and the elegant 12,000-foot sacred cone of Mount Fuji was visible 70 miles away.

A proverb says: When the sky is blue, Fuji is angry. And indeed the meteorological report confirmed that vicious Force Nine winds were stripping the clouds from Fuji's slopes. They were blowing

*HMSO CAP 286.

from the northwest, so that the aircraft would be in the dangerous lee of the mountain on its route.

The pilot decided he would fly VMC, Visual Meteorological Conditions, meaning that he was not under strict control but could choose his own route, until he was past Fuji. He would then fly on to Hong Kong on the more normal IFR, Instrument Flying Rules, sticking to a controller's orders.

A movie film taken by a passenger survived intact. It showed the aircraft climbing over Gotemba City into the turbulent area, 14 miles from the top of Fuji, until at a height of 15,000 feet and a speed of 400 mph, the film showed a whirl of seats and carpet. Then it stopped.

First the starboard wing and then the front of the plane broke away as the aircraft disintegrated in midair. The turbulence was too great for the stresses to be taken. All on board were killed. The inquiry reported that "the aircraft suddenly encountered abnormally severe turbulence over Gotemba City which imposed a gust load considerably in excess of the design limit." A strong mountain-wave situation existed over Japan. Wave clouds were detected to the west and southwest of Fuji by satellites three-quarters of an hour before the accident.

If the airplane stays in one piece, if the pilots do not become disoriented so that their vision gets tunneled onto a single instrument, and if they do not lose their sense of the aircraft's attitude and become dizzy, then severe turbulence should be merely frightening.

The first thing the pilot does is to switch on the "Seat Belt" and "No Smoking" signs: unstrapped passengers can be killed, and in bad turbulence it is very difficult even to hold on to a cigarette. He checks his weather radar through the storm. He must not try to climb over it, for the turbulence extends higher than the aircraft can fly. He removes the height and speed locks from the autopilot, which will try too hard to keep the height and speed that it is locked into. If the plane is caught in an updraft, the autopilot will immediately stab the nose down and increase power to lose height. This mechanical overreaction could destroy the aircraft, so planes are normally "hand flown" in bad conditions.

The cockpit lighting is turned up to full brilliance, even by day. One pilot will normally wear dark glasses. It prevents temporary blindness after lightning strikes—modern aircraft are bonded together, so lightning should run harmlessly through to discharge wicks at the tail, although one jet is thought to have been destroyed by it.

The speed will be cut back to the "rough airspeed," so the engine note changes and the air brakes may go up on the wings. Radios spoiled by static are turned off. Deicing equipment is switched on. Ice dislodged from the air intakes can damage engines and cause flameouts, so engines are deiced singly or in pairs. All loose equipment in the cockpit is stacked away. When the storm hits, the pilot simply tries to "ride" it. He ignores even large "height excursions," as he calls the sickening drops and rises of thousands of feet. He maintains only a rough height and course. All his concentration goes to the attitude indicator, keeping the aircraft fairly straight and level in attitude. Even if the storm makes the aircraft drop, the pilot will keep it straight and not climb. It takes some eight seconds before the thrust from the jets is effective, and by then the aircraft may be rising again.

Only in mountain-wave turbulence, where there is a danger of being sucked down onto the mountains, will the pilot pour on full engine power to fight for height.

Even that may not be enough. The Uruguayan plane that crashed in the Andes was on full power but the downdrafts still sucked it down into the mountains. The Andes and the Sierra Nevadas are the most notorious mountain-wave areas, followed by the Southern Alps in New Zealand and the Pyrenees.

If the crew try to do too much, all of them can eventually be trying to fly the plane at the same time, with the power going straight from idle to full, and with elevators, ailerons, speed brakes and rudders being used in a totally uncoordinated way. Control must be positively in the hands of the captain alone.

The passengers may notice the engines being eased off as the aircraft hits turbulence. The speed brakes may also be used, as they are very efficient in cutting back speed rapidly. But from then on, there should be few power changes. The rudder will not be used. At high speeds, the rudder is ineffective, and may reverse its effect, leading to violent yawing and the danger of structural damage.

Aircraft can also suffer from jet upset in turbulence. This is due to the speed and clean design. Because a jet develops a huge amount of thrust and yet has very low drag, it can fly far too fast. This is called "gross overspeed potential." It means that an aircraft which is designed never to exceed 650 mph could reach 1,500 mph in a dive.

Turbulence is the main initiator of an upset. A jet has reduced maneuverability in the thin air at altitude and can become unstable in rough weather. If it stalls it has poor lift and will lose a great deal of height before it can recover.

Thus a jet at cruising altitude can be "upset" and start losing height, either at runaway speed or in a stall. Once an upset starts, it will very rapidly escalate because of the bulk of the aircraft. Jets have lost 25,000 feet in pulling out of upsets.

In a stall, the pilot will be warned by the stick shaker. He pushes the stick full forward to get the nose down and airspeed up. Full power goes on the throttles to keep the height loss to a minimum. The nose has to be kept down in a deep dive for some time for the speed and clean airflow to build up.

If the plane goes steep nose up, the pilot pushes the stick forward and puts on full power. This is a very unpleasant maneuver, as it brings temporary negative g, or weightlessness, as the aircraft noses forward. However, when the nose goes up more than 50 degrees, the elevator is probably not effective enough to get the nose pushed down. So the pilot has to put the plane into a 90-degree bank—the wing pointing directly down—and let the nose fall.

Recovery from a large angle of bank takes time, because the nose drops as the aircraft turns. If the pilot tries to pull the aircraft straight too quickly, it will sideslip and tend to roll. He must ease it level with ailerons.

A high-speed dive is counteracted by full-speed brakes, and then the plane is pulled out of the dive. It will buffet badly as the nose comes up and speed begins to drop off. In a typical upset, an aircraft could dive from 35,000 feet to 22,000 feet. Its speed would increase greatly. As it pulls out of the dive, it will try to get back to its lower speed by lifting the nose. The pilot must counteract this by pushing firmly forward on the stick to keep the aircraft level. The speed will gradually drop off. When he is back to cruising speed, the pilot can start climbing back to altitude.

In fact, there are recovery drills from even the most severe positions. If the artificial horizons collapse during an upset, for example, recovery is still possible. A spin can be recognized by sloppy controls, noise and a low airspeed, and a high rate of turn. Rudder is put on in the opposite direction to the spin, the ailerons centered, and the stick pushed forward. As the aircraft steadies in the dive, the nose is eased up.

A spiral also sends the turn indicator haywire, and the airspeed rapidly increases. Aileron is used against the turn, and again the aircraft should settle down in a dive.

It is even possible to survive an upside-down dive without an artificial horizon. The pilot realizes he is upside down when he is hanging in his straps and pencils and briefcases fly around him. The aircraft is rolled for eight seconds—that being the rule of thumb for a jet airliner to roll through 180 degrees. It should then be right side up, in a spiral.

A total loss of all altitude information can be coped with for a short period. The pilot steers straight by the compass and the turn indicator. He keeps level by checking the airspeed and altimeter for height.

Turbulent and gusty conditions can be dangerous on takeoff as well as at height. A 727 of Continental Airlines was taking off from Stapleton International Airport at Denver. The aircraft was expected to have a head wind on the takeoff runway of 20 knots. The aircraft started its roll with a slight tail wind, which then changed to gusting head winds of 20 knots. But as the aircraft started to lift off, the winds changed to a violent 90-knot tail wind.

No aircraft is designed to cope with such a tail wind on takeoff and the 727 stalled and crashed, overhwelmed by a wind shift of 180 degrees and more than 100 mph in seconds. Although the aircraft was seriously damaged, there was no fire and all aboard escaped.

22

Ditching

Another emergency that passengers brood about on flights across the sea is a forced landing on water, "ditching" as pilots call it. It is reassuring to know that even heavy modern jets can ditch without harm. Indeed, one did it by mistake. A Japan Air Lines DC-8 was making an approach in bad visibility to San Francisco airport.* The pilot thought he was close to the airport when he was still over the bay. Calmly and with great precision, he let the great aircraft down through the murk to a pillow-soft landing in the Pacific. All the 107 passengers and crew clambered out and sat on the wings as the tide went out and the aircraft settled on a mudbank.

If this can be achieved accidentally, think how much better it should be done if the pilot is doing it on purpose.†

With the reliability of modern jet engines, ditching is now extremely unlikely: most aircraft that get into the sea have

*NTSB AAR 70-2.

†A National Airlines crew emulated the Japanese in May 1978. They landed in Escambia Bay near Pensacola by mistake. Six crew and 49 passengers were rescued from the warm Florida waters by a passing barge captain, though three drowned. The flight crew had failed to monitor the aircraft's height and rate of descent, thus landing in the sea three miles short of the runway and sinking in 12 feet of water. National fired all three. *The New York Times*, November 12, 1978.

overshot runways or have aborted takeoffs at airports close to the sea. This is why a few aircraft each year wind up in the sea at Hong Kong and Tokyo.

But it still happens with propeller aircraft, and many ditchings are survivable—a DC-3 with engine failure went into the sea off Majorca, and only one person, an old lady who could not swim, was drowned.

An Olympic Airways propjet was put in the sea off Athens after extreme turbulence, with survivors. And 48 out of 76 survived when a Lockheed Constellation ditched near a ship 560 miles west of Shannon in the Atlantic. Any aircraft flying 400 nautical miles or 90 minutes' flying time from the nearest land must carry life rafts and life jackets.

Much depends on how the pilot touches down in relation to the surface of the sea. If there is a swell running, the pilot must land parallel to it, preferably along its crest. Ditching into the face of a swell would break up the aircraft. So pilots aim to land along the crest, just as in the desert they land parallel to sand dunes. Ditching has much in common with desert landings. During the Yom Kippur war, sophisticated fighters, like Russian MiG-21's and American Phantoms, were landed with little more than scratched paintwork and sand in the engines.

But when wind speeds are between 25 and 35 knots, the aircraft will drift so much that it will need correction. There are also medium-sized waves with long foam crests, and a welter of whitecaps. Here the pilot compromises: he heads partly into the wind, landing across the swell tops but avoiding rising waves. He keeps the nose almost into the wind to stop drift before yawing away from it with a heavy kick on the rudder just before touching the water.

Above 35 knots the wind and waves have to be faced straight on if there is enough space between the waves. The wave crests have broken into spindrift and large streaks of foam cover the sea. This is miserable weather for yachts, let alone Boeings, but by firmly landing into the wind, which cuts the speed and thus impact of landing, and down the back of a large, clearly defined wave, there is a good chance of survival.

In more normal weather, a landing along the crest or on the windward side parallel to waves or swell is the procedure.

As soon as the emergency starts, the pilots are drilled to immediately put out a MAYDAY. Typically, this would be "MAYDAY, MAYDAY, Flight One, 24 West 21 North estimated, course 140 degrees, speed 220 knots, altitude flight level 300 [30,000 feet]. Fire on No. 4 engine. Ditching on present course, descending immediately. Please intercept . . . ."

The transponder which identifies the aircraft on radar screens at air traffic control is set to the emergency code, 77. If possible, the nearest ship is located and course set for it. The example is rather charitable, because the aircraft is about halfway between New York and London and is very near a weather ship. Pilots get to know weather ships and their crews well, becoming "postmen" to them and passing messages on to them. The amount of chat in mid-Pacific or mid-Atlantic is vast.

A famous British Airways captain, O. P. Jones, tried to get through to weather ship *Charlie* in the Atlantic one night. But an American stewardess on another aircraft was already talking to it. "I'm twenty-two, five feet four, 35-22-35, blond hair, blue eyes. My apartment is at 16 Brooklyn Park, my telephone number is . . ." "Can you cook?" asked the sailor on *Charlie*'s radio. "Everyone says my apple pie is something," said the stewardess.

Captain Jones finally got through in a gap in the conversation. "I'm fifty-one years old," he said, "five feet nine, 42-32-35, blue eyes, a torpedo beard. I'm interested in breeding bulldogs and I live in Sussex, England. My cooking is well known. Do you want my telephone number?"

The sailor gasped "No-o." "Then," said Captain Jones, "can I have the wind at nineteen thousand feet?"

To get back to a situation when a plane's engines go quiet and stay quiet.

The cabin staff and passengers are warned. The passengers are moved forward as far as possible, brought into first class, and strapped in away from the tail, because the tail is where the captain is planning that first thump of water be felt. As the passengers move, he retrims. The cabin staff should be getting food, water and blankets tied down around the exits. Life-raft positions are assigned.

This preparation is vital. An Overseas National DC-9, operated as Dutch Antillean Airlines' Flight 980 from JFK to Juliana Airport, St. Maarten, was diverted to St. Thomas after three attempts to land in poor weather. It was low on fuel and made for St. Croix. It ran out of fuel and ditched. Although a Pan Am flight confirmed the ditching site on radar, and Coast Guard, Navy and Marine helicopters were quickly on the scene, one crew member and 22 passengers of the 63 aboard were drowned.

The National Transportation Safety Board found that "the probability of survival would have been increased substantially if there had been better crew coordination prior to and during the ditching. The Board has recommended that action be taken to improve passenger safety through adequate warning, proper briefing, standardized seat belts and more accessible stowage of life vests for emergencies."

The engineer starts dumping fuel if he can. With Flight One he cannot, because there is a fire on the right wing—but enough fuel has been used so that the aircraft will float.

As the aircraft comes down from 10,000 feet to 3,000 feet, the engineer methodically goes through his emergency checklist. The crew work out the landing speed after estimating weight.

On the approach the captain determines sea conditions and his final ditching heading on the sea. Life vests are put on. Landing speed will be normal.

The first officer transmits a final position. The emergency exit lights go on. The captain checks that the landing gear is up—if down it would drag the aircraft nose down, puncture the belly and let in water through the undercarriage doors. The flaps go to 50 degrees.

At 500 feet, the first officer warns the passengers that ditching is imminent. The captain keeps the rate of descent at 200 feet a minute, a gentle approach, and makes sure he does not stall.

At 50 feet, the copilot warns passengers "Brace . . . Brace." The throttles come fully back. The pilot pulls firmly back on the stick to get the aircraft 10 degrees nose up. Like this, it hits slightly tail first—not too much, or it will bring the nose crashing into the water as the plane pivots; not too little, or the aircraft may bounce and then plow in nose first. The wings must be level as the plane goes in; if one wing tip is down it will dig into the water and drag the aircraft around.

If most of the fuel has been used, the aircraft will float indefinitely. During the late 1930's a Lockheed twin, the *Stars' Special,* which carried Hollywood stars over the Atlantic, had its wings filled with Ping-Pong balls for buoyancy. A Junkers which ditched off Newfoundland in 1931 floated for a week before the crew were rescued.

If there is a ship the aircraft will land ahead and to one side of it: even a 5,000-ton steamer needs half a mile to stop, and if the chosen savior is a supertanker it will need six miles.

The rafts are complicated affairs: a 30-seater life raft costs several thousand dollars. It comes with heliographs for flashing at search aircraft; radio beacons that transmit automatic positions on 121.5 and 243 MHz, the emergency frequencies, and that have a duration of 40 hours; rocket flares; compasses; insect repellent and seasick tablets. Aircraft flying over desolate land with snow and ice, such as the Polar Routes between Europe and the U.S. West Coast and Japan, must carry sleeping bags for a third of those aboard, polar suits for the crew, a stove for every 75 aboard to melt snow, and snow shovels and ice saws.

It has taken months for airliners to be found after they have crashed on land, but wartime pilots have survived for 50 days in very small rafts. Fish always follow dinghies: brightly colored fish, fish that "puff up," fish with human-looking teeth or mouths like a parrot's, or fish covered with spikes or bristles should be avoided as they are poisonous. Protein absorbs a lot of fluid, so people should not eat much if there is little water. Wastes should be thrown overboard only at night if there are sharks or swordfish around.

The experienced ditcher will also be aware of such tricks as avoiding "immersion foot" by removing his footwear, drying and loosely wrapping his feet with cloth, and exercising his feet and toes. He will reduce thirst by sucking a button and make sure he eats very little so as to preserve digestive fluids.

When he drifts to land, he will know the search and rescue signs to stamp in the sand or snow. I means that he requires a doctor, II that he needs medical supplies. F will get him food and water, L fuel and oil. LL means that all is well; N is no, Y is yes. W means an engineer is wanted, $\vee$ that firearms are needed. A triangle, $\triangle$, means that it is probably safe to land. If he leaves his camp, he leaves an arrow, $\uparrow$, pointing in the direction he has gone.

23

Pilot Error

The three-engine Boeing 727 took off from Frankfurt half an hour after midnight. It was on a scheduled flight to London's Gatwick from Kabul, Kandahar, Beirut and Istanbul. Estimated flight time to London was one hour.

The weather over northern Europe was mainly brilliant; a cold and very clear night with almost unlimited visibility in the frosty air. Here and there patches of freezing fog stubbornly refused to shift. One hung over Gatwick airport. It was not thick, perhaps only 250 feet. People on the ground at Gatwick could see the halo of the moon through it.

But it had cut the visibility on the runway to 100 meters. Nothing had landed there, and the controllers did not think anything would. They had reckoned without Ariana Afghan Airways, Flight 701 and its Captain Rahim Nowroz.

There were 54 passengers aboard, and eight crew—Captain Nowroz, copilot Abdul Attayee, a flight engineer, a ground engineer and four cabin staff.

The aircraft was virtually brand-new and, apart from a warning light on the autopilot, was to perform perfectly that January night.

Captain Nowroz had 10,400 flying hours. He had been trained in England, with Boeing in America, and in Beirut and Brussels. He was reckoned a thoroughly satisfactory pilot, although his Belgian instructor had noticed a tendency to do routine duties on the flight deck himself rather than ask his crew. The Belgian's report was made three months before Flight 701: it noted that the routine duties were done at the expense of "handling the controls."*

Copilot Attayee was thought by a Boeing assessor on a training course he had recently completed to be "weak on instrument cross-checks. Forgets checklist."

At 1:13 A.M. the Boeing was at 24,000 feet over Wulpen, in Belgium. The few passengers who were not dozing had the choice of a drink or coffee. They could see clear to the Channel coast. Flight 701 passed into the London airways control zone.

"Gatwick's runway visual range is 100 meters . . . er . . . confirm your point of landing now," radioed the airways controller. The patch of fog at Gatwick was still refusing to budge. All night the controller had been diverting aircraft to London's Heathrow.

The weather at Heathrow was sharp and good—the sky was clear and the visibility on the runway 2,500 meters.

"Roger, we are trying . . . er . . . to Gatwick; we'll see later," Nowroz radioed back from his Boeing.

The controller was surprised: "701. I didn't get that. Again, please."

Still without much conviction, Nowroz repeated: "I say again . . . er . . . we are trying in Gatwick, 701." The controller caught it this time. He asked 701 to maintain height and course to the Mayfield beacon in East Sussex and then on to Gatwick.

To be certain that the pilot knew conditions, the controller repeated: "Gatwick visual range 100 meters." He told him to land on runway 27.

Nowroz acknowledged: "Gatwick. The runway 27." He did not repeat the visibility. It was well beneath limits. He needed a minimum visibility of half a mile and a cloud ceiling of 200 feet before company regulations allowed him to make an approach. The cloud was down on the runway. The visibility was 100 meters.

*HMSO CAP 244.

Flight 701 flew on. The controller gave it permission to descend to 8,000 feet. It was 1:20 A.M. The throttles on the Boeing were eased back. The engines hushed a little, and a few passengers stirred in their sleep as the aircraft slipped down over the Channel. The flight was smooth and routine.

The airways controller was still worried. The conditions at Gatwick nagged him. Did the pilot of 701, with that hint of a foreign accent, understand what things were like at Gatwick? He checked with Gatwick for the actual weather at the minute.

At 1:23 A.M. he called up Nowroz again. His voice was conciliatory. No British airport can be closed. Any pilot who wants to try to land, may do so. If it was of interest, though: "701, London. I just checked with Gatwick. The runway remains . . . the range remains at . . . er . . . 100 meters and there's no sign of improvement at the moment."

He expected Flight 701 to pull up and divert to starlit Heathrow. All the other flights had diverted—Gatwick was as silent and empty as the tomb. Most of the nonessential night staff had taken advantage of the fog and gone home.

But Flight 701 was continuing. "We'll try Gatwick . . . er . . . if we cannot make it at Gatwick will it be OK if we go to Heathrow?" Nowroz felt a little uncertain. He'd try Gatwick. If it was as bad as the controller said, he could always pull up and make for Heathrow. But it looked beautiful out of the cockpit window. As clear as a bell.

The controller acknowledged and cleared 701 down to 5,000 feet, with a direct course to the beacon at Mayfield. The red warning lights on the beacon flashed brightly over the Sussex countryside. Gatwick was only 20 miles away.

The radio circuits clattered in the cockpit as Attayee transferred to the frequency for Gatwick approach. London airways continued to take an interest in the flight, however, checking it on the radar screen. The aircraft had now slid down to 5,000 feet. The passengers were waking up as the warning signs for seat belts and no smoking lit above their heads.

Flight 701 was three minutes away from the Mayfield beacon. It was 1:27 A.M. When Captain Nowroz called up the approach controller, he had hoped for an improvement at Gatwick. It looked so clear everywhere else.

"Gatwick weather—surface wind is calm. Weather visibility is five zero 50 meters in freezing fog. Runway visual range is equal to 100 one zero zero meters. Temperature is −3." The controller dispelled the cockpit hopes. Gatwick lay under a pall of freezing fog bad enough to reduce traffic on the London–Brighton road a few yards away to a crawl.

Nowroz acknowledged the runway number and the barometric pressure, which he set into his altimeter. The controller was puzzled and uneasy. He had thought he would have an empty night, at least until the fog shifted. It was damp and cold. Even planes from the big airline based at Gatwick, now part of the international airline British Caledonian, whose pilots knew every nook and cranny of the airport, were heading elsewhere without a second thought this night.

"Er . . . 701, do you wish to make an approach?" he asked.

"That's affirmative," said Nowroz. The Gatwick controller cleared the tri-jet down to 2,000 feet.

The crew settled to their approach checks. The chief steward warned the passengers to put their seats upright, extinguish their cigarettes and tighten their safety belts. They were expecting to land in seven minutes. The steward did not mention the weather, but they could see the lights of Heathfield and the stars.

Altimeters were set and cross-checked. The crew chatted. "It's ground fog, not air fog," said Nowroz. "Yeah, once you get in it you have to be very f——ing slick."

The engineer was interested in the fog. He had heard the controllers going on about it in his headphones. "I suppose it'll be known as freezing fog, not moving," he said.

At 1:28 A.M. the controller turned the aircraft to the right. It had been winding down England parallel to the coast. Now it turned inland toward the runway.

"Alter course," said the captain. He banked to the right, steadying until the compass was pointing due north.

"What's the minimum?" he asked the copilot.

"Minimum?" said Attayee.

"Yeah," from the captain.

"Gatwick," said Attayee, flipping to Gatwick approach in his navigation manual. His finger found the Gatwick minimum, which he was supposed to abide by.

"Er, minimum two hundred [cloud base] and a half mile [visual range]," Attayee reported. They had zero and 100 meters.

"Two hundred and a half," Nowroz acknowledged. He fretted a little. How high was Gatwick above sea-level? "What's the elevation?" he asked.

"We don't see the . . ." Nowroz was interrupted by the worried approach controller again. "701 . . . er . . . in event of an overshoot will you be wishing to go back to Mayfield or proceed to London?" he asked.

"Er . . . proceed to Mayfield then proceed to London, 701," replied Nowroz. He set a cursor on the compass to 270 degrees, the heading he would take if he overshot.

At 1:29 A.M. the controller told the pilot that the flight had 13 miles to run to touchdown. At 1:29 A.M. and 44 seconds, the captain ordered "Flaps two." Attayee moved the flap lever low by his left hand to two degrees. The passengers heard the roar of the flap drives and the aircraft sunk its nose a little. The speed was 223 knots. It should have been 190.

At half past one, the approach controller ordered the aircraft to turn left and head west northwest. It would pick up the Instrument Landing System signals as it closed from the left. It had 11 miles to run. Nowroz banked the aircraft to the left. As it turned he coupled the automatic pilot to the ILS and selected "Glide-slope auto." The aircraft would automatically fly down the radio beam being sent out from the runway at an angle of 3.7 degrees.

"Flaps five." Again the flap drives clattered, and in the cockpit there was a burst of loud clicking as the stabilizer automatically countered the change of altitude as the flaps were lowered to five degrees. The speed was 40 knots too high at 200 knots.

The copilot saw the ILS instruments come alive as they neared the glide slope: "Outer marker number one identified," he called. Nowroz was content. Flight 701 was on the right profile, even if the speed was a little high.

"Roger, put flaps one five," he called.

As the flaps came to 15 degrees, the stabilizer ticked again, as it trimmed the aircraft. The flight was as near to the standard approach as it was to get. Height was almost perfect, the heading good, the speed coming back to 143 knots.

One hundred and forty three knots was the lowest speed to be recorded on the flight.

At 1:31 A.M. and 10 seconds, Attayee told Gatwick that he was established on the localizer. The plane was picking up the ILS properly. The controller cleared him to descend—he had been steady at 2,000 feet, with the automatic pilot on Hold Altitude. But he added: "In the event of . . . er . . . overshoot, climb on runway heading to 2,000 feet." The plane was eight miles from touchdown. There was the normal staccato of pilots concentrating on a blind approach.

"What is the flap?" asked Nowroz.

"Flaps at fifteen . . . glide slope alive," said Attayee as the plane flew into the narrow beam of the ILS glide slope.

"Gear down," said Nowroz.

"Gear is coming down." A rumble and bump jolted the cabin as the undercarriage started to extend. The speed was high but the flight profile otherwise good.

The throttles came back as power was reduced from 40 percent of takeoff power to 20 percent. The noise in the cabin died away as the undercarriage thumped into place.

"What's that red light?" Attayee had seen a single red light above the fog. "Yeah, that's the light at the end of 09." Nowroz thought it was a light at the end of the runway. It was not; it was a hazard warning light on a hill short of the runway. Flight 701 was still flying in clear air, but the fog was under it now.

Nowroz asked the engineer to see if the "stabilizer out of trim" warning light went on, as it had in Frankfurt, and to set the "bug points" on the airspeed indicator—144 knots, the minimum approach speed, on his ASI, and 124 knots, the ground or overshoot speed on Attayee's.

"V Ref set at 114 on your side," the engineer confirmed.

"OK, 124 set," said Attayee.

"Anti-skid five releases." The engineer checked the brakes of the wheels.

"Gear down and three green lights." Attayee confirmed that the undercarriage was locked in place.

"Standby for the flaps," said the engineer. It was 1:32 A.M. and 22 seconds. The plane had five and a quarter miles to run to touchdown.

Height and course were good as the autopilot began to fly the aircraft down the glide slope. Power was at "flight idle." The flaps were at 15 degrees. As the engineer spoke, they should have been going to 25 degrees, and shortly after to 40 degrees.

Nobody touched the flap lever. Nothing happened.

Little was said as the pilots scanned the fogbank beneath them for a clue, a reference. The autopilot had to push the nose down hard to get the aircraft onto the glide path, since the flaps were not extended enough for it to descend at the normal angle. The Altitude Hold switches had clicked off.

The increased airspeed demanded more nose-down trim to keep the aircraft on the glide slope. The passengers near the tail felt the upward swing as the nose went down. It was still very quiet.

It was quiet, too, in the cockpit. The pilots were looking out the windows. Gatwick approach gave final clearance to land at 1:32 A.M. and 42 seconds—"runway visual range still 100 meters."

The autopilot had used so much down elevator that it could no longer trim out the load on the stabilizer. The system was overloaded. The "stabilizer out of trim" light went on. The engineer spotted it at once.

Captain Nowroz punched a button on his control column, disconnecting the autopilot. He retrimmed the aircraft and continued the approach himself. His headphones buzzed as the aircraft crossed the outer marker at exactly 1:33 A.M.

Flight 701 was less than three miles away now, at 1,300 feet.

Gatwick acknowledged 701 over the outer marker. There was no further conversation. Gatwick was being called up by a British pilot based at Gatwick, asking, "I think we'll have to divert to . . . er . . . Luton. Could you just give me your last . . . er . . . RVR, please?" "One hundred meters," "Roger. That clinches the matter then. Thank you very much." He diverted.

"Flap three zero," Nowroz commanded. "Three zero coming

down," Attayee acknowledged. There was a stir in the cabin as the flap drives started to run, and the nose sank. The aircraft seemed to be going nose down, but with no lights below it, it was difficult to tell.

There was silence in the cockpit for the next 41 seconds. That is a long silence on a flight deck during an approach. Both pilots were searching outside the windshields. The flight instruments ran on their own.

These showed, in the soft red cockpit lighting, that Flight 701 was beginning to go amiss. The flaps moved from 15 degrees to 30, without the usual intermediate 25-degree stage.

This caused a marked pitch, which reached an attitude of 7 degrees nose down. The rate of descent accelerated. The aircraft sank below the radioed glide slope, leaving it at 1,200 feet with three and a half miles to run.

The plane was coming down at 1,200 feet a minute, twice the normal rate. It was 1:33 A.M. and 10 seconds, and the passengers could hear the increase in the engine noise as Captain Nowroz put on a little power.

For more than 40 seconds, the plane dropped farther beneath the glide slope. There was no comment from the crew. The landing lights bounced off the fog now, glistening back at the cockpit. They were still in clear air, descending from 1,000 feet to 500 feet in 22 seconds.

They entered the fog.

The crew strained forward, peering out the windshields. The runway lights had been switched on to 100 percent high intensity, and the red and white lights of the VASIS system, which tells the pilot if he is too high or low, were at 80 percent. Flight 701 never got near enough to see them. Precision Approach Radar, which pinpoints height, would have warned the crew that they were too low at 1:33 A.M. and 18 seconds. There was no Precision Approach Radar at Gatwick. It had been withdrawn 11 months before, on economy grounds; only military airfields normally have PAR nowadays.

The aircraft sank below 500 feet. It moved in the fog across two farmhouses. The nose was still well down at 6.5 degrees and the speed was 153 knots, where it should have been 125 knots for a serious attempt at landing.

At 1:33 A.M. and 46 seconds, Attayee broke the silence. "Four hundred feet." Nowroz queried it at once: "Four hundred feet?" He had not noticed it himself. As his Belgian instructor had noticed, he had been concentrating on other things at the expense of handling the controls. Attayee confirmed: "Yes, we have four hundred feet." Nowroz suddenly and acutely realized he was in danger. He had let himself be lured into the fog, and he had not been slick enough. He wanted out.

He tried to get the nose up, but the aircraft was nose-heavy. Attayee helped him pull on the control column, but they could only pull it back about an inch. Nowroz slammed the throttles wide open.

The passengers heard the roar as the engines opened up to takeoff power. In the field below, cattle scattered, and a power line slipped by invisible in the fog.

It took Nowroz six seconds to decide to abandon the landing and get up to a safe height. During that time, the aircraft lost another 120 feet.

As the nose slowly began to come up, the horrified Attayee saw trees filling the windshield. "We're finished," he screamed at 1:33 A.M. and 57 seconds.

A second later, Flight 701 brushed through treetops. It knocked a chimney pot off a house. Attayee saw more trees rushing toward him. One or two passengers had noticed the trees below them, but had not had enough time to take it in.

Panic started only when the right wing hit the tree trunks and was severed. The plane began to roll to the right. It broke clear of the trees and the undercarriage touched along a grass field.

It became airborne again, rolling to the right, the nose high now. The crew were shouting but the noises were unintelligible. The engines were still at full power, scorching the field, and the noise was shattering.

The tail of the aircraft, heavy with three engines, slammed into the bedroom of a house. The occupants, Mr. and Mrs. Jones, died instantly, as the house collapsed. The central engine and the stabilizer were trapped in the ruins of the house. They pulled down a ceiling, and the Joneses' baby's cot dropped to the ground floor. Rubble covered it, keeping the flames off the baby. The baby lived.

The rest of the plane started to spread itself over two fields. The wreckage trail was 1,395 feet long. The passengers in the back of the cabin were dying rapidly now.

Fire broke out. It was fed by the spray of fuel from the ruptured tanks and started to eat away at the wings and fuselage. Several passengers were thrown clear into the fields. Only seven had been killed by the crash impact, but the fire went through the survivors rapidly.

The crew leaped out of the window exits in the wrecked cockpit. As the flames reached the cockpit, the radio crackled: "Ariana 701. This is Gatwick Approach. Do you read? . . . Ariana 701. This is Gatwick Approach. Do you read?"

London airways' controllers were worried too: "I've lost sight of him now at about two miles from the runway," said one. "See if he pops up the other side or stays down . . . I reckon he's either landed or crashed."

Only 11 passengers and the 2 pilots and flight engineer survived; 43 passengers, 4 cabin staff and the ground engineer died. It was 1:34 A.M.*

The most common cause of crashes is pilot error. Some of the mistakes pilots make are chillingly simple, like the Ariana pilot forgetting to use his flaps in the correct sequence and thinking that the autopilot was not working properly when in fact it was overloaded.

Three incidents show that the crews of even a leading international airline are subject to making the most simple errors. The airline is British Airways and the aircraft in each case was a 747.

Flight BA 029 was a scheduled service between Heathrow and Johannesburg, stopping at Zurich and Nairobi.† It had a three-

---

*Captain Nowroz was grounded after the crash, and now works as an operations training superintendent for Ariana on the ground in Kabul. A. Z. Attayee, the copilot, is still flying Ariana 727's, and the flight engineer, M. H. Formuly, is on Boeing 720's.

†AIB Bulletin 16/74.

man flight crew, the captain, copilot and a flight engineer. There were 15 cabin staff to look after the 281 passengers.

The flight went smoothly until the aircraft was 172 miles from Nairobi, about half an hour out. The captain briefed the copilot and the engineer for the approach and landing. He noted the airport's height. Nairobi is 5,327 feet above sea level.

At 4:45 A.M. on September 3, 1974, the aircraft started its descent. It leveled off at 12,000 feet 20 minutes later, with 36 miles to run. The sky was clear and the Ngong hills spread out beneath the crew. Beyond the hills, the plateau surrounding Nairobi Airport was covered by low cloud. The big plane slipped down to 10,000 feet.

At 5:08 A.M. and 59 seconds, the Nairobi radar controller called them again: "Speedbird [the BA call sign] 029 . . . descend seven five zero zero feet."

Neither pilot heard this right. The copilot called back without hesitation: "Roger. Speedbird 029 cleared to five thousand feet." The radar controller did not remark on the error.

Flight 029 was now headed for disaster. The pilots thought they had been cleared down to 5,000 feet—which, given Nairobi's height, was 327 feet *below* the runways. The clearance was to "seven five zero zero feet," 7,500 feet.

The aircraft was losing height at 1,900 feet a minute. It entered the bank of low cloud which obscured the Nairobi plateau. The crew could no longer see the ground, nor would they expect to until they were almost at the airfield.

At 5:10 A.M. and 38 seconds, the aircraft "captured" the Instrument Landing System. But Flight 029 was flying far below the ideal glide slope. The ILS deviation light flashed on. The flight engineer noticed that the glide-slope pointers on the ILS were pointing "UP" so much that they were out of view. "We have no glide scope," he said. "We have," said the captain, who thought the engineer meant that the system had failed.

At 5:11 A.M. the aircraft was 10 miles from touchdown, and was cleared to land. It was still sinking at 1,650 feet a minute. At 5:11 A.M. and 42 seconds it was only 270 feet above the ground and the decision height warning began to sound automatically.

The engineer called "Two-hundred-foot decision height." Normally it comes immediately before landing at the height at which pilots must be able to see the runway if a landing is to be continued.

Almost at once, the aircraft broke out of cloud. The captain saw dark rocks and the ground. He pulled back on the controls and put on power. It was 5:11 A.M. and 50 seconds. The aircraft sank to within 70 feet of the rocks and thornscrub as it struggled for height. It was eight miles short of the airfield.

Two hundred and ninety-nine souls poised on the edge of eternity. Then the engines bit into the air, and the captain took the plane back to a safe height and on to a correct landing. He remained convinced that the controller had cleared him to 5,000 feet until the tapes of the conversation between the plane and the ground were replayed. The controller was heard to say: "seven five zero zero feet." In any event, the captain must have known that 5,000 feet in this area was below ground level.

Experience is no guard against this type of error: the captain had been with the airline for 32 years and had more than 18,000 flying hours.

(British Airways has been singularly lucky at Nairobi. On February 2, 1964, a BA Comet was approaching the airport when the pilot set his altimeter at 938 millibars instead of 839. This made the aircraft appear 3,000 feet higher than it was. The error was not checked, and the aircraft touched down in Kitengele game park, nine miles from the runway. Miraculously, the pilots managed to fly it away.)

In the second incident, a BA 747 was on a final approach to Bahrein when the captain leveled off too high. The aircraft came down tail first, banging the tail on the runway. It was night, and the aircraft took off for Bombay without the tail having been properly inspected. On arrival, having crossed the waters of the Indian Ocean, it was found to be damaged. Such damage to the tail could lead to rapid decompression of the cargo and passengers' cabins.

The third accident was at Kuala Lumpur on May 12, 1976.*

*AIB Bulletin 6/76.

Flight BA 888 left Heathrow on a Monday night bound for Melbourne with three stops on the way. Shortly after midnight on Tuesday it started its approach to Kuala Lumpur airport, Malaysia. It was a fine calm night and when the Jumbo was within 15 miles of the airfield the runway lights were clearly visible to the pilots. The captain, in the left seat, decided to make the landing himself from the northwest.

From this direction the airport has no ILS. Instead, pilots use the less accurate kind of radio beacon, VOR, which is sited to the north and is not exactly in line with the runway.

This means that the pilot must calculate his own rate of descent from the airport landing chart. As he passes over the VOR beacon he starts his stopwatch and monitors the times and heights until he reaches the final radio beacon, called NM, which lies four and a half miles from the runway.

The normal angle of descent is three degrees. Pilots use a rough rule of thumb to check their height on the slope at set points on the approach by simply multiplying the distance from the runway (in nautical miles) by three. This gives the correct height in hundreds of feet.

When BA 888 was six miles from touchdown it should therefore have been at a safety height of 1,800 feet. But it was at only 980 feet and its sinkrate was too fast and steep for a three-degree slope.

The pilots still had a full view of the runway lights ahead and remained unaware of their dangerous rate of descent. As they passed the final radio beacon NM with four miles to run, they were distracted by a misunderstanding about the amount of landing flap that had been selected.

The plane should then have been at 1,200 feet with a speed of 168 mph. Its actual height was 600 feet and traveling at 204 mph—well beyond the safety limits.

A few seconds later the captain called: "Can anyone see the runway?" Almost at the same instant his copilot called "One hundred feet above ground"—a routine call that normally comes during the last seconds before touchdown. They were still three miles away from the runway and should have been at 800 feet.

The captain applied full power instantly and started to climb. As he radioed to the airport controller that he was overshooting, two heavy thumps shook the plane as it hit the tops of the forest trees 150 feet above the airport level, and two miles from the runway.

When they had climbed to a safe height, the crew checked for damage, particularly to the undercarriage, which had been lowered before impact with the trees. Luckily, they were able to land safely 18 minutes later.

All these incidents took place during the approach and landing. This is by far the most dangerous part of a flight, accounting for up to 87 percent of crashes in some years, and almost always for more than half. Takeoff accounts for a further third or so, with en route accidents never exceeding one in ten.

The great bulk is caused by pilot error. IATA's senior safety officer, Lawson C. White, carried out a special investigation.* Of 63 jet crashes during landing, 44 were caused by pilot error, 16 were for undetermined reasons, 2 were caused by weather, 1 by a ground controller, and none resulted from mechanical faults.

Lawson C. White analyzed the crashes and pointed out: "Many of the accidents classified as pilot error I am convinced were the result of another human error other than the pilot's. Someone who forgot that pilots are normal. There is only so much information a pilot can receive and integrate at a given time. Anything in excess of this is not conducive to human reliability."

White noted that most of the accidents followed a deviation from normal operating practices. "Flying is the type of occupation which encourages free expression . . . There still seems to be a few who cannot resist the free expression and cause so much concern, especially to the other crew members who fly with them."

He emphasizes the need to fly by the book: "Clearances are meant to be adhered to, discipline is all important and accurate flying is essential in order to survive."

Accidents would be avoided if greater use was made of the flight data recorder, the "black box" which records what happens on a

---

*"Safety in the Accident Prone Flight Phases of Takeoff and Approach and Landing," by Lawson C. White, IATA, November 1972.

flight.* White was disappointed by safety exchange information between the airlines. This has been due to the legal problems that could arise if an airline admitted to the cause of an accident in a safety report: "It seems iniquitous that because of this liability problem, airlines are forced to withhold information which could help to prevent a future and perhaps catastrophic accident."

White also found that pilots were unwilling to contribute to safety by noting their mistakes. "Looking through 1,400 or so reports . . . one is also struck by the lack of pilot input, reports on incidents which the pilot knew were only a hairsbreadth away from being an accident. There is a natural reluctance to admit one's failings, nevertheless, the pilot profession demands a high degree of responsibility and this responsibility should be taken to include a requirement to inform others regarding one's own mistakes."

Pilots literally do not own up to incidents for fear of the sack even though the transmission of those incidents among other pilots would help prevent their repetition. The fear is justified, since pilots have been fired on the spot after admitting incidents.

White's descriptions of landing accidents make dispiriting reading for those who put their faith in gold stripes. The prominent cause is given and fatalities to crew and passengers: "Pilot failed to arrest excessive descent. Neglected altitude-speed control." United Airlines Boeing 727. No crew, 43 passengers killed. "Aircraft entered steep rate of descent as a result of pilot maneuvering the aircraft to execute approach at a lower altitude in bad weather. Pilot misjudged approach." CPA DC-8. Ten crew, 54 passengers killed. "Crew failed to monitor altitude of deteriorating visibility." American Airlines Boeing 727. Six crew and 52

---

*The "black box," in fact red, stores information on steel tapes. It records time, speed, course, acceleration and height. It is normally installed in the tail, which has the best chance of surviving a crash. It is built to withstand fire of more than 1,000 degrees Centigrade, acceleration of 1,000g and immersion in sea water for a month. Many are fitted with beacons for underwater recovery: the black box from a Boeing 707 was found 10,000 feet under the Mediterranean four weeks after the crash. Cockpit Voice Recorders are standard on most airliners. They record all conversation in the cockpit. Pilots were worried about them as "spies in the cockpit" so the tapes are wiped clean every 30 minutes and are played back only after an incident.

passengers killed. "Pilot attempted night visual approach in deteriorating weather, over a partially lighted terrain without altimeter cross-reference." TWA Convair 880. Five crew and 60 passengers killed.

The litany goes on: "Pilot deviated from prescribed track. He was too high for straight approach." Varig 707. Seventeen and 80. "Premature descent during a visual approach by night initiated from an incorrectly identified point." Air France 707. Eleven and 52. "Lack of crew coordination and inadequate monitoring of aircraft position in space." SAS DC-8. Three and 12. "Pilot miscalculated his position and collided against mountain." Air India 707. Eleven and 106. "Navigation error on the part of the pilot. Premature descent." Alitalia DC-8. Nine and 85. "Pilot failed to execute approved instrument safety procedure." Mexicana 727. Seven and 72.

White found that takeoff accidents were totally different. They are much rarer than those on landing. White computed an accident rate which makes a crash on takeoff a two million to one chance. Most were caused by mechanical failure, particularly to the engine or engine-powered systems rather than pilot error. Other causes varied from detached tire treads, to an Air India 707 whose undercarriage collapsed after hitting a cow, to a PIA Trident which hit a vulture at Lahore and a Delta DC-9 which hit a buzzard at Savannah.

Crashes on small and financially rocky airlines have been caused by pilots flying in poor conditions simply because the company needed the revenue. A DC-3 of General Airways* took off into low cloud, bad visibility, snow, freezing precipitation and icing conditions over Texas. The wings began to ice up and fuel ran low. The captain, who was killed in the ensuing crash, was attributed with "indifference to elementary rules of flight safety, coupled with severe economic compulsion." If he had not taken off, the airline would have had to pay board and lodging for the passengers.

Errors in reading altimeters have killed as many pilots as

*ICAO Accident Digest, No. 11, p. 79.

anything by confusing them into fatal error. Altimeters often have three hands on the face, one pointing at hundreds of feet, one in thousands of feet and the other in tens of thousands. Muddle the three and the aircraft is flown straight into the ground when the crew think it is several thousand feet up.

This has happened several times: to the passengers and crew of an Iberia Airlines Caravelle in Sussex; a Lockheed Electra in New York; a DC-6 at Acapulco; a Viscount at Prestwick; a Britannia in Hampshire; a VC-10 in Nigeria; another Britannia in Yugoslavia; an Air India Boeing on Mont Blanc; an Air France Caravelle; a Pan Am Boeing; and many more. Millions of dollars and hundreds of lives have been lost because altimeters, like watches, have two hands. Like watches, in the dark or when the owner is new to the model, they are misread.

Moreover, the pilot has to juggle with two different altimeter settings. During the cruise, he will use a standard barometric setting. But for greater accuracy while landing, he will adjust to the exact barometric pressure of the area. He sets the QNH, which gives his height above sea level, and which at a high airport like Nairobi will read 5,300 feet even after he has landed. For height above the ground, he uses the radio altimeter. He concentrates on this below 2,500 feet.

Pilots, not unremarkably, are prone to the same failings as the rest of us, such as indecision. The only difference is that they are severely punished for this. A pilot spends his working life making decisions—it is what distinguishes his job and justifies his high salary. Very occasionally, a pilot does not really make up his mind and drifts into an accident.

Captain Nowroz is an example. He never really decided to land at Gatwick. "We'll try Gatwick . . . er . . . if we cannot make it at Gatwick will it be OK if we go to Heathrow?" He had only decided to have a look, which is a different thing.

Friction between captains trained in the rigorous days of wartime flying and their young, commercially brought-up copilots can be predictably severe. Some captains refer to their crews as "milk runners," with their easy and noncombative lives. The crews react by calling ex-wartime pilots the "bomber buggers."

The captain of a DC-8 at Heathrow, also on a foggy night, taxied slowly out for takeoff.* He could not decide which runway to use. Twice he started a takeoff but aborted and stopped. On the third attempt, he thought the controls had locked when the aircraft had reached takeoff speed. He slammed the throttles shut and braked, but the aircraft crashed into a cabbage field at the end of the runway. There was nothing wrong with the plane.

There is a known copilot problem, called the "Captain God Complex." Here the man in the right-hand seat, the copilot, develops an inferiority complex to the captain on his left. It is entirely at the captain's discretion whether to allow him to fly a takeoff or landing. Copilots can be airborne for months without getting any real handling experience.

A pattern of errors is established. Copilots make particular mistakes when they do fly a sector: they are prone to takeoff swing and landing veer, to very bumpy landings and to crashing short of the runway through getting too low on the approach. Captains, on the other hand, handle things wrong when they act as copilot. They are responsible for "premature withdrawal of the undercarriage" (official terminology for pulling up the gear before the plane is airborne) and wrong selection of flaps and undercarriage on landing.

It is difficult to change concentration. A pilot often has to change from flying his aircraft from instruments a few inches in front of him to looking at a rain-soaked runway half a mile away. That runway has to make immediate sense—its distance, its angle relative to the speed and descent of the plane, all judged by eye.

It may be night and raining, gusty with crosswinds on the runway so that he has to crab the aircraft into the wind. On a long-haul route, the pilot may not have seen the ground or flown the aircraft by eye for eight hours or more.

Take a pilot flying into Bombay when the monsoon is on. The controllers talk to him in heavily accented English. His aircraft bumps and swings in the cloud. He scans the instruments for speed, rate of descent, engine power, compass heading, height.

*CAA 21/63. All on board survived.

He watches the model on the artificial horizon, trying to anticipate it as it lurches in the turbulence. It is raining in the cloud and the windshield wipers are going, but nobody is looking out through the windows.

His left hand and his feet control the aircraft with small, coordinated movements. His right hand must be free for other tasks, such as stroking the throttles back. The other pilot is busy selecting flap, changing radio circuits, flipping the "No Smoking" and "Seat Belt" signs on, setting the altimeters, putting the undercarriage down.

His eyes are totally adjusted to the soft red lighting of the cockpit. He has not seen the ground since he left Europe nine hours before.

Slowly the aircraft lets down from the cloud. With 800 feet left on the altimeter, his copilot says he can see the airport. He looks up from the artificial horizon. There is no real horizon. Rain is drumming off the windshield and the wipers distort the glass as they clear it. The forward speed is 180 mph, as fast as a Grand Prix car flat out. There is half a mile to go. The wind is gusting off the Indian Ocean.

Touchdown will be in 15 seconds. He has just 15 seconds to decide whether he has satisfied the demands of three dimensions for a safe landing, and to set it down, 15 seconds of sight after hours of instruments. It is asking a great deal. Sometimes it is too much.

Any pilot will opt to fly by sight rather than on instruments when he can. It's easier; he can cut corners and get through more quickly. There has been a fatal tendency for a pilot who has carried out an instrument approach in cloud to go visual as soon as he is below the cloud. He will try to maintain visual flying even if he has to overshoot: instrument overshoots are complicated. But he may well go back into cloud while circling, and in the involuntary transition from eyes to instruments while close to the ground there is great danger.

At least sixty major accidents have been caused by pilots trying to fly visually in instrument weather.

A special committee of the British Air Line Pilots' Association examined flight fatigue in great detail, producing a lengthy report.* It accepted that "pilot error" was the biggest single cause of aircraft accidents but said that fatigue is the most readily rectifiable component of pilot error.

Some of the cases the committee recorded are highly disturbing. A VC-10 captain wrote to his flight manager: "At chocks under [end of flight] at Hong Kong I had been on duty 14 hours and had been without sleep for 25 hours and 15 minutes. In my opinion the condition of the flight deck crew on arrival at Hong Kong was totally unfitted for duty. Both my first officers fell asleep more than once during the flight from Darwin, and in fact I had to waken one of them to give him the approach briefing."

Other pilots reported extreme fatigue. "About an hour after takeoff from Manchester, at about 0900 GMT, the navigator stated that he was the only one awake." "Two serious errors—flaps called for and not selected—and no one noticed till a dangerously low airspeed. The approach was low." "Both the first officer and the engineer were falling asleep during the last two hours prior to descent. The first officer forgot to call final heights from radio altimeter and I was finding difficulty in keeping eyes open on final approach."

Pilots complain of disorientation through time-zone changes. "To start with, the four days it takes to get to Tokyo [from Europe] with a time difference of eight hours leaves one with a colossal inability to sleep in Tokyo," one wrote to BALPA. "During the 40 hours off there, I would say that 75 percent of the crew were snatching the odd few hours sleep their body would allow them during the rest period.

"Consequently, out of Tokyo, everybody was more than a little disoriented. From here follows the Hong Kong–Delhi–Hong Kong–Delhi shuttle. . . . This necessitates a stop at Rangoon for refueling. Weather at Hong Kong and on route was pretty diabolical, coupled with temperatures of 115 degrees Fahrenheit in Delhi (monsoon starting shortly, with similar problems), all combined to produce a very tired crew.

*Flight Fatigue, Report of the Special Committee. BALPA. London, 1973.

"Finally the last straw; Delhi, Beirut, Frankfurt, then as passenger home on the same aircraft, was 14 hours 30 minutes duty time. Thus three night duties and one day duty stretching into night within the last five days, coupled with an eight-hour time change."

The pilot ended: "This doesn't make Jack a very safe boy." This is far from reassuring for any passenger.

The pilots claim that there has been evidence of pilot fatigue in many crashes involving pilot error. The crew of a BAC 111, which crashed at Milan after they shut down the good engine after an engine failure to the other, had been on duty for 13 hours 53 minutes. A DC-4 on a vacation charter from the Mediterranean crashed at Stockport, killing 72, the pilot having been on duty for 12 hours 55 minutes. A VC-10 crew slammed into the ground near Lagos, killing all 87 aboard, after 10 hours 35 minutes on duty.

Fatigue often leads to tension between pilots and airline management, who consider that demands for shorter hours are sparked off by industrial reasons and not safety. A pilot wrote of his airline doctor: "He just took my pulse and said that if I was trying to get at the management, then the medical people did not want to be involved."

The worst-affected pilots tend to be those whose day-night-day work patterns are superimposed on the effect of continual time-zone changes as the crews cross and recross the Atlantic or the U.S.

All of us are prone to regression, particularly when tired: under stress we tend to go back to what we were first taught. Thus pilots can try to fly a jet in an emergency as they would the turboprop or propeller aircraft they learned on. This has serious implications on the approach, where pilots miss the immediate response in power when the throttles are opened that the prop planes had, and the slowing effect of idling propellers. Crashing short of the runway has been an all-too-common accident for jet pilots trained on props.

Some pilots have "left-right" problems. Confusion between left and right is not uncommon. For years the British Army would put a piece of straw on a recruit's left foot and would order "straw foot forward," so the recruit could look down to determine his "straw foot." One Norwegian fighter pilot flies with his watch clearly visible on his left arm to help him.

Nevertheless, crashes occur. A Dove, a twin-engine propeller aircraft, was landing at Heathrow when it suffered falling oil pressure. The pilot stopped the port engine, bringing the pitch control back through the feathering gate. When the propeller had stopped he switched off the port engine switches. It was the starboard engine that had a fractured crankshaft. He had identified it correctly on the radio to the tower, but then he shut down the wrong engine.

Aircraft can survive a wide range of potential disasters. One four-engine passenger jet has even survived a total engine failure, when all four stopped at 37,000 feet. The British Airways Super VC-10 was cruising from Hong Kong to Tokyo at 37,000 feet when the No. 3 engine failed and was shut down.*

Almost immediately, the No. 1, 2, and 4 engines ran down. There was a complete electrical failure, since the generators are run off the engines. The crew managed to establish the aircraft in a dive of 3,000 feet a minute at an indicated airspeed of 290 knots. It would take the powerless aircraft 12 minutes to fall into the dark sea beneath it. They were flying on emergency lighting, standby instruments and limited flying controls. There were no yaw dampers to prevent the nose swinging from side to side, and the aircraft started to roll badly.†

The divergent Dutch roll became serious, with bank angles of 45 degrees as the plane rolled wing up, wing down out of control. The yaw was also considerable. The crew turned the aircraft 90 degrees to get it off the airway: it might otherwise have slammed into aircraft below it as it made its rapid descent.

Partly extended speed brakes were used to assist in controlling the Dutch roll. The transponder was tuned to the emergency setting and an attempt was made to transmit a MAYDAY distress

---

*AIB Bulletin 20/74.

†The VC-10 is very prone to Dutch roll. Its three-section rudder has a yaw damper on each section. With the yaw dampers inoperative, a VC-10 at cruising speed will roll to 45 degrees of bank within 12 seconds.

call. The crew lowered the electrical ram air turbine, the ELRAT. This is a turbine which is driven by the rush of air when it is lowered under the wing. The airflow of 290 knots was enough to get it spinning and generating power, exactly as a windmill produces electricity. The crew got power back on the flying controls and on the standby yaw damper.

As the aircraft came back under control, the crew established the cause of the engine failures. They restarted all four engines with the help of ELRAT and got the aircraft back to normal at 28,000 feet, three minutes after it had first plunged down. They climbed back to 37,000 feet and flew on safely to Tokyo.

The cause of the incident was simple. The No. 4 fuel tank had been allowed to empty at a time when all four engines were being fed from that tank in order to correct an imbalance between left and right wing fuel quantities. The engines stopped because they ran out of fuel, a classic case of crew error.

In a similar case, all three engines stopped on a 727 off the Florida coast. The National Airlines flight, with 111 aboard, was cruising at 33,000 feet on the run from Fort Lauderdale to Newark. Suddenly, one after another, all three engines stopped.

In all, five minutes elapsed between the loss of the first engine and the successful restarting of the third and last. The flight engineer had forgotten to turn on the boost pumps needed to help feed fuel into the engines at that height. National disciplined him.

Pilots have pushed aircraft beyond their limits and broken them up, although fortunately this is restricted to training flights. Thus a Braniff captain was flying a 707 with a Boeing test pilot as instructor. During one of a series of Dutch rolls, which were beyond the maximum bank angles permitted for the aircraft, the aircraft went out of control. The No. 1, 2 and 4 jet pods were torn off by loads beyond the design strength. The aircraft, on fire and with only one engine left, was crash-landed along a river.*

Five years later, in 1964, a Lufthansa Boeing was flying in the **Winerzburg-Ansbach area.**† The three-man crew was on a training

*CAA 21/59.
†CAA 16/64.

flight at 13,000 feet, flying VFR. The aircraft rolled right over once, far beyond the design maximum. On the second roll it went out of control while upside down, and it became overstressed and disintegrated.

The crew died. The accident report revealed that "there were no signs of any technical defect or technical failure of any unusual nature of the aircraft or of weather influences as causative or contributive factors. There is nothing to say that the two rolls were not intentional."

There can be no training against error or recklessness. Pilots are symbols of stability and stern sense. They can be frighteningly different from their image, even with the very best airlines.

This is part of the radio communication between ground control and the crew of a DC-9 jet landing at Fort Lauderdale, Florida.* The plane is on a flight for Eastern Airlines, Flight 346. A thunderstorm is taking place.

Flight 346: "Hello, approach man, Eastern 346, maintaining three [thousand feet]."

Miami Approach: "Roger, Eastern 346, fly heading 300, maintain 3,000 to runway 9L final approach course, following a Northeast DC-9." (This identical aircraft decided rightly that the weather was below limits and did not attempt to land.)

346: "OK, how about a 320 heading here? We're just trying to stay clear of some showers."

Miami: "Yes, sir; that's good enough . . . Eastern 346 descend and maintain 2,000 [feet altitude]."

346: "Out of three for 2,000, Eastern 346."

Miami: "Roger, new weather at Lauderdale estimated 700 overcast, one-half mile, thunderstorm, heavy rain showers . . . The glide slope is out of service [for the Instrument Landing System]."

346: "Ah, f——."

Miami: "Eastern 346, what do you need to shoot at it with

*NTSB AAR 72-31.

the glide slope out? [What weather minima to attempt a landing?]"

346: "Ah, moment . . ."

Miami: "Eastern 346, turn left heading 270."

346: "Two seven zero, 346. Can we get lower?"

Miami: "Ah, are you going to make the approach?"

346: "Four, four-sixty we need [460 feet height of cloud ceiling above the runway]. If we got 700, it's enough."

Miami: "OK, sir, ah, descend to 1,700, turn right heading 360."

346: "Three-sixty down to seven—say again."

Miami: "Descend to 1,700, reduce to 160 knots now, please."

346: "OK."

Miami: "Eastern 346, turn right heading 070, cleared straight in, ah, localizer runway 9—left approach Fort Lauderdale airport. Glide slope inoperative."

346: "Three-forty-six, right."

Miami: "Eastern 346, contact the tower 119.3 [radio frequency]."

346: "Nineteen-three, and have a happy. Tower man, Eastern 346."

Fort Lauderdale Tower: "Eastern 346, Fort Lauderdale Tower, report the marker inbound for nine left, wind 180 degrees at 10 [knots]. Estimated 700 [feet cloud ceiling], overcast, half mile [forward visibility], heavy rain shower over the airport."

There was to be more air-to-ground talk, but cockpit talk continued:

Captain: "Get it lined up with . . ."

Copilot: "Put the VOR on yours [for an instrument approach]."

Captain: "Right, you got the localizer on yours?"

Co: "Yeah."

Co: "Gimme 25 [degrees of flap]."

Captain: "No, you'd better get over there, get on the localizer."

Co: "That's 460 feet. I haven't heard that marker come in yet . . . see if they can give us a radar fix to find out how far we're out."

Co: "50 [degrees of] flaps."

Captain: "I'd use . . . 25."

The captain took over the controls.

Co: "There's the runway, right under us."

At this point the aircraft crashed. It broke apart at the tail and was destroyed by fire, although nobody was killed. The pilots had begun the approach after another DC-9 had turned back because of bad weather. They did not carry out landing checks. They never reported passing the outer marker and never got clearance to land. When they crashed, the flaps were fully down and the throttles at idle—a combination giving the plane its maximum rate of sink.

Most chilling, they were both fully qualified pilots flying with a highly respected airline.

24

Mechanical Failure

Mechanical and airframe failure accounts for most nonpilot error crashes. A pilot must never exceed his aircraft's specifications or disaster will result. The values on modern jets are fine and they must be flown accurately: if a minimum approach speed of 143 knots is given and the pilot comes in at 110 knots, he will crash.

Each aircraft type has a limitations book, which the pilot must adhere to or his machine will be in instant distress. The limitations are broad-ranging, as a look at a 707's book shows.

The machine is sensitive to weight. The maximum taxi weight is 160 tons (a 747 is 358 tons). This weight would be dangerous in flight after the flaps are brought in and wing lift is reduced. The in-flight maximum is four tons less with flaps in—the aircraft will have lost weight anyway through burning off fuel on taxiing and takeoff. Maximum landing weight is 110 tons, so 50 tons of fuel have to be burned off or dumped before a fully laden aircraft can land again.

The aircraft must only be operated when ground temperatures are between −54 degrees Centigrade (−65 degrees Fahrenheit) and 49 degrees Centigrade (120 degrees Fahrenheit). The takeoff altitude limits are from 1,000 feet below sea level to 10,000 feet above. Runway slopes must not exceed two degrees; tail winds must not exceed 10 knots. En route maximum altitude is 42,000 feet.

The engine exhaust gas temperature reaches a maximum of 555 degrees Centigrade on takeoff for five minutes; the maximum continuous temperature is 490 degrees Centigrade. Oil pressures must keep within 35 and 55 pounds per square inch, with an upper temperature limit of 143 degrees Centigrade.

There is a host of maximum airspeed limitations. With flaps fully extended, the pilot must not exceed 195 knots; with takeoff flaps at 14 degrees he can go up to 223 knots. The undercarriage can be put down at 270 knots. Flaps cannot be extended above 20,000 feet.

Emergency drills are set out on yellow cards. Engine failure on takeoff is the most commonly practiced. If it occurs before V1—the computed decision speed at which a takeoff can still be abandoned—the pilot immediately applies full brakes and closes the throttles. The speed brakes on the wings are put up at 60 degrees, and reverse thrust is used on the operating engines.

After V1 the pilot has to continue, building up speed and taking off. As soon as he is climbing, the pilot gets the undercarriage up. V2 is the lowest safety speed. The flaps come in at V2 plus 30 knots at a height of 800 feet. The aircraft is then flown level until the speed builds up to V2 plus 50 knots.

At V2 plus 50 knots the aircraft can fly up to a safe height to dump fuel, at 8,000 feet and above. The flaps and speed brakes must be in during dumping. The dump chutes, pipes that extend under the aircraft, are lowered at a maximum speed of 240 knots. Once the chutes are down, the aircraft accelerates to 275 knots as the aircraft load is lightened as the fuel is pumped out. Normal dump time is from 10 to 20 minutes.

An engine-out landing involves a slightly higher approach speed to maintain lift. Modern jets can land with two engines out. An aircraft with two engines out is set up in the approach somewhat above the normal landing speed. The turbocompressors and bleeds are switched off to keep maximum power. Six miles out 14 degrees of flap are selected.

A speed 30 knots above normal has to be maintained all the way in now. The gear goes down as late as possible. Rudder trim has to be zeroed at 500 feet. The loading on the rudder, carried by the asymmetrical engine thrust, could be trimmed out during the cruise and approach.

The commit point is at 300 feet. If the crippled plane is off line and height for the runway, it can go around for another try as long as it stays above 300 feet. The thrust is increased slowly, because it increases the asymmetric yaw from the engines, which must be controlled with the rudder. The flaps come in, and slowly, very slowly the aircraft will creep back to a safe speed to circle around again.

Below 300 feet, the aircraft is committed to land; if it veers off course, nothing can be done about it. The speed is very fast, 30 knots above normal, and the crew will be sweating with the exertion of keeping the aircraft straight. Even with rudder boost, preventing yaw on the rudder will take all the strength in their legs. The throttles have to be played with delicately as the plane drifts crabwise across the runway. When the gear hits, maximum braking is necessary straightaway to compensate for the lack of reverse thrust.

A failure of the hydraulic system also causes abnormal landings. Flaps, undercarriage, spoilers, speed brakes and nosewheel steering are all normally hydraulically operated. The pilot first makes sure that he has "dumped," or turned off, the hydraulics on these to prevent them working unintentionally.

The approach is made at 15 knots above normal speed. The undercarriage has to be extended manually, by turning a cranking handle, a slow and laborious job. Once it is down, it cannot be gotten up again, so the aircraft cannot divert easily to another airport. The flaps are worked electrically. The aircraft is lined up very carefully on the runway since there is no nosewheel steering and the aircraft has to be running straight when the rudder ceases to steer at 80 mph.

Reverse thrust is put on immediately on touchdown. The reservoir in the brakes should stop the aircraft although emergency pneumatic brakes can be used in the last resort.

A problem of the modern pilot is the stuck, stalled or runaway stabilizer. Most jets have variable incidence stabilizers, where the tail moves up and down to establish the rough angle of climb or descent, and smaller elevators are used for accurate trim.

A runaway stabilizer is when the tail starts moving of its own accord. When it happens, the manual trim wheel spins in the cockpit and the pilot must immediately cut out the stabilizer switch and circuit breakers and grab the trim wheel with his hand and stop it.

When this wheel spin is stopped, the pilot can wind the stabilizer by hand on the wheel or adopt the procedure for a stuck stabilizer. With a stuck stabilizer, the pilot must keep a constant speed for as long as possible in order to maintain his trim.

He then makes a jammed stabilizer landing. This is again physically exhausting, with constant pulling needed on the control column. The basic nose-up and nose-down pitch of the aircraft is controlled by the flaps and speed brakes. The flaps put the nose down, since they are under the back of the wings, and the speed brakes above push it up. Fine trim is maintained with the elevators.

By pulling circuit breakers, the pilot isolates the inboard flaps to use for the landing. He uses the outer flaps to keep the nose down. The inboard flaps go down to 50 degrees at an early stage, and the trim is maintained with the speed brakes. The aircraft must only bank gently, or the nose will be pulled down too far for recovery. If, as is most likely, the tail jammed while cruising, any reduction in speed will tend to put the nose down. Pulling back on the stick could exhaust the pilots. This is checked by moving the aircraft's center of gravity aft, either by moving the passengers or by transferring fuel to the back.

Stabilizers can also stall, when the load on the stabilizer is so great that the motor drive cannot move it. An aircraft can recover from a full nose-down stall or runaway, although it requires great courage and skill from the pilot.

Against all natural inclination, the pilot must not pull back on the stick even though he is hurtling earthward. This makes things worse since the stabilizer cannot recover while the controls are forcing on it. It will recover only when it is relieved of pressure. Neither must the pilot throttle back, even though his speed in the dive will be approaching the design limit. Throttling back simply puts the nose even farther down.

The speed brakes are pulled fully up, and very slowly as the aircraft loses height, the nose starts to come up and the speed drops off. Gradually the forces on the stabilizer reduce and the controls are effective again.

Two aircraft which suffered structural failure in flight were the Hawker Siddeley Comet and the Lockheed Electra. The Comet suffered from metal fatigue in the fuselage and was grounded after a series of crashes in 1954. Later it was modified and made fully safe.

An accident report on an Electra which crashed in Indiana in 1960, killing 63, said that there had been an "in-flight separation of the right wing because of flutter induced by oscillation of the outboard nacelles." In simple English, the wing fell off through strain and vibration. The Electra was also modified safely.*

Structural failure is often associated with a particular type of aircraft. But it can also affect an individual plane. The last message from a British Airways Vanguard en route to Salzburg came as the plane cruised over Belgium. "We're going down, Flight 706, we're going down vertically . . . out of control." The rear pressure bulkhead ruptured, helped by corrosion from the lavatory. It tore off the stabilizer and the aircraft nose-dived into the ground.†

If the cabin suddenly depressurizes, the pilot goes through an immediate emergency check: oxygen mask on, communications with crew and passengers established, and passenger oxygen switched on. Passengers must put out cigarettes at once and breathe from the oxygen masks that drop down above their heads.

The captain announces the emergency descent to a lower altitude where there is air. He has 15 seconds to lose height before the passengers start to become unconscious. He closes the throttles, the "thrust levers" as he calls them. The speed brakes

*CAA 9/60. It cost Lockheed $118 million to strengthen the wings. A worrying factor was that the wing condition became evident after only 132 hours of flight. The test program should surely have discovered this.

†CAA 20/71.

are extended; the autopilot is canceled. The aircraft banks and turns to lose height more quickly, although the angle of bank must not exceed 45 degrees.

The undercarriage goes down. The airspeed must not creep above Mach .83 or 320 knots on most aircraft or there will be structural damage. The pilot levels out at 14,000 feet after the emergency descent.

Depressurization should be survivable. An Aer Lingus 707 was at 25,000 feet with 112 aboard when the main cargo door partially blew out.*

The aircraft at once decompressed. The copilot, who was flying the aircraft, flew an immediate emergency descent to 11,000 feet. There was noise and buffeting, but the aircraft landed quite safely with nobody injured.

But tragedy followed during another flight when the port rear freight door of a DC-10 blew out.† Turkish Airlines THY Flight 981 was a scheduled run from Istanbul to London via Paris. As it climbed through 13,000 feet on takeoff from Orly, it disappeared from the radar. It crashed in woods, and all 346 aboard died instantly, making it the world's biggest air disaster at the time.

The freight door, together with a number of bodies, was found nine miles from the main wreckage. When it blew out and the cargo hold decompressed, the cabin door distorted and disrupted the cables of the main flying controls in the tail. The huge plane went out of control and crashed. There was much bitterness when it was discovered that a similar accident had already crippled another DC-10, though not fatally, a fact which should have prevented repetition.

McDonnell Douglas, the DC-10 manufacturer, alleged that an employee at Paris Orly had not latched the door by the correct procedure. The manufacturer also alleged that Turkish Airlines might have added unauthorized shims to the lock-limit warning switch, to correct a flickering warning light, and misrigged a lockpin in the mechanism.

*CAA 25/70.
†AIB Bulletin 5/74.

McDonnell Douglas had good reason to mitigate its own liability. The original door-lock design was unquestionably poor—though McDonnell Douglas further alleged that this was the fault of its design-and-manufacturing subcontractor responsible for the door lock. And McDonnell Douglas had delivered the aircraft, DC-10 ship 29, to Turkish Airlines without some safety modifications that McDonnell Douglas had itself recommended in its *Service Bulletin* SB 52 37.*

The *Service Bulletin* followed two carbon-copy incidents. The same freight door had blown out on American Airlines DC-10 ship 1 above Windsor, Ontario, more than a year before. The pilot managed to land the stricken airliner, but American Airlines was not to be so fortunate during another post-takeoff emergency six years later at Chicago.

The Federal Aviation Administration did not emerge unscathed from Paris. The FAA had not made the Windsor-incident modifications mandatory by issuing an Airworthiness Directive. Neither had it ordered floor-venting modifications to prevent the floor from buckling and jamming the controls. Yet modifications had been recommended by the National Transportation Safety Board after the Windsor incident, and would have saved the Turkish airliner.

As for the legal aftermath of the crash, lawyer Lee S. Kreindler, who specializes in this area, said, "Intelligent laymen can only have contempt for what lawyers, governments, and airlines have created."

There were grotesque differentials in liability limits. This was a Turkish flight from France to England by an American aircraft containing passengers of several nationalities. That is complex, but no more so than any average international flight. Where the airline's limited liability was concerned, some passengers were on a 1929 Warsaw Convention compensation limit of $10,000, others on a 1955 Hague Protocol limit of $20,000, and yet more on the Montreal Agreement limit of $75,000.

The wise had bought airport insurance for $100,000 and up, for a cost comparable to that of an in-flight movie.

*The Safe Airline. London, J. M. Ramsden, 1976.

Another DC-10 crashed shortly after takeoff at Chicago in May, 1979, killing all 273 aboard. An engine broke away as it was developing full takeoff power. As it tore upward and back, it damaged the leading edge of the wing and cut hydraulic power. The leading-edge droops on the wing withdrew, causing it to stall. The other wing continued to produce high lift, and the aircraft banked and crashed.

The FAA took the unprecedented step of grounding all 138 DC-10's operated by American carriers for five weeks. Inspections of DC-10's revealed cracks in the pylon mountings that attach the engine to the wing. The ban was ended on condition that the mountings be checked, with inspections required every 100 to 3,000 flying hours on different parts. The major inspections take up to 50 man-hours and involve ultrasonic scans to find small metal cracks.

McDonnell Douglas, the maker, was also ordered to redesign parts of the pylon within two years.

The accident also involved instrumentation. Had the pilot known that the wing had stalled, it is possible that an emergency landing could have been made.

Despite the FAA ban and investigation, no clear reason for the second DC-10 disaster emerged. McDonnell Douglas said that the cracks in the pylons had resulted from slipshod maintenance procedures. The FAA appeared to side with this, stating that "the DC-10, properly maintained and inspected, is a safe aircraft." During routine overhauls, mechanics had sometimes detached the pylon and engine together, instead of disassembling them separately.

American Airlines, operator of the ill-fated Chicago–Los Angeles flight, suggested that there might have been a design fault.

The attitudes were all too predictable. McDonnell Douglas had a vested interest in blaming airline employees. It thus turned on American Airlines mechanics, just as it had earlier blamed a Turkish Airlines cargo loader for misfastening the cargo door during the Paris tragedy. That attempted to switch the onus from maker to operator.

The FAA has an interest in going along with the manufacturer. The FAA gives manufacturers a Certificate of Airworthiness that presumes the design to be sound. The FAA had certified the DC-10, and it must have been tempting for the agency to single out nonapproved maintenance procedures rather than McDonnell Douglas.

And, naturally, American Airlines at once started speaking of a design fault to shift responsibility off its own mechanics and onto the makers.

Whether it deserves it or not, the DC-10 has got a bad name. When the wings fell off the Electra and the tail off the Comet, the manufacturers ultimately took the responsibility and fixed their products so that it did not happen again. The aircraft were restored to confidence.

The DC-10 has been different. There was haggling between airline, manufacturer, and safety authorities after Paris, and again after Chicago. The only beneficiaries have been the lawyers, who have seen a fresh cornucopia of fees slide into their grasp as their clients fight to evade responsibility.

The public has simply been told that the DC-10 is safe— provided the pylons are looked at every 100 hours.* The FAA may have been entirely justified in praising the DC-10's safety record, though in concentrating on its 1,500,000 safe landings the FAA lays itself open to the obvious charge that it has been on takeoff that things have gone wrong.

But the airlines can hardly expect passengers to be entirely convinced when it has apportioned no blame, least of all to itself, and when it still treats the pylon with suspicion.

The DC-10 has raised some serious questions about safety. The Paris crash showed that despite the procedures for the instant

---

*I once flew on a Royal Air Force Puma helicopter in the Central American colony of Belize. Every hour and a quarter, the pilot would head out of the jungle from resupply missions and land on the beach. He switched off the engines, waited a bit for the rotors to stop, jumped out, walked around, got back in, and flew off.

The third time he pulled the stunt, I asked him what he was up to.

"We had some trouble with the blades, old boy. Started disintegrating in the air. Awkward. So there's a dye we use to spot the cracks. Should take a lot more than seventy-five minutes for a crack to get critical. So we just stop and have a look. Perfectly all right."

Well, it was perfectly all right. But it didn't feel that way.

notification of faults and incidents between airlines operating the same aircraft, carbon-copy accidents still occur. There were suggestions that McDonnell Douglas had rushed through the design in order to compete with the Lockheed 1011.

Both Paris and Chicago revealed the aircraft to be remarkably vulnerable to the whims of junior airline employees, at least in some reports. A cargo handler allegedly mis-shut a door at Paris; mechanics allegedly used a forklift to remove engine and pylon at Chicago. A great airliner should not easily fall prey to mishandling at this level.

And both incidents showed the fail-safe capability of the DC-10 in a bad light.* The Paris crash occurred only because decompression jammed the control lines under the cabin floor. Had the controls been differently sited, there would have been no accident. The DC-10 can be flown on two engines, even if the third has fallen off. But the loss of electrical and hydraulic power that followed the loss of the engine at Chicago doomed the aircraft, since the lift devices on the wing retracted and the pilot had no information that the wing had stalled. A similar accident on a 747 or 1011 is, in theory at least, impossible.

Airline reaction to Chicago was not reassuring either. The grounding was enormously expensive, with 12 percent of all airline seats in the U.S. being removed from the market and some airlines losing over $20 million in revenue. U.S. airlines honored the ban. They had little option. But foreign airlines lobbied immediately, powerfully, and often successfully at home to continue flying their DC-10's. One might have thought that an aircraft that was banned in its place of manufacture would be banned elsewhere. But restrictions were quickly lifted in Europe, including those on Freddie Laker's famous Skytrain DC-10's which were serviced by American Airlines.

Pilots love the DC-10. It is, one said, "an enormously forgiving

---

*The fail-safe standard of the *crew* on American Airlines DC-10's has been dramatically upheld on one flight. An FAA flight inspector was carrying out flight checks on an A.A. DC-10. The first officer was flying. Just after takeoff rotation, he died of a heart attack. Although the aircraft was in a critical phase of flight, at night, turning over water at low altitude, the captain took the controls and landed safely.

aircraft." Perhaps it should be more forgiving to a cargo door and a pylon and to those who either close them, maintain them, or design them.

The DC-10 was the result of a particularly bitter marketing war against Lockheed. The development of very powerful fan-jet engines in the 1960's made it obvious that wide-bodied aircraft capable of seating several hundred passengers would dominate the industry in the future.

Boeing scooped the long-range intercontinental market with the 747, which it developed early and well. That left the other two major U.S. manufacturers, Lockheed and McDonnell Douglas, to fight for the medium-range market.

Many in the industry thought it was absurd to develop both the Lockheed 1011 and the McDonnell Douglas DC-10. The two aircraft are virtually identical in terms of speed, range and capacity, if not in design detail. To get both manufacturers into profit, five hundred aircraft have to be sold. This means that they must not only compete with each other, but must also penetrate the 747's intercontinental market.

Lockheed and McDonnell Douglas knew that it made more sense for only one aircraft to be developed, but both were adamant that it should be theirs. Thus both proceeded. TWA was so convinced that only the 1011 should be developed that it offered United Airlines some of its delivery positions if United would buy 1011's. United was the last big U.S. airline to decide which airliner to buy.

In April 1968, United decided on the DC-10 and thus the DC-10 program got under way. The decision was perhaps inevitable. The DC-10 has General Electric engines. General Electric's allied bank is Morgan Guaranty. Morgan Guaranty has one of the largest single shareholdings in United.

McDonnell Douglas had the motto "Fly before they roll." This meant getting the DC-10 into the air before the 1011 was rolled out of its hangar. They succeeded triumphantly, with a nine-month lead. This gave the DC-10 a clear commercial edge, and at the time of the Chicago crash McDonnell Douglas had sold 277 DC-10's and was into profit. Lockheed still had a long way to go with the 163 1011's sold.

There is no evidence that McDonnell Douglas developed the DC-10 too quickly. Nevertheless, the DC-10 has been involved in two total disasters that are directly attributable to the aircraft and not to the pilot. In both, the DC-10's fail-safe record has been shown to be skimpy.*

Cabin ventilation should be able to cope with even severe smoke. Although the crew all go on oxygen and wear goggles, putting the turbocompressors on maximum and altering the cabin altitude to the rarer atmosphere of 10,000 feet will deal with dense smoke. The aircraft must never be depressurized to get rid of smoke as the ventilation system is better than any combination of open windows and doors. In the very rare event of flying unpressurized, the copilot's window is opened.

Fire in the cargo compartments can spread very quickly. When it is suspected, the flight engineer puts on a smoke mask and takes a "walk-around" bottle of oxygen and a portable fire extinguisher. He is lowered through the nose compartment on the cockpit escape rope.

The first move with an engine fire is to cut off the warning Klaxon. All the crew shout out the number of the engine on fire, since pilots have been known to shut down the good engine by mistake. The throttle is then shut. The aircraft goes onto essential power, since one of the generators will have had its engine stopped. If necessary the pilot can switch off radar, galley heat, window heat, fuel boost pumps and the reserve hydraulic pump to save power.

The engine fire handle is pulled, the boost pumps switched off

---

*The Chicago DC-10 had seven emergencies before its final crash. In February 1975, the rear engine overheated in Acapulco. The same month, the right engine burned out after takeoff, again at Acapulco, and then the rear engine failed on takeoff at Dallas. That August, the airliner made an unscheduled landing at Phoenix after the slats failed. There was only one emergency in 1976, a forced landing after the loss of hydraulic fluid at Dallas. The aircraft made another forced landing the next year in Los Angeles when the right engine overheated. A takeoff at Chicago was aborted in 1978 for the same reason.

and the manifold valve closed. If the first warning light stays on, the bottle discharge button is pushed, and the extinguisher is sprayed into the engine. If the warning light is still on after 30 seconds, Phase II starts—another foam bottle sprays the engine.

If that does not work, Phase III begins. This is literally an attempt to blow the fire out. The aircraft has to be flown at a minimum of 250 knots, the faster the better since there is no Phase IV.

The chances of surviving a crash are much reduced on aircraft using JP4 fuel. This is a "wide-cut" gasoline like regular automobile fuel, needed by piston engines because it is volatile. However, this makes it ignite readily in a fire. JP1 fuel, as kerosene is known, is much less inflammable.* A study by A. F. Taylor and Lin Beow Hong showed that in 130 JP1 accidents, under 30 percent of those aboard died, of whom 10 percent died through fire rather than the crash itself. In 28 JP4 accidents, more than half of the 40 percent on board who died were killed by fire. A passenger should not fly with an airline that uses JP4: it is saving money at the greater risk of his life. JP1 is, however, used by all major airlines.

The odds against a two-engine-out landing have been calculated at 1,000,000 to 1. But sometimes, in training, it is done on purpose. Ten percent of all airliner crashes occur on training flights. A Delta Airlines pilot, Jim Morton, with 16,000 hours' experience, was being checked out as a captain on a DC-8.† During the takeoff run from New Orleans International, the instructor, Maurice Watson, chopped one engine. Morton took off and started to climb out. A minute later Watson chopped a second engine. Number 1 and 2 engines were dead—there was no power

---

*JP4 can ignite down to −10 degrees Fahrenheit (−23 degrees Centigrade). JP1 kerosene has a flash point of around 100 degrees Fahrenheit (38 degrees Centigrade). The advantages of JP4 are that it is cheaper and lighter, at 7.6 pounds to the gallon compared to 8 pounds for JP1. Lord Brabazon, when Chairman of the British Air Registration Board, suggested a "fuel duel" to JP4 adherents. He would stand in a pool of kerosene lighting matches. They should do the same in JP4. He had no takers.

†CAA 8/67. Quoted at length in *Safety Last,* by Captain Brian Power-Waters, Millington, London, 1974.

on the left wing. The altitude was only 1,200 feet and the speed a meager 200 knots.

To lose power at this most critical stage in takeoff on two engines is so unlikely that it could only happen on a check flight. Even so, Morton might have made it. But Watson cut the rudder boost, the hydraulic aid that was helping Morton keep the nose straight against the asymmetrical thrust of the engines on the starboard wing.

The altitude was down to 800 feet. Speed was deteriorating. "Don't get below 160 . . ." said Watson.

Watson called the landing checks and looked at the runway lights. It was after midnight. "OK, looks good. How 'bout that now, we're straightened out."

The good humor did not last long.

The runway was only a mile away and coming up fast.

"Call my airspeed for me," said Morton.

"One four zero."

Too slow. Power was put on the engines on the right wing. The plane immediately turned left.

"One three five is your airspeed . . . see you're getting near . . ." Watson shouted. "Put the rudder in there . . . you're getting your speed down now. . . . You're not going to be able to get it."

"I can't hold it, Bud." Morton had no rudder boost. Watson had chopped it to add realism to the check.

Watson shouted: "Naw, don't. Let it up! . . . Let it up!"

It exploded into the ground and smashed through three houses and a hotel. Six crew and 13 on the ground died.

The incident list of a major airline shows what happens short of accidents. Behind the unblemished record of British Airways in one year lay 442,904 hours of flight and 264,324 takeoffs and landings. The passengers at the back would be amazed at the dramas they lived through. There were 99 stall warnings and 230 abandoned takeoffs and 625 engines were shut down in flight. Lightning struck 127 flights, and birds hit 153. The same airline registered 35 air misses in the first six months of 1976.*

*British Airways Air Safety Review, February 2, 1977.

These statistics are for a notably safe and large airline. An average airline would have clocked up more incidents. The reader should note that BA shows exceptional frankness in revealing its operational details. The reluctance of some other airlines to exchange accident information lessens safety standards. The reader should not fall into the trap of regarding BA as dangerous because it is frequently mentioned. The reverse is the truth: a frank airline is generally a safe one.

Appendix One

What Goes Up . . .

World airlines work through emergencies at a fair rate. Take a typical January, this one in 1976, and the accidents noted during it.*

New Year's Day itself saw two. A DC-10 of SAS took off from Copenhagen's Kastrup Airport into a flock of gulls. The crew heard a loud bang and saw a flash in the big tri-jet's No. 1 engine, which lost power.

The emergency landing was successful, although it was found that 15 birds had been through the devastated No. 1 engine, and had also damaged the No. 3. A further 28 gulls were found on the runway.

Later that day, a Boeing 720 of Middle East Airlines took off from war-scarred Beirut for the Persian Gulf. It disintegrated at 37,000 feet over the Saudi Arabian desert, killing all 81 aboard. The cause was a bomb in the forward cargo compartment. The terrorist has not been found.

On January 2, a DC-10 of the big American carrier Overseas National careered off the runway at Istanbul after a heavy landing. The next day an Aeroflot Tu-124 crashed after takeoff from

*CAA Supplement No. 28, July 1976.

Moscow, killing 87. As with all Russian crashes, no details were given.

On January 4, a Lear 24A jet of Winship Air Service crashed at Anchorage, Alaska, killing six, for the fourth straight day of accidents.

A lull ended on January 7, when a Viscount propjet of Mandala Airlines in Indonesia overshot the runway and ended up in a monsoon ditch. Three days later, an F-27 of Burma Airways suffered a collapsed nosewheel on landing. Passengers survived both these incidents.

On January 15, nobody survived the crash of a Colombian DC-4 into mountains near Bogotá. Nor did the passengers escape the crash of a C 47 in nearby Bolivia on the 18th, after the right engine failed on takeoff.

Again in South America, an HS-748 crashed into mountains in Peru, killing 33. A Russian-built An-24 crashed on the approach to Canton on a flight from Shanghai on the 21st, killing all 40 aboard. Back in South America, an Emb-110 of Transbrasil crashed fatally on takeoff the following day.

The final victim for the month was an L 188 of Panarctic which crashed on landing at Edmonton in Canada. That ended an average month.*

The reasons for crashes of airliners since 1946 have been worked out by the British Civil Aviation Authority. They make interesting reading, although it should be remembered that they include more than 30 years of crashes.

Airframe failure, through metal fatigue or turbulence, accounts for 154.

Aquaplaning on wet runways, where the tires have no bite and braking is useless, has led to 58 crashes, although they are not usually fatal.

Bird strikes have downed 38 aircraft—although nobody has yet

---

*An increase in the accident rate seems to be taking place. An analysis by Dr. Shaw, technical director general of IATA, indicates that the loss rate of jet airliner hulls, having declined up to the mid-1970's, is now creeping up again. Approach and landing crashes, having dropped to almost one per million in the early 1970's, have now returned to the 1960's rate of between two and three per million.

been killed on a jet airliner. The cargo has broken loose on 20 flights. A massive 536 aircraft have hit high ground, and 300 water—almost always with fatal results. Crew incapacitation, ranging from food poisoning to death, has affected 18 flights.

Seven aircraft have crashed after a member of the crew has been shot.

Doors and windows have opened or failed in flight on 45 aircraft. These accidents can be eerie. The pilot of an Egyptian Viscount on the Luxor to Aswan tourist run reported: "After takeoff from Luxor at an altitude of approximately 9,000 feet a sudden explosion occurred and three-quarters of the front entrance door blew out. The aircraft returned to Luxor, and on landing, one of the stewardesses was found to be missing."

The main passenger door also blew out on an Aerolineas Argentinas Avro 748. The stewardess was left desperately hanging on to the inside of the lavatory with her left hand, while almost the whole of her body was outside the aircraft. The steward caught her blouse, but could not stop her being sucked out and falling 11,000 feet. An Air France passenger was sucked from his seat to the Iranian desert when a window failed.

Electrical faults have contributed to 45 airliner accidents, and the failure of all engines to 164. Flying controls have jammed or gone wrong on 89. Dirty or incorrect fuel has affected 19 flights.

Fuel starvation or mismanagement and running out of fuel have contributed to 79 incidents. The most common error is for pilots to switch to empty tanks.

Hail damage has caused 23 accidents, and the buildup of ice and snow 87. Almost all these are to propeller aircraft. Jets produce huge quantities of hot air which can be piped to places where ice can form.

Hidden bombs have exploded on 34 flights. PAL of the Philippines has had three aircraft sabotaged. British Airways lost a Comet into the Mediterranean, killing all 66 aboard in a 1967 attempt to kill the Cypriot guerrilla leader General Grivas. A TWA Boeing 707 with 88 aboard also plunged into the Mediterranean after a bomb blast in 1974. Swissair lost a CV-990 jet and 39 passengers near Frankfurt in 1970 and Continental a 707 with 45 aboard over Mississippi in 1962.

Twenty-four have been shot at by ground fire, or shot or forced down by fighter aircraft. Most incidents were in the Taiwan area and Vietnam, although a Boeing jet of Libyan Arab Airlines was forced down by Israeli fighters and crashed in the Sinai desert. There is an international code for military aircraft to use to airliners. The fighter rocks its wings from a position in front and to the left of the airliner. This means: "You have been intercepted. Follow me." The fighter then circles an airport, lowering its undercarriage and overflying the runway in the direction of landing. This means: "Land at this airport." Had this procedure been followed, there would have been no tragedy in Sinai.

In-flight fire has a bad record—316. Many fires start in the toilets, most commonly from cigarette butts. Alitalia Jumbo, Pan Am and American Airlines 707's have all been forced to make precautionary landings after fires in the toilets. In one extraordinary incident on a DC-10 of National Airlines en route to Miami at 39,000 feet, a passenger deliberately burned himself to death in the right aft "blue room," or toilet. The toxicity of fires is due to a wide range of materials used in aircraft toilets and cabins—vinyls, honeycomb, a variety of plastics, stainless steel, aluminum and fiberglass.

Instruments, either missed, misread or failed, account for 63 incidents. Lightning strikes are held responsible for 13 accidents.

Major power-plant disruptions and the loss of propellers in flight have caused 184 accidents, marginally above the figure for midair collisions, at 137.

The biggest category of all, only to be expected since takeoff and landing are the most dangerous parts of flight, is over-running and veering off the runway, a total of 1,226.

Tire bursts are low, at 11. "Third party" accidents, which means hitting anything from a hotel to a coconut tree, measure 102.*

*A DC-8 on a training flight hit a hotel at St. Louis. A Garuda F 28 hit a coconut tree at Palembang in Indonesia. The impact was severe enough to kill 26, including the crew, although another 36 survived. The tree was destroyed. A Hughes 500 helicopter suffered tail-boom damage when it was hit by a London Transport bus at the exclusive Dorchester Hotel in London's Park Lane. A 1011 of All Nippon Airways had two flight deck windows broken when it hit volcanic rock thrown up by the eruption of Mount Usu. Smoke and ash were reported up to 40,000 feet on

It is also possible to work out which aircraft have been involved in the most accidents. DC-3's, also known as Dakotas, have been involved in some 1,600 accidents. The Curtiss C 46 Commando has been in 720 and the DC-4 in 201.

Of jets, 194 Boeing 707's, 84 Boeing 727's, fifteen 737's and twenty-three 727's had been listed by the CAA as involved in accidents up to 1976. An accident is defined by ICAO as an occurrence where there is death or injury to those on board, or substantial damage to the aircraft. The DC-8 had reached 85, the DC-9 had 61 and the DC-10 had 19. The Fokker Friendship had 13. The Comet 4 series had 43 accidents and the Trident 15. The Lockheed TriStar had 8, the Caravelle had 54, Convair 880's and 990's had 32, the VC-10 had 12, and the BAC 111 had 30.

The most abused aircraft in the world undoubtedly have been United Arab Airlines' Comets. Things were bad enough with SU-AII and SU-ANI. The former first crashed into snowbanks at Geneva, and then collapsed its undercarriage and went off the runway again at Khartoum. SU-ANI's first off-runway excursion came at Kuwait, after it had landed on its starboard wing tip, setting it on fire. Its second came in 1970 at Addis Ababa, when it touched down halfway along the runway. This time its port wing tip and fuel pod hit the ground.

But the Egyptian airline managed to crash poor old Comet SU-ALD not twice, but thrice.

On Christmas Eve, 1960, while landing in Libya, the pilot put SU-ALD straight into a drainage ditch. The plane was repaired. Less than two months later, on February 15, 1961, it was landed heavily, tail down, at Damascus. It was again badly damaged and repaired.

For a little while, it led a charmed life, with no incidents. Then on July 27, 1963, while trying to land at Bombay in bad weather, the pilot put the plane into the sea in severe turbulence, writing off himself, his passengers and poor SU-ALD.

August 7, 1977. The big jet landed safely at Sapporo. And on November 15, 1977, an Ethiopian Airlines DC-3 collided with a donkey and was written off in the subsequent crash landing. History does not relate what happened to the donkey. ICAO Summaries, 1976, 1977.

But, to end on a more optimistic note, take the case of a Constellation of F. and B. Livestock Airlines. As those other aircraft were crashing in 1976, the Connie's No. 1 propeller ran away when the plane was 65 miles east of Belize in Central America. The pilot could not control the rpm or feather the prop and 25 miles east of Belize, out over the Caribbean, it flew off. It hit the No. 2 engine, which also stopped. The aircraft was now flying on the starboard engines alone.

The undercarriage was lowered for an emergency landing at Belize. The left main gear failed to extend. The crew couldn't get it down even manually. By now the oil temperatures on the two remaining engines were dangerously high. The pilot decided to put the Connie down at once, without one propeller and two engines, with faulty landing gear and oil temperatures well in the red on the now faltering starboard engines.

Not a soul aboard was scratched.

Appendix Two

Pilot Aptitude Test

Devised by the author and based on RAF Pilot Selection at Biggin Hill.

Pilots need special skills for their job, with a flair for mathematics, obtaining information from instruments, and physical coordination, applied to a machine rather than a sport. They must also have a reasonable intelligence on a general basis. This IQ test is designed to screen out those whose general intelligence is not up to pilot standards.

There is a strict time limit of 20 minutes.

GENERAL INTELLIGENCE TEST

1. Which one is wrong, if

are correct?

2. What should x be?

$$5 \quad 11 \quad 23 \quad 47 \quad x$$

3. What number goes into the brackets?

$$24 \quad (47) \quad 42$$
$$35 \quad (52) \quad 14$$
$$32 \quad () \quad 16$$

4. What number is missing in this sequence?

$$6 \quad 36 \quad 18 \quad 324 \qquad\qquad 26244$$

5. Which is wrong?

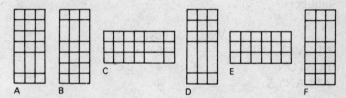

6. Which is the odd man out in these anagrams?

   YONWAR   NIPAS   RECNAF   GIBLEUM   ANDAAC

7. If MDSDQ becomes JAPAN and SRODQG becomes PO-LAND, what is WXUNHB?

8. Which piece fits the missing section?

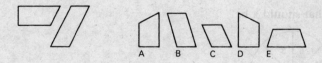

9. Which diagram continues this pattern?

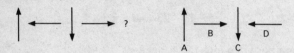

10. What is x?

4   5   16   25   256   x   65536

11. What word does not belong here?

COW   DEER   SNAKE   MAN   DOG

12. If these results are in the relationship of the letters to numbers:

	Won	Lost
CLEVELAND	3	6
BOSTON	2	4
ATLANTA	3	4

How has DETROIT done?

13. Which pattern is inconsistent?

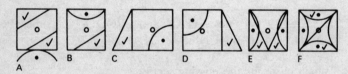

14. What should x be?

15. If CHILE = 37 and ITALY = 67 and ZAIRE = 59, what is SPAIN?

ANSWERS

1. F. It is the wrong pattern for an obtuse angle.

   2 points.

2. 95. Each number is doubled, and one added.

   2 points.

3. 42. In the first line, the numbers outside the brackets are divided by 6, in the second by 7, in the third by 8.

   2 points.

4. 162. The first number is squared for the second number, halved for the third and squared again, and so forth.

   3 points.

5. D. It has only six horizontal bars.

   1 point.

6. CANADA. All the others are in Europe.

   2 points.

7. TURKEY. Each letter moves back three places in the alphabet.

   2 points.

8. C.

   1 point.

9. A. It turns ¼ of a revolution each time.

   1 point.

10. 625. There are two sequences, alternately squaring from 4 and 5.

    2 points.

11. SNAKE. All the others are mammals. A snake is a reptile.
    1 point.

12. Won 3, Lost 4. Each vowel is a win, each consonant a loss.
    1 point.

13. F. One semicircle has no dot in it.
    1 point.

14. 7. Each number triples its opposite lower number and adds one.

    2 points.

15. 59, like ZAIRE. Each letter is given its number in the alphabet and the totals are added. Thus A = 1, Z = 26, and so forth.

    2 points.

Average score　　14
Good score　　17
Excellent score　　22

The pass mark is 15, just above the average. With jobs hard to get at the moment, many airlines would insist on at least 17. But historically it has been 15 and that, rather than today's intake, is likely to be flying you.

ERROR RECTIFICATION TEST

First read the Instrument Explanation (no time limit).
A pilot has to be quick and firm about rectifying errors, whether

from his instruments or from mechanical failure such as an engine shutdown. Select the appropriate description.

There is a strict time limit of 5 minutes.

Instrument Explanation

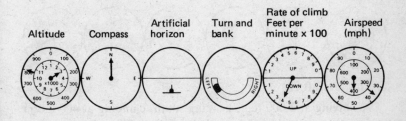

Altitude. The inner pointer indicates thousands of feet. The outer gives the hundreds. Thus the altitude shown above is 3,800 feet: 3,000 on the inner pointer and 800 on the outer.

Compass. The course is self-explanatory. Here it is north.

Artificial horizon. If the model plane is above the line of the horizon, it is climbing. If below, it is descending. Here it is descending.

Turn and bank. The bubble is to the left, so there is a left turn here.

Rate of climb. The pointer shows how many hundred feet per minute the plane is climbing or descending. Here it points at 400 feet, in the down section. The aircraft is thus descending 400 feet per minute.

Airspeed. The inner dial shows the hundreds of miles an hour, the outer in tens. The inner here points to 400, the outer to 35. The airspeed is thus 435 mph.

Simply write down your answers in sequence. The case above would be:

> 3,800 feet, north, descending, turning to the left, down at 400 feet a minute, at 435 mph.

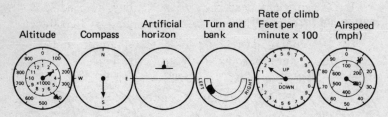

1. This aircraft is:

   A. Flying at 3,000 feet, heading south, climbing at 400 feet a minute, banking left, and climbing at 300 mph.

   B. Climbing at 400 feet a minute, banking right, climbing, flying at 3,400 feet, heading south, at 340 mph.

   C. Flying at 350 mph, climbing at 300 feet a minute, banking right, climbing, heading south, at 3,500 feet.

   D. Flying at 3,400 feet, at 310 mph, heading south, climbing at 200 feet a minute, climbing, banking left.

   E. Flying at 310 mph, heading east, at 3,400 feet, climbing at 200 feet a minute, banking left, climbing.

   F. Flying at 320 mph, heading south, at 3,400 feet, climbing at 200 feet a minute, banking left, climbing.

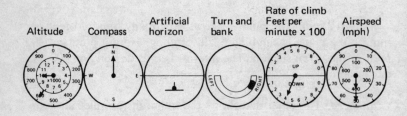

2. This aircraft is:

   A. Flying at 540 mph at 6,100 feet, heading north, descending at 400 feet a minute, descending, turning right.

   B. Turning right, heading north at 540 mph, descending at 400 feet a minute, turning right, descending, at 10,600 feet.

   C. Descending, descending at 400 feet a minute, at 450 mph, turning left, heading south, at 10,600 feet.

   D. Flying at 450 mph, at 10,600 feet, heading north, descending at 400 feet a minute, turning right, descending.

   E. Flying at 10,600 feet, heading south, descending at 400 feet a minute, at 540 mph, turning right, descending.

   F. Flying at 450 mph, at 9,600 feet, heading north, descending at 400 feet a minute, turning right, descending.

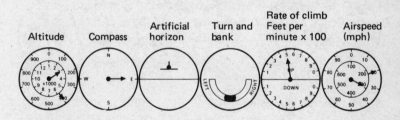

3. This aircraft is:

   A. Flying at 4,300 feet, at 320 mph, climbing, heading east, climbing at 500 feet a minute, climbing, no turn.

   B. Flying at 320 mph, climbing at 500 feet a minute, turning left, climbing, heading east, at 3,000 feet.

   C. Climbing at 400 feet a minute, heading south, no turn, altitude 3,400 feet, at 300 mph, descending.

   D. Climbing at 500 feet a minute, at 4,300 feet, heading east, climbing, no turn, at 320 mph.

   E. No turn, climbing at 500 feet a minute, at 3,400 feet, climbing, at 320 mph, heading east.

F. Flying at 230 mph, climbing at 500 feet a minute, at 3,400 feet, no turn, climbing, heading east.

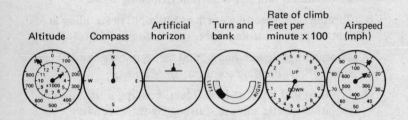

4. What is wrong with these instruments?

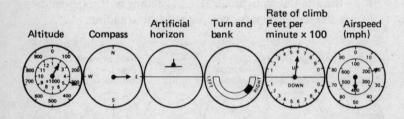

5. The aircraft above is:

A. Flying at 3,200 feet, at 420 mph, climbing, turning left, climbing at 600 feet a minute, heading east.

B. Climbing, flying at 2,300 feet, at 440 mph, turning right, climbing at 600 feet a minute, heading east.

C. Heading east at 420 mph, climbing, climbing at 600 feet a minute at 420 mph, turning right, at 2,300 feet.

D. Flying at 240 mph, heading east, climbing at 600 feet a minute, at 2,300 feet, turning right, climbing.

E. Heading east at 640 mph, climbing at 600 feet a minute, at 2,300 feet, turning right, climbing.

F. Flying at 420 mph, heading east, climbing at 800 feet a minute, climbing, turning right, at 2,300 feet.

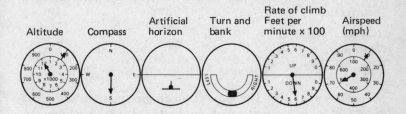

| Altitude | Compass | Artificial horizon | Turn and bank | Rate of climb Feet per minute x 100 | Airspeed (mph) |

6. The aircraft above is:

   A. Flying at 11,200 feet, descending, at 510 mph, descending at 600 feet a minute, no turn, heading south.

   B. Descending at 400 feet a minute, heading south, at 510 mph, descending at 12,100 feet, no turn.

   C. Flying at 510 mph, descending at 600 feet a minute, heading east, at 12,200 feet, turning left.

   D. Flying at 11,200 feet, descending, at 420 mph, heading south, no turn, descending at 600 feet a minute.

   E. Heading south at 510 mph, descending, no turn, at 12,100 feet, descending at 600 feet a minute.

   F. Descending at 600 feet a minute, heading south, left turn, descending, at 510 mph and 12,100 feet.

ANSWERS

1. D

2. D

3. E

4. The artificial horizon shows the aircraft is climbing, but the rate-of-climb indicator shows it descending at 400 feet a minute.

5. C

6. E

Score 2 points for each answer that is correct. No points unless it is correct.

Average score   8
Good score   10
Excellent score 12

The pass mark is 8. The rapid grasp of instruments is extremely important for pilots, particularly on short-haul and vacation routes, where traffic is dense, aerial traffic jams common, and ground controllers are issuing frequent orders. Although 8 would be acceptable initially, and for an airline with long routes such as the transatlantic, pilots for vacation flights should score at least 10.

INSTRUMENT COMPREHENSION TEST

It has been a long time since pilots flew by the seat of their pants. They are now taught, in fact, totally to ignore what the seat of their pants or any other part of their bodies is telling them. It is common for a pilot flying in cloud to feel he is upside down when in fact he is the right way up, or to feel he is turning to the left when in fact he is turning to the right.

Unlike birds, which can fly in blinding conditions of fog or cloud with no trouble, man needs an artificial horizon and instruments to tell him what he is doing. Pilots learn to trust their instruments without hesitation. They scan them constantly. The ability to interpret this information from instruments quickly and accurately is vital. After reading the introduction about instruments, start the test. Write down the altitude, course, attitude of the aircraft from the artificial horizon, the turn, the rate of climb and the airspeed for each question.

There is a strict time limit of 4 minutes.

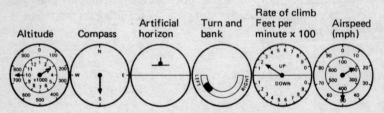

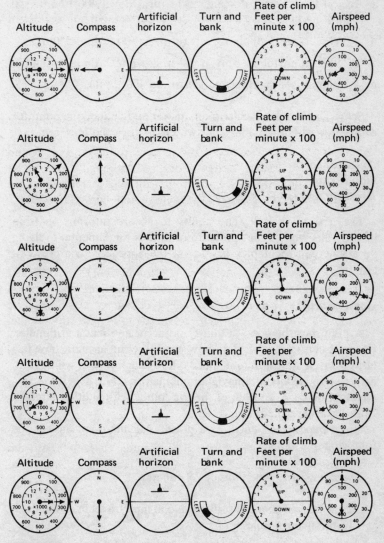

ANSWERS

1. 3,750 feet, south, climbing, left turn, up 200 ft/min, 250 mph
2. 10,250 feet, west, descent, no turn, down 400 ft/min, 565 mph

3. 12,150 feet, north, descent, right turn, down 600 ft/min, 150 mph

4. 3,500 feet, east, climbing, left turn, up 500 ft/min, 530 mph

5. 9,250 feet, north, descent, no turn, down 600 ft/min, 670 mph

6. 4,250 feet, south, climb, left turn, up 400 ft/min, 400 mph

Score 2 points for each correct answer and deduct one point for each error with a maximum of two errors for each question.

Average score   8
Good score   10
Excellent score   11

The pass mark is 9. The ability to absorb information from instruments while under pressure of time is fundamental to flying an airliner on a complex course on the approach to a crowded airport.

MATHEMATICAL TEST

A pilot must be good at quick and accurate mental arithmetic. He must constantly calculate how much fuel he has left, how fast he is burning it at different speeds, how much time it will take to arrive at an airport or a navigational beacon. If he gets the wrong answers, he could run out of fuel or collide with another aircraft. Both have happened.

Use a paper and pencil, or a pocket calculator, to answer the following questions.

There is a strict time limit of 15 minutes.

1. How far will an aircraft flying at 550 mph travel in 25 minutes, to the nearest mile?

2. An aircraft is 90 miles from an airport and flying at 470 mph. How long will it take to reach the airport at this speed, to the nearest half minute?

3. An aircraft flies at constant 200 mph for 10 minutes, then at 300 mph for 20 minutes and then at 400 mph for 30 minutes. How far will it fly in this hour?

4. An aircraft flies at 100 mph for 20 minutes, 200 mph for 10 minutes and 250 mph for 30 minutes. What is its average speed in miles per hour, to the nearest two decimal places?

5. An aircraft takes off from London Airport at 12:45 and flies toward Frankfurt at 550 mph. Another aircraft takes off from Frankfurt at 12:50 and flies toward London at 600 mph. The distance between the two cities is taken as 400 miles. Will they be nearer London or Frankfurt when they meet?

6. Your car does 30 miles to the gallon at 50 mph and 25 mpg at 70 mph. You drive 40 miles at 50 mph and 125 miles at 70 mph. How much gas do you need?

7. How much gas do you save by driving 90 miles at 50 mph rather than at 70 mph, on the fuel consumption shown in Question 6?

8. How much longer will the journey of 90 miles take if you drive at 50 mph and not 70 mph?

9. The car in front of you is driving at 50 mph. You are moving at 75 mph. It is 5 miles ahead. How many minutes will it take you to catch up?

10. Your car does 35 miles to the gallon. It has 2½ gallons in the tank. How far can you go?

ANSWERS

Score 1 point for each correct answer.

1. 229 miles.

2. 11½ minutes. 11 or 12 minutes acceptable.

3. 333.33 miles. 333 miles acceptable.

4. 191.66 mph. 190 mph acceptable.

5. Nearer Frankfurt.

6. 6.33 gallons or 6⅓.

7. 0.6 or ⅗ gallon.

8. 31 minutes. 30 minutes or ½ hour acceptable.

9. 12 minutes.

10. 87½ miles. 87 acceptable.

Average score   6
Good score   8
Excellent score 10

The pass mark is 8. Pilots have to be above average in mathematics. This is an area where people improve with practice, so do not be too disappointed if you fail it the first time. It can be worked on.

MECHANICAL COORDINATION TEST

Coordination is very important. Despite advanced controls and systems, a modern airliner still has to be flown with sensitivity and accuracy. This is particularly true in landing, when the pilot has to bring a 200-ton machine moving at 150 mph out of the sky onto the first 1,000 feet of a narrow runway. He uses his feet and hands for totally different purposes—his feet to yaw left or right, one hand to steer and the other to move throttles and levers—so he must be well coordinated.

With a pencil in each hand, trace a line within the patterns *simultaneously* and *continuously*. Thus, in the first example you must draw a cricle between the two existing circles with your left hand, and a square with your right. Your drawing must NOT touch the existing lines. You must move both your hands at the same time and you must not stop and restart. There are penalties for this. This is a high-scoring test.

There is a strict time limit of 2 minutes.

Make sure the paper is *firmly weighted down* and *cannot move* as you draw on it.

ANSWERS

Start with 15 points, and subtract one point each time you have crossed the lines to a maximum of three points per problem. Thus you cannot lose more than three points in any problem, even if you cross the lines four or more times.

Average score   6
Good score   10
Excellent score   13

The pass mark is 8. Below this, you are unlikely to have the natural aptitude in coordination for flying. (With helicopters, which require a very constant and high standard of coordination to keep them in the air, the pass mark goes up to 10.)

PERSONALITY TEST

Personality plays as important a role in flying as it does in anything else. The airline pilot needs to be stable, self-confident, extroverted and able to fit easily into a team. Flying can impose considerable emotional strain, particularly on long-haul pilots who are constantly jetlagged, far from home and close to pretty stewardesses. Pilots have been known to develop a severe fear of flying and to crack up. Pilots are screened intensively before they are accepted. Stability and team spirit are the qualities which rate high. There is no time limit on this test, but the questions should be answered yes or no fairly rapidly. It is impossible to be totally accurate about one's emotions. So settle for what you generally think is the right answer, and not what is precisely right.

No 1. Do you ever feel exhausted by problems?

Yes 2. Do you ever wonder what you're doing with your life?

No 3. Do you put things down to "luck" or "fate"?

Yes 4. Would you say you are happy?

Yes 5. Do you like planning for the future?

No 6. Do you always wear a safety belt?

Yes 7. Do you always keep your word, even on trivial matters?

No 8. Were you afraid of ghosts as a child?

No 9. Are you frightened of failure?

Yes 10. Do you believe you are the master of your own destiny?

No 11. Are you gloomy about the prospects for the world?

Yes 12. Do you buy things on impulse?

No 13. Would you shelter under a tree in a thunderstorm?

No 14. Do you ever "switch off" for a bit?

Yes 15. Did you sleep with your door open as a child?

Yes 16. Were you quite popular at school?

Yes 17. On the whole did you obey your parents as a child?

No 18. Do you feel you are unlucky?

Yes 19. Do you weigh things carefully before making a decision?

No 20. Do you bet on long shots in horse races?

No 21. Do you keep up to date with your personal correspondence?

No 22. Are you afraid of spiders, grass snakes and other harmless things?

Yes 23. Do you ever wish you were as successful as somebody else?

Yes 24. Will you stick out for your own ideas even when you are in a tiny minority?

Yes 25. Have you been successful in life?

No 26. Do you often change your hobbies?

No 27. Do you get bored with dull, if safe, routine?

Yes 28. Do you have your car regularly serviced?

No 29. Do you ever get worried about trivial things?

Yes 30. Do you stick to a decision once you have made it?

No 31. Do you do a lot of things just to please other people?

No 32. Do you feel lonely even when there are other people around?

No 33. Do you prefer spontaneous events to planned ones?

Yes 34. Do you have life insurance?

No 35. Do you often have to rush to catch a train or bus or plane?

Yes 36. Do you get embarrassed if you make a social blunder at a party?

No 37. Do you hate looking at holiday pictures of yourself?

Yes 38. Could you give up smoking or begin a diet if necessary?

Yes 39. Does somebody love you?

Yes 40. Do you get to know people quickly?

Yes 41. Do you think that a good pension is a vital part of a job?

Yes 42. Do you consider yourself to be a responsible type?

Yes 43. Can you relax and sit without fidgeting?

No 44. Do you mind your ideas being laughed at?

No 45. Do you know where you want to end up in life?

Yes 46. Do you usually feel calm and satisfied?

YES 47. Do you plan a car trip carefully, with maps and so forth?

YES 48. Have you ever done something impulsive for a dare?

No 49. Are you always forgetting little things to do?

No 50. Do you ever have to take sleeping pills?

No 51. Is there any feature of your body—skinny legs, protruding ears—that you would like to change?

YES 52. Would you walk under a ladder?

No 53. Do you usually drop straight off to sleep?

No 54. Do you blurt things out without thinking?

YES 55. Would the details of a guarantee influence your choice of car?

No 56. Do you often keep people waiting?

YES 57. Do you like everything to go exactly according to plan?

YES 58. Are you reasonably attractive to the opposite sex?

YES 59. Do you read horoscopes in the paper?

No 60. Do you feel the fates are against you?

No 61. Do you often think it over for a day or two before a decision?

YES 62. Have you ever thought of going into business on your own account?

No 63. Do you find it difficult to concentrate for long periods?

No 64. Do you worry about the future a lot?

YES 65. On the whole, are you a useful member of society?

YES 66. Do you decide what to watch on TV, and not the person with you?

No 67. Do you ever feel like giving it all up?

YES 68. Do you know your birth sign?

YES 69. Do you think that "better safe than sorry" is a good motto for life?

YES 70. Do you think that the world is basically a serious place?

The questions are designed so that those who are not suited to flying airliners will score higher than those who are. It is worth noting that the qualities needed by a fighter pilot are often the opposite of those an airline pilot should have: thus a fighter pilot should score fairly high in the impulsive, risk-taker and irresponsible sections. An airline pilot would be rejected if he had a similar score.

In each case you score one point if your answer is the same as those given below. The questions are divided into sections to cover the important aspects of personality as far as flying passenger transports is concerned.

Impulsive to Controlled

Impulsives are inclined to act on the spur of the moment. They make hurried, often premature decisions and are unpredictable. Airline flying is very much a routine business, and so systematic and controlled people are necessary, who look before they leap.

 5. No

12. Yes ✓

19. No

26. Yes

33. Yes

40. Yes ✓

47. No

54. Yes

61. No ✓

68. Yes ✓

High scorers are impulsive.

Anxious to Calm

Although many high achievers are anxious types, anxiety is not conducive to good airline pilots. Anxious people are easily upset by things that go wrong and worry unnecessarily.

Flying is littered with delays, alterations and minor technical problems that would wear out an anxious pilot's nerves. Serene types, immune to irrational fears and upsets, are wanted.

1. Yes
8. Yes
15. Yes ✓
22. Yes
29. Yes
36. Yes ✓   3
43. No
50. Yes
57. Yes ✓
64. Yes

High scorers are anxious, worried types. Those with low scores are calm.

Inferiority to Self-esteem

Feelings of inferiority can lead to sloppiness and nervous strain. Self-confidence and self-esteem are positive characteristics for the safe pilot. A pilot with an inferiority complex might be unable to translate his decisions into action for fear of being wrong. This is potentially hazardous.

2. Yes ✓
9. Yes
16. No   ✓
23. Yes ✓
30. No
37. Yes

44. Yes
51. Yes
58. No
65. No

High scorers have a feeling of inferiority. Low scorers are proud of themselves.

Dependent to Independent

Although a pilot must not be too much of an individual, and should blend easily into a team or crew, he should have plenty of self-reliance and independence of thought and action. Pilots must monitor each other continuously to avoid the sort of errors that, unchecked, have caused many disasters—mis-set altimeters, wrongly selected flaps, even forgetting to lower the undercarriage. A pilot who is unquestioningly obedient to authority might sit by while his captain flew the aircraft into the ground.

3. Yes
10. No
17. Yes
24. No
31. Yes
38. No
45. No
52. No
59. Yes
66. No

High scorers are overdependent on others.

Depressed to Happy

If a pilot is overly depressed, his state of alertness and anticipation will be affected. Depression also affects powers of concentration and can induce a state where the pilot's arousal point becomes so suppressed that he ignores safety checks.

 4. No
11. Yes
18. Yes
25. No
32. Yes
39. No
46. No
53. No
60. Yes
67. Yes

High scorers are depressed. However, those who score only 1 or 2 on this section will be just as suspect as the person with 8 or 9. To be that happy suggests complacency and smugness, equally incompatible with good flying.

Risk-taker to Careful

Those with a gambling instinct, always prepared to take a chance, make good fighter pilots and very bad airline pilots. Nothing in airliner flying should be taken by chance and the risk-taker should not be in the cockpit of such an aircraft.

 6. No
13. Yes
20. Yes

27. Yes
34. No
41. No
48. Yes
55. No
62. Yes
69. No

High scorers are gamblers who should stick to combat planes.

Irresponsible to Responsible

It is clearly vital for a pilot to be responsible and not to indulge in flying tactics that are unorthodox if fun. Irresponsible people can be expected to be casual, unpredictable, careless of regulations. That is a recipe for a serious crash. Pilots must be conscientious, trustworthy and reasonably serious-minded.

 7. No
14. Yes
21. No
28. No
35. Yes
42. No
49. Yes
56. Yes
63. Yes
70. No

High scorers are irresponsible, although they are good passengers.

The following people would be eliminated as unsuitable:

1. Those with 9 or 10 points as impulsive, feeling inferior, dependent, irresponsible.

2. Those with 10 points as depressed, anxious.

3. Those with 8, 9 or 10 points as risk-takers.

4. Those with one point as anxious, feeling inferior, depressed (they are so calm, full of self-esteem and happy that they are so complacent that an engine could drop off without their noticing it).

5. Those whose total is over 58 points, since they tend to instability.

6. Those whose total is less than 15 points, since they tend toward torpor and overweening self-pride.

The average score is 45, and scores up to 58 are unremarkable. Personality testing is still very much in its infancy. Many airlines and air forces are reluctant to use it since it is still controversial. They use interviews and observation of would-be pilots at selection centers. However, the criteria and the qualities they are looking for are similar to the ones in this test.